THE SAILOR IN ENGLISH FICTION
AND DRAMA

THE SAILOR IN ENGLISH FICTION AND DRAMA

1550-1800

BY

HAROLD FRANCIS WATSON

PROFESSOR OF ENGLISH IN SIMPSON COLLEGE

The bowsprit got mixed with the rudder sometimes.

—THE HUNTING OF THE SNARK

AMS PRESS, INC.
NEW YORK
1966

TO

ARTHUR HUNTINGTON NASON

PREFACE

This study had its inception many years ago when a small boy listened with wonder to selections from an anonymous fiction appropriately entitled *Through Arctics and Tropics;* and I wish to express my gratitude to my father and mother, who made the student's life possible for me. More immediately these chapters are the result of researches carried on for five years under the kindly direction of Professor A. H. Thorndike of Columbia University, to whom my especial thanks are due for encouragement, for many helpful suggestions, and for detailed criticism of the entire manuscript. To Professors H. M. Ayres, E. H. Wright, and S. L. Wolff of Columbia University, my thanks are also due for reading and criticism of the manuscript. To Professor J. W. Draper of West Virginia University for valuable suggestions, and to Professor C. H. Grandgent of Harvard University for bibliographical assistance, I wish to acknowledge my obligations. To the officers of the libraries of Columbia University, New York University, and Harvard University, and to the Director and officers of the Columbia University Press, I am grateful for many courtesies.

To my former teacher Professor A. H. Nason of New York University for inspiration, to my present colleague Professor W. C. Hilmer of Simpson College for linguistic assistance, and to my old friend Thomas O'Malley, Esq., of Bushwick High School, Brooklyn, for what he would call *colloquia de natura rerum,* I am also deeply grateful. And to my wife, Martha Tucker Watson, without whose clerical assistance this study might never have been brought to completion, I owe more than I can well express.

Whatever of virtue there may be in the following chapters is largely owing to those who have advised me, and the defects are due to my own limitations. Without pretending to have read every piece of nautical literature produced during two centuries and a half, I have endeavored to point out the most significant developments between 1550 and 1800. That I have made neither errors nor omissions, I cannot hope: the motto on the title page may have a more immediate application than was intended.

Simpson College   H.F.W.
May 25, 1931

CONTENTS

CHAPTER I

INTRODUCTION

THE SAILOR IN THE VOYAGE NARRATIVES

1550-1660

The following study aims to discuss in some detail the presentation of the sailor in English fiction and drama from 1550 to 1800. Only one existing work purports to deal with the entire subject in much the way contemplated here, Robinson and Leyland's beautiful volume *The British Tar in Fact and Fiction*, which suffers from several faults. It aims "to contrast the real with the ideal,"[1] and contains a wealth of material obtainable only by a professional mariner; but, perhaps because the whole evolved from notes to accompany a series of nautical prints,[2] it lacks definite organization, makes illogical generalizations, and reveals deplorable carelessness as to the details of literary history.

"Disorders arose mostly from men who had not the right spirit of the sea."[3] Raleigh's *History of the World*, which presents the mariner in a decidedly unfavorable light, "is merely a partial picture."[4] Real sea officers did not neglect the interests of the common sailors.[5] The "whole history of the Navy proves" that the seamen must have been superior to the records of them given by the diarists and satirists.[6] In short, the general impression made by Robinson and Leyland is that the mariner must always be a noble fellow because, if he is not a noble fellow, he is not a mariner.

Worse, however, than the attempts to whitewash, or perhaps one should say to holystone, Jack Tar, are the many specific errors. Chaucer's Shipman is represented as actually a good fellow, and his making prisoners walk the plank is deleted to leave the picture intact.[7] *Robinson Crusoe* is dated 1717.[8] The simile, "as fast as we heave men overboard in a sea fight," is transferred from a speech in which Captain Durzo comments on the rapidity with which the heroine's dimples can ensnare men, to another in which the Captain promises to make haste in changing his clothes.[9] The command *yare* in *The Tempest* is derived, not from the Old English *gearu*, ready, but from a contraction of "Ye are to take care!"[10] The whole fairly bristles with this sort of thing. Yet, because of its scope, the *British Tar* is prerequisite to further study.

A number of articles on special parts of the subject have been listed in the Bibliography, and will be referred to in the proper places. One of the most impressive of these is Professor Secord's masterly discussion of Defoe's literary method, which pretty well settles Hoti's business for *Robinson Crusoe* and *Captain Singleton*.[11] With this may be compared Professor Eddy's study of *Gulliver's Travels* and Professor Cawley's unpublished dissertation on the influence of the voyage narratives on English non-dramatic literature 1550-1600.[12] Schneider's *Die Entwickelung des Seeromans in England im 17. und 18. Jahrhundert*, Ross's *The Development of the English Sea Novel from Defoe to Conrad*, and Treneer's *The Sea in English Literature from Beowulf to Donne* are too general to have much significance. And Mr. De la Mare's beautifully written and inspiring essay on desert islands touches lightly a tremendous subject.[13] There seems room, then, for a fairly comprehensive survey of the sort suggested at the beginning of this chapter.

The year 1550 is a convenient point of departure in that it marks a lull in maritime interest between two periods of expansion.[14] The tradition of the vikings and their Anglo-Saxon cousins had been overwhelmed by the romances of chivalry five centuries earlier, and all scholarship cannot reconstruct the tale of Wade and his boat "Guingelot." Despite the occasional sea experiences of the Crusaders, the cycles of romance had either avoided salt water altogether by placing Saracens at convenient cross roads, or had borrowed nautical incidents from the Greek novels of Heliodorus and Achilles Tatius. Chaucer's Shipman, the last great realistic sailorman, had gone west of Dartmouth a hundred and sixty-five years earlier, and nothing like him would appear for fifty more. Elizabeth was uncrowned, Drake unknighted, the King of Spain's beard unsinged, the Armada unfought, and Hakluyt's *Voyages* unpublished. Save for a little realistic satiric interest carried over from the *Ship of Fools*, some mystery play Noahs with shrewish wives, and an occasional figure of speech in a Renaissance poem, the influence of the sailor had disappeared from English literature.

The half century following saw the rise of the voyage narratives which culminated in the mighty tomes of Hakluyt; and beside them, but owing little to them, the pirate attacks and shipwrecks of Arcadian fiction. From the beginning of this development to the present time, the sailor has practically always been an important character; and the closing date 1800 has been chosen rather arbitrarily because of the exigencies of space. The concluding chapter will suggest possibilities for further investigation.

To avoid repeating long explanations, I shall employ a number of general terms in a limited and somewhat technical sense; and, although these terms will ordinarily be defined as they occur, I shall summarize them here for the convenience of the reader. The designation "heart of oak" will be given to the boisterous, hard drinking, brave, and loyal seaman who apparently represents the real thing somewhat exaggerated. Petruchio and the swearing boatswain of *The Tempest* are hearts of oak. Later, this figure becomes unendurably sentimental, with much talk about the "honour of Old England." From him must be distinguished the "humours captain," a thoroughly despicable officer, presented against a background of landsmen as a subject for contempt and mirth. Such a character is Jonson's Captain Shunfield. The "plain dealer" owes more or less to both the other conceptions of the mariner, but prides himself particularly upon his bluntness, honesty, and bad manners. Of course, Wycherley's Captain Manly suggested this designation. The expression "noble pirate" is almost self-explanatory.

The term *"Tempest* school" will be applied to all dramas which present a realistic scene aboard ship, regardless of actual borrowings; and, in the same way, the term "humours school" will be applied to all plays containing only a humours captain. The authentic records of voyages will ordinarily be called "voyage narratives." Novels dealing with the sea will be designated "imitation voyages" if they follow the technique of the voyage narratives, and no attempt will be made to classify them as "philosophic," "fantastic," "extraordinary," etc. The term "naval episode" will be applied to the tales of naval warfare inserted in the novels of the last half of the eighteenth century. *Robinson Crusoe* and *Gulliver's Travels* are imitation voyages; whereas *Roderick Random* contains a naval episode. For the rest, it should be remembered that frequent borrowings among the various types tend to break down the classifications almost as soon as they are set up.

The study of the presentation of the sailor in English literature should begin with the narratives of actual voyages, for it is from them, especially in the earlier periods, that our knowledge of the facts must be obtained. Such a work, for example, as William Laird Clowes' monumental seven volumes on *The Royal Navy* would be most inadequate in the Elizabethan chapters did it omit all the contributions made by Hakluyt, Purchas, and their colleagues; and, although the mariners' tales become less essential as official documents become more complete, the former continue to supplement the latter to a surprising degree. The voyage narratives, moreover, as any student of literature knows, contribute details to such diverse productions as Shakespeare's *Tempest,* Defoe's *Robinson Crusoe,* and Coleridge's *Ancient Mariner.* Not so well known is the fact that voyage accounts also contribute a considerable element of technique to the nautical novels of the eighteenth century, which in many cases purport to be travel books.

From the last viewpoint the narratives of actual voyages may be considered a type of literature. Although the superficial reader obtains from Hakluyt, Dampier, and Anson a sense of varying styles, purposes, and attitudes, careful examination of a large number of these accounts gives one a distinct impression of unity. Naturally most of the authors are seamen or men closely connected with the sea. Whether a certain type of humanity tends to follow the nautical profession, or whether following it tends to produce a certain type, the fact remains that the sailor has a definite personality of his own, and differences are further reduced by the fact that these authors are nearly all officers or landsmen whose sympathies are largely with the officer class. The ability to read and write, in times when it was less usual to be literate, may also be considered something of a definite characteristic. The purpose of most of the writers is informational, with a strong leaning toward the economic, so that stress is placed on useful rather than interesting details; and on the other hand there is the human tendency to tell a good story. Probably the fact that many of the narratives are based on log books or journals also has considerable influence on their form and content. With a few exceptions such as Johnson's *General History of the Pirates,* a collection of short biographies intended primarily for entertainment, the voyage accounts have a fairly definite technique.

Partly because they are all much alike and partly because the influence of the sea tales on creative writing may be felt within a few years, as Bulkeley and Cummins' story of the "Wager" on *Roderick Random*,[15] or after centuries, as Hawkins' water snakes on the *Ancient Mariner*,[16] there is little value in making the discussion of them fall into periods corresponding to those of literary history. This chapter will survey the voyage narratives 1550-1660 and the presentation of the sailor given by them.

The object of the expedition, trade with China, the discovery of new land, or the acquisition of gold from the natives, tends to give the narrative of a voyage a definite plot. There is a much desired end, the mariners set forth to accomplish it, and they succeed or fail. Unity of action in the dramatic meaning of the term is an element in most voyages. The journal method of recording events from day to day, on the other hand, tends to neutralize the effect of the unifying force, and the reader loses the thread of the story in a jumble of soundings, islands, anecdotes, and climatic peculiarities. That John Davis's expedition of 1585 aimed to discover the Northwest Passage and failed, is lost sight of in the vivid description of how Master Ellis of the "Mooneshine" succeeded in making friends with the natives.[17] In some of the narratives it is almost impossible to discover the purpose of the voyage without reading a summary in a naval history. This disproportion between unimportant details and the main event is further emphasized by the fact that many of the former are purely informational and deadly dull. Many of them, moreover, have little to do with the sea.

At the risk of seeming to contradict a statement made earlier that the authors of voyage narratives are nearly all sailors or landsmen interested in maritime activity, I must digress long enough to explain that the amount of such Elizabethan interest is usually overestimated today. The following quotations, which can be paralleled by others from less authoritative sources, indicate the extent of the misconception:

The spirit of overseas discovery and maritime expansion had permeated national life.—*Shakespeare's England*, I, 141.

Seamen had begun to speak in literature, and the thoughts and language of the sea, by tongue and by writing, were being grafted into the conceptions and language of men who never knew the salt breath of ocean. —*Cambridge History of English Literature*, V, 90.

The preceding chapter has shown how the great race of Tudor seamen left their mark on the literature of the country of their birth.—*Ibid.*, V, 100.

There is considerable excuse for this impression. The naval history of the period has an importance out of all proportion to the interest actually shown by contemporaries. The great exploits of the sea knights are suitable material for novels such as *Westward Ho, Drake in California,* or the more recent *Dark Frigate,* and have been often used, so that a reader of fiction has a hazy recollection of quantities of literature concerning the Spanish Main. Scholarly articles on a subject like *The Tempest* sometimes bring together scattered material in such a way that a false emphasis is given. And overgrown bibliographies of works dealing with the sea contain mathematical treatises, reports on the profits to be made in the Balkans, descriptions of the inhabitants of Florida, and letters to foreign potentates. William Warner explains that in giving accounts of "English voyages" he will tell about the "countries" but not the "customs."[18] With the most liberal interpretation of the term, less than half of Hakluyt is concerned with maritime activity, and in Purchas the proportion is much the same. It is significant that there is no "character" of an old salt until Overbury's (?) *A Sailor* (1614), that there is no formal treatise on ships and sailors before

Smith's *Sea Grammar* (1626), and that Sir Walter Raleigh hated the water so thoroughly that he would walk around by London Bridge rather than be rowed from Westminster across the Thames.

The following journey is sufficient to classify Coryate's *Crudities* under Elizabethan Literature of Sea Travel in a modern bibliography:

> I Departed from Venice in a Barke to Padua about eight of the clock in the evening of the eighth day of August being Munday after I had made my abood there sixe weekes and two dayes, and came to Padua about nine of the clocke the next morning.[19]

Granted that the Elizabethan interest in the sea is limited to a smaller group than is usually supposed, there is enough maritime material in Hakluyt to make some generalizations possible. Despite the fact that this collection is unusually heterogeneous, nearly all the authors of voyage accounts are sea captains or landsmen directly interested in the sea. As indicated by the diary method so frequently used, by the presence of unimportant details, by the stress on position and soundings, and by the instructions included in the companies' articles, ship's logs are the principal sources.

> Also that you take with you paper and ynke, and keepe a continuall journall or rememberance day by day, of all such things as shall fall out worth the knowledge, not forgetting or omitting to write it, and note it, that it may be shewed and read at your returne.[20]

The content according to another reference is to be

> . . . the Navigation of every day and night, with the points and observation of the lands, tides, elements of the sunne, course of the moon and starres. . . .[21]

Pages of dull facts and figures such as the following are accounted for on this ground. Much of the sea material indicates that the voyagers themselves regarded the sea merely as a road and recorded their experiences only because custom—and the various Honourable Companies—required the keeping of the log.

The next day being the first of June, we set saile at 3 a clocke in the morning, and set our course North, the wind at the Southwest, and at Southsouthwest.

The 10. day about one of the clocke in the afternoone, wee put into Norway to a place where one of the headlands of the sound is called Bottel: the other headland is called Moile. There is also an Island called Kene. Heere I did find the pole to be elevated 62. deg. it doeth flowe there South, and it hieth 7. or 8. foote, not above.

The 11. day in the morning the winde came to the South and to the Southeast: the same day at sixe in the afternoone we set saile, and bare along the coast: it was very foule weather with raine and fogge.

The 22. day the wind being at west, we did hall the coast East northeast, and East. The same day at 6. in the morning we did double the north cape. Aboute 3. in the afternoone wee past Skites beare nesse, and hald along the coast East, and East southeast, and the same night wee halled Southeast, and Southeast by East.[22]

This sort of thing continues for seventeen pages and is paralleled by hundreds.

On the other hand, some of the writers are persons of considerable literary ability like Sir Walter Raleigh or Hakluyt himself, and even where aptitude is lacking, the irresistible impulse to tell a good story tends to improve the narrative method. That many of the writers are conscious of their technique is indicated in a variety of ways. Once in a while there is a Latin quotation or literary allusion. The "excellent Mathematician and Enginier" Master Edward Wright, in describing the Earl of Cumberland's voyage to the Azores, adds to his account of a storm in terms of Psalm CVII this conclusion:

. . . we had just cause to pray a little otherwise then the poet, though marring the verse, yet mending the meaning.

Deus maris & Coeli, quid enim nisi vota supersunt,
Solvere quassatae parcito membra ratis. [sic][23]

Sir John Hawkins concludes the story of his voyage to the Indies in 1567-1568, an account making some pretensions to literary style, with an allusion to John Foxe:

> If all the miseries and troublesome affaires of this sorrowfull voyage should be perfectly and thoroughly written, there should neede a painefull man with his pen, and as great a time as he had that wrote the lives and deathes of the Martyrs.[24]

This implied apology for not being more elaborate falls in line with several others.

> . . . The discourse of our whole proceeding in this voyage wil aske more time and a person in better health then I am at this present. . . .
>
> . . . I pray you be not offended with these my rude letters for lacke of time. . . .
>
> . . . But because such things are impertinent to the matter, I will returne (without any more mentioning of the same) to that from which I have digressed and swarved. . . .[25]

Although I can find no passage having all the characteristics of Euphuism, there are many with carefully balanced structure and either parallel or antithetical ideas. The matter from which Master Ellis has "swarved" above continues:

> . . . our ship now sailing on the surging seas, sometime passing at pleasure with a wished Easterne wind, sometime hindered of our course againe by the Westerne blast, untill . . . we fell with Frizeland, which is very hie and cragged land and was almost cleane covered with snow, so that we might see nought but craggie rockes and the tops of high and huge hilles, sometimes (and for the most part) all covered with foggie mists.[26]

Surely the alliteration is introduced consciously. Raleigh uses increased parallelism without the alliteration:

> . . . the pitifull object of so many bodies slaine and dismembred could not but draw ech mans eye to see, and heart to lament, and hands to helpe those miserable people, whose limnes were so torne with the violence of shot, and paine made grievous with the multitude of woundes.[27]

With the rather elaborate writing quoted above should be compared Richard Johnson's "unperfectly written notes," which for nearly fifty lines average more than one *and* to the line, the dull account on page 9, or the involved if vivid phraseology of Steven Burrough's *Discovery toward the River Ob*:

Although the harborough were evil, yet the stormie similitude of Northerly winds tempted us to set our sayles, & we let slip a cable and an anker, and bare with the harborough, for it was then neere a high water: and as alwaies in such journeis varieties do chance, when we came upon the barre in the entrance of the creeke, the wind did shrink so suddenly upon us, that we were not able to lead it in and before we could have flatted the shippe before the winde, we should have bene on ground on the lee shore, so that we were constrained to let fall an anker under our sailes, and rode in a very breach, thinking to have warped in.[28]

The more usual method, however, is neither the fine writing represented by the first group of examples nor the awkward phraseology illustrated in the second, but a straightforward simplicity suggestive of the King James Bible. This can best be shown, I think, by calling attention to the figures of speech most common in the voyage narratives. Ten chosen at random make vivid comparisons. The wood is as even "as if it had beene cut with a paire of gardeners sheeres."[29] A tuft of trees on the brow of the land shows "like a Porpose Head."[30] Friesland rises "like pinacles of steeples."[31] The natives make "great outcries and noyses, like so many Buls."[32] The wind from the hollows of the hill produces "such a breth of heate . . . upon our faces as though we were entred within some bathstove or hotehouse."[33] Davis compares the noise of the surf near Lumlie's Inlet with "the fall of some great water through a bridge."[34] A flock of cranes make a noise "as if an armie of men had showted all together."[35] Rockweed appears like "clusters of grapes."[36] The ashes fall so thick from Tierra del Fuego that "you might write your name with your finger upon the upper deck."[37] Lice are

said to be as big as "peason, yea and some as big as beans."[38]
I can find no Elizabethan conceits, and only one nautical simile,
"Sprang their luff," in the whole collection.

Probably such details as the appearance three times of a sea
monster "like a mulato or tawny Indian,"[39] the discovery of a
venomous two-headed worm as big as a man's arm,[40] the anecdote of how one of Drake's followers had his bed shot from under him,[41] and the account of the bolt of lightning which killed
four men and temporarily disabled many more,[42] are not included entirely for didactic purposes. Most of the attempts at
humour seem rather pathetic to our eyes; but the astonishment
of the Russian bishop at Master Killingworth's five-foot beard
("This is God's gift!"),[43] and the successful attempt of Frobisher to cure an Indian of lameness by shooting over his head,[44]
have their human appeal today. Better, although not legitimately
discussed in connection with conscious attempts at literary technique, are the probably unintended humorous touches such as
the euphemistic account of the capture of the French vessel by
Hore's men: "such was the policie of the English, that they be-
came masters of the same,"[45] or the authority Mercator gives
for his maps of New France in a letter to Frobisher: "they were
taken out of a certaine sea card drawn by a certaine priest out
of the description of a Frenchman."[46]

The Purchas collection of 1625, although larger and less well
chosen, does not differ materially in the impression it gives
from that of Hakluyt. Of the comparatively small group of accounts dealing primarily with the sea, many are obviously based
on log books; several, notably those of Barents and Strachey,
are written in rather elaborate literary style; and a few are en-
livened by anecdotes such as the one from Captain John Smith's
Historie of Bermudas:

One Henry Long, with six others being on fishing, a sudden storm arose
with terrible thunder, and the Boat was tossed over the Rocks, the fish

tossed over-boord, and Long with two others escaped (the rest drowned) one of the three being demanded what he thought in the present perill, answered, hee said nothing, but Gallowes claime the right, which within halfe a year fell out accordingly.[47]

Knivet's account of Candish's second voyage contains the following grim detail concerning the cold:

Here one Harris a Goldsmith lost his Nose: for going to blow it with his fingers, cast it into the fire.[48]

Surprisingly little direct information is given in Hakluyt about the common sailor. Human interest details of the kind so frequent in later nautical fiction are comparatively rare in the accounts of actual sea fights and shipwrecks contained in the collection. Probably the chief characteristic of the foremast hand as described in the voyage narratives is his lack of discipline. Indeed, the commissioned group themselves seem to be no models in this respect: even the great Sir Walter deliberately disobeys his orders. Furthermore it should be remembered that the sailor has to look out for his own interest or no one will. Life is cheap. One company stresses in its orders that the captain is not to risk a man lest the profits of the voyage be endangered, but rarely is any provision made for the mariner's care. Apparently individual deaths were not recorded in the logs, unless unusual. Men lost overboard are mentioned casually and frequently. In one place the statement is made that "the [prisoner] was heaved over boord, because he was sore hurt,"[49] and only when the casualty list reaches "only thirty sound men in three ships" or five hundred dead out of seven hundred and fifty, is any stress laid on it. It is true that eight captains are included in the latter terrible figure, but against that should be set the record of two sound men in a ship's company, of which one was the ship's boy and the other the captain.

So we placed other men in the roomes of those that we lost, and set saile.[50]

Punishments must have been frightfully severe, as indicated by Boteler's imposing list of tortures: lashing to the capstan bar, the bilboes, ducking from the mainyard arm, and "keel-rakinge" later to be known as keel hauling, "if the offense be very fowle." Minor infractions of discipline were punished by whipping at the capstan, and the boatswain must beat the ship's boys once a week with his cane, said the sailors, or the wind would fail. The rules of the Council for Fenton's voyage to the East Indies sound reasonable enough,[51] with jury trial by members of the crew after a review of the case by members of the company, when the death penalty was to be given for "treason, mutinie, or other discord"; but while little is said of these matters in Hakluyt, we know that Drake exercised high justice, middle, and low in the case of mutineers, and that repentance could not save the ringleader from the headsman's axe.

Discipline nevertheless was poor, particularly when some question of loot was involved.

Hereupon they mutined and at last grew into such furie, as that they would have it or els breake downe the cabbine . . . whereby I was forced to yield. . . .

The company, which were in all but 33 men and boyes, being in mutiny, and every day ready to go togather by the eares (the captaine being sicke and like for to die) would not stay, but would needs go home.[52]

The next day our capitaine calling upon the sailers to finish a foresaile which they had in hand, some of them answered that unlesse they might goe directly home, they would lay their hands to nothing; whereupon he was constrained to follow their humour.[53]

"Our mariners, contrary to their captaines direction" may almost be considered the characteristic "Once upon a time" for an Elizabethan sea incident.

An element closely connected with the general lack of discipline is carelessness: "our men partly having no rule of themselves" ate, drank, and bathed to excess, and died of "swellings" and agues.

The Gunner being carelesse, as they are many times of their powder, in discharging certain pieces in ye gunner roome, blew up the Admirals cabbin, slew the gunner with 2 others outright, & hurt 20 more, of which 4 or 5 died.[54]

". . . our hulke . . . fell afire by some great negligence and perished. . . ."[55]

The "Merlin," "through the negligences of one of their gunners," was blown up and sunk. The "Ayde" however suffered less melodramatically in being set on fire "by the negligence of the Cooke," and was saved by a ship's boy. While the master of the "Tyger," in defiance of the curse of the weird sisters, was sleeping, "by the ill worke of his men" she collided with the "Minion." How much of this negligence is due to drunkenness is difficult to say.

May's *Brief Note* makes it clear that liquor was responsible for the wreck which gives us *The Tempest*, and there are one or two references to it as a maritime necessity, notably the pathetic statement that "to their great griefe . . . all the way homewards they dranke nothing but water."[56] A carpenter gets drunk and drowns himself. Drunkenness is not, however, among the "contagions of vices" forbidden by the company rules. After all it is reasonable to suppose that, as in other ages, the sailor of this time did his serious drinking when ashore and out from under authority, a phase of his life not represented in Hakluyt. There is no reference to the sailor's amorousness or to the proverbial frailty of his wife, again probably because these phases of his life did not concern his officers. Gambling is forbidden in one set of rules as leading not only to the poverty of the player but to strife and murder.

The only direct quotation from anyone below the rank of

boatswain is in Spanish, and the paraphrases of actual conversations convey little information. The speeches of officers, which, as today, may possibly have caught some reflection of the sailor's vocabulary, are formal and almost literary, with no sprinkling of the technical terms appearing in the accounts of taking in sail and hoisting the anchor. As indicated in creative literature, the Elizabethan mariner had a technical vocabulary for business purposes, but he did not use it to ornament his ordinary speech. On the other hand, it should be noted that the only suggestion of the profanity which the plays indicate that he used also, is found in the rule against it, so that this negative evidence should not be given too much weight. Strong disapproval is expressed of blasphemy, swearing, and filthy tales. In no case is an incident recorded dealing with the forbidden vice.

Against the lack of discipline, carelessness, and, perhaps, wickedness of the Elizabethan sailor, may be set his courage. Again and again his superiority to the other nationalities is suggested. One company provided that, as far as possible, only English sailors be used on their ships. Pressed on a foreign vessel, a tar refused to fight against ships of his own country, but would do valiant service otherwise.[57] One swam under water to fix a broken rudder; another fought off icebergs with a capstan bar; another defeated overwhelming odds; and still another refused to surrender till his ship sank under him. There is record in Hakluyt of only two English warships actually falling into Spanish hands.

But chiefly the boatswaine shewed himself valiant above the rest: for he fared amongst the Turks like a wood Lion; for there was none of them that either could or durst stand in his face, till at last there came a shot from the Turkes, which brake his whistle asunder and smote him on the brest, so that he fell downe, bidding them farewell, & to be of good comfort, encouraging them likewise to winne praise by death, rather than to live captives in misery and shame. . . .[58]

Another element noticeable throughout the collection, but probably a reflection of captain and owner rather than of ordinary mariner, is piety with an eye to the main chance. After all the chief aim of the explorations is traffic rather than discovery, and this economic interest colors most of the activities, as when William Burrough instructs Pet and Jackman to carry a large map of London with "the river drawen full of Ships of all sorts, to make the more shew of your great trade."[59]

. . . [The mariners are] not to disclose to any nation the state of our religion, but pass it over in silence, without any declaration of it, seeming to beare with such lawes, and rites, as the place hath, where you shall arrive.[60]

And principally see that you forget not dayly in all the voiage both morning and evening, to call the company within boord to prayer, in which doing you shall please God, and the voiage will have better successe thereby, and the company prosper better.[61]

There is always the suggestion that, if one serves God, one is likely to escape drowning and increase the profits of the company.

Thanks to the frequently quoted complaint of Sir Richard Hawkins, Purchas contains a rather more vivid account of the lawlessness of Jack ashore than does Hakluyt.

I beganne to gather my companie aboord, which occupied my good friends, and the justices of the Towne two dayes, and forced us to search all the lodgings, Taverns, and Ale-houses. (For some would ever bee taking their leave and never depart:) some drinke themselves so drunke, that except they were carried aboord, they of themselves were not able to goe one steppe: others knowing the necessitie of the time, faigned themselves sicke; others to bee indebted to their Hosts and forced mee to ransome them; one his chest; another, his Sword; another, his Shirts; another, His Carde and Instruments for Sea: And others to benefit themselves of the Imprest given them, absented themselves; making a lewd living in deceiving all whose money they could lay hold of.[62]

A little farther along, he refers to the tendency for discipline to go to pieces in sight of loot:

But the Mariner is ordinarily so carried away by the desire of Pillage, as sometimes for very appearances of small moment, he looseth his Voyage, and many times himselfe.

And Nicholar Downton cites an example:

. . . like disgoverned pilfering-people, they runne all into the ship, not forbearing to breake open Chests, tumble into the Frigat, and make spoyle of all things that liked them, forbearing no ill language to such as I had sent to restraine them.[63]

One wishes he had recorded the "ill language!"

That drink may have had something to do with the fairly common mutinies, as well as with carelessness of consequences, is indicated by Richard Cocks' account of rebellious sailors. The Purser, having gone ashore, found

. . . divers drinking and domineering; he bestowed blowes amongst some of them, and notwithstanding the Master had commanded Lambart and Colphax to retire aboord, yet they staid ashoare all day . . . and being drunke, went into the field and fought, Lambart being hurt in the arme, and remained drunken ashoare all night, as Boles did the like, and so had done two or three nights before, and quarrelled with Christopher Evans, about a whoore.[64]

Courage is again stressed, as in the characterization of the captured pirate who, freed to help guide the ship in an emergency, announced, "I had rather here drowne with so good company, then bee hanged at home alone."[65] Piety also appears in many of the Purchas narratives.

Sir Richard Hawkins' account mentioned above contains a formal discussion of the ranks and duties aboard ship much in the fashion of Captain John Smith's *Sea Grammar* (1626) or Boteler's *Six Dialogues about Sea-Service* (written 1634). This material is almost entirely didactic and adds very little to our knowledge of the personality of the sailor. In general, the Elizabethan voyages present the mariner as lawless and brave amid terrible hardships; and as having a trace of the characteristics with which he is endowed for stage presentation.

The Civil War put an end temporarily to the production of voyage narratives, perhaps because the potential authors were too busily engaged with the national crisis, or perhaps because the Navy was commanded by landsmen. At all events, a new cycle began with the Restoration.

CHAPTER II

THE SAILOR IN THE VOYAGE NARRATIVES

1660-1800

In the Restoration period, the chief authorities for the personality of the English sailor are Teonge's *Diary* and Esquemeling's *Buccaneers of America*. Henry Teonge (pronounced Tong) was a country parson who, apparently to escape extreme poverty, served as chaplain on board English war ships in cruises to the Mediterranean 1675-1676 and 1678-1679. An educated man, he sprinkles his writing with tags of Latin and ofttimes bursts into poetry of a rough and ready sort. Leaving out of account a fairly respectable Latin epitaph, the following is a fair sample of the reverend gentleman's muse, and incidentally shows his almost Dickensian obsession with food and drink:

> Our stay, though short, got provender good store,
> Beef, pork, sheep, ducks, geese, hens, chickens galore.
> Cider, beer, brandy, bread—and something more
> I could have told you had I gone ashore.[1]

"Deus vortat bene!" from its frequent repetition seems to be his favorite saying and amounts almost to a "humour." He describes points of historic interest in detail and discusses their importance in pedantic fashion. It need scarcely be said therefore that the worthy chaplain composed his diary with some attempt at literary style.

How far the gay spirit of the author, suggestive of the devil-may-care attitude of a cavalier lyric, is a personal reaction due to his temporary escape from worldly care, and how far it represents the spirit of the officers of the Royal Navy, is difficult to decide. Presumably Teonge, like Hakluyt's authors, has the viewpoint of the officer class. Since he is essentially a landsman, however, he records details usually missing from the Elizabethan accounts. One of the best of these describes Jack taking leave of his Polly:

Hither many of our seaman's wives follow their husbands and several other young women accompany their sweethearts, and sing *Loth to depart* in punch and brandy; so that our ship was that night well furnished, but ill manned, few of them being well able to keep watch had there been occasion. You would have wondered to see here a man and a woman creep into a hammock, the woman's legs to the hams hanging over the sides or out at the end of it. Another couple sleeping on a chest; other kissing and clipping; half drunk, half sober or rather half asleep; choosing rather (might they have been suffered) to go and die with them than stay and live without them.[2]

And later the officers' wives are also pictured:

[The captain's lady] like a woman of great discretion, seems no whit troubled that her husband might have the less. But our Lieutenant's wife like weeping Rachel or mournful Niobe; as also was the Boatswain's wife. . . . Only our Master's wife, of a more masculine spirit—or rather a virago—lays no such grief to her heart, only, like one that hath eaten mustard, her eyes are a little red. . . . But [he concludes, apparently of both groups] they were no sooner out of sight but they were more merry; and I could tell with whom, too, were I so minded.[3]

Since the first part of *Buccaneers of America* is a translation, the style has little significance for this discussion. The occasional lapses into the first person suggest that the author was present during much of the activity he describes so vividly, but there is nothing to indicate that he derived his account from a ship's log. Ringrose's story, however, the publisher refers to as the "present narrative or Journal." This source is confirmed by the careful dating, the recording of unimportant details, and, in the last chapters, the inclusion of sea marks, soundings, and ship's position. Ringrose attempts to adorn his writing with bits of human interest. Because of different atmosphere, his story makes an interesting contrast to that dealing with Morgan. At the outset there is something like comic opera in the detailed description of the pirate ensigns, among which the Jolly Roger of tradition does not appear:

First, Captain Bartholomew Sharp with his company had a red flag, with a bunch of white and green ribbons. The second division led by Captain Richard Sawkins with his men, had a red flag striped with yellow. The third and fourth, led by Captain Peter Harris, had two green flags, his company being divided into two several divisions. The fifth and sixth, was led by Captain Edmund Cook, with red colours striped with yellow, with a hand and sword for his device.[4]

In the eighteenth century there are so many voyage accounts that any sort of detailed consideration of them is impossible. The pictures they give of the English mariner and the methods of presentation are similar to those of the preceding century. Most of the narratives are based largely on journals and, at the same time, make some pretensions to literary style. Says Captain William Dampier (1703):

As to my Stile, it cannot be expected, that a Seaman should affect Politeness; for were I able to do it, yet I think I should be little sollicitous about it, in a work of this Nature. I have frequently, indeed, divested my self of Sea-Phrases, to gratify the Land Reader; for which the Seaman will hardly forgive me: And yet, possibly, I shall not seem Complaisant enough to the other; because I still retain the use of so many Sea-Terms.[5]

Woodes Rogers, writing in 1712, explains that

Tho others, who give an Account of their Voyages, do generally attempt to imitate the Stile and Method which is us'd by Authors that write ashore, I rather chuse to keep to the Language of the Sea; which is more genuine and natural for a Mariner. And because Voyages of this sort have commonly miscarried, 'tis necessary that I should keep to my Original Journal. . . .[6]

Is there a trace of the Plain Dealer characteristic in this? Both Dampier and Rogers adorn their writings with details of human interest, such as the former's account of the sailor who drowns himself to save three hundred dollars,[7] or the latter's sniggering reference to the friar and the female slave.[8] Perhaps as amusing as anything is Rogers' anecdote of how the English offer to compromise with their Portuguese friends on toasts to the Pope and the Archbishop of Canterbury respectively, by drinking to William Penn.[9]

Whether Johnson's *History of the Pirates* (1724) should be classed with the voyage narratives, since it is a collection of about twenty somewhat apocryphal biographies of famous pirates, is doubtful. The best known of these probably—I remember reading a summary of it as a long footnote in my grammar school history—is the story of Teach or Blackbeard,[10] a villain with as great audacity as Morgan and considerably more imagination, witness his battening down hatches and filling his ship with sulphur fumes to see whether hell was really going to be so bad after all. Shooting Israel Hands for amusement, he crippled him for life, and perhaps immortalized him, for Stevenson has given the name to a character in *Treasure Island*. Avery and Low also appear in creative writing.

George Shelvocke (1726), whose melancholy attitude toward life in general makes him a forerunner of the sentimental romanticists, gives the following elaborate description of the island of Juan Fernandez, on which he was wrecked:

In short, every thing that one sees or hears in this place is perfectly romantick; the very structure of the Island, in all its parts, has a certain savage irregular beauty, which is not to be expressed; the many prospects of lofty inaccessible hills, and the solitariness of the gloomy narrow valleys, which a great part of the day enjoy little benefit from the sun, and the fall of waters, which one heard all around, would be agreeable to none but those who would indulge themselves for a time, in a pensive melancholy. To conclude, nothing can be conceiv'd more dismally solemn, than to hear the silence of the still night destroy'd by the surf of the sea beating on the shore, together with the violent roaring of the sea-lions repeated all around by the ecchoes of deep valleys. . . .[11]

Coleridge, it will be remembered, received several suggestions for the *Ancient Mariner* from the vivid writing of the Captain of the ill-sped "Speedwell" (notably from the black albatross which follows the ship and which all assume will bring bad luck).[12]

The "Wager" cycle, from which Anson's *Voyage* will be excluded for the present as containing only slight mention of the disaster, gives the same impression of literary attempts on the basis of journals. The earliest and least elaborate account is that of Bulkeley and Cummins, whose principal aim, as they admit, was to defend themselves from accusations of mutiny. They refer many times to the use they are making of their journal; and apparently quote directly at length. They add that they are carrying out the tradition of publishing the accounts of voyages that are regarded as extraordinary.

We don't set up for Naturalists and Men of great Learning, therefore have avoided meddling with Things above our Capacity.[13]

They also claim somewhat sarcastically that their story differs from other voyage accounts in that it contains no fiction: this protest, as Professor Atkinson has pointed out, is a convention of voyage writing, whether real or fictitious. The apology suggests that some attention is to be paid to literary style; and, as I shall show later, the account of the disaster is sufficiently vivid to become the source for a wreck in *Roderick Random*.

The Honorable John Byron's version, representing the other half Rome, is that of a cultured gentleman who, in neo-classical diction, attempts to defend the commissioned officers from the accusations made by Bulkeley and Cummins. He speaks of the "ungovernable herd," "the licentious crew," "superfluous conceits," and, for that matter, of "uncouth, desolate, and rugged" country containing a range of "deformed broken rocks."[14] Isaac Morris while almost choking with indignation at the way he and his companions were marooned by the others "for whose preservation we had risqued our lives, in swimming ashore for Provisions,"[15] obviously enjoys joining the fray to show how great the sufferings of his group were, and tells a straightforward narrative of adventure by land. The anonymous narrative of 1751 calls a plague on both houses, although in general the author's attitude toward the commissioned group is not so contemptuous as toward the others. He tends to wise saws, Latin quotations, literary allusions, heavy humour, and philosophy. The sun rises "gilding with its rays the eastern horizon." Captain Cheap shows "all the Prudence and Fortitude becoming a brave Officer." "The genuine Spirit of marine Brutes, which *Bulkeley* had charmed for a few Minutes, broke forth."[16] His snobbish ridicule of Bulkeley's pretensions to intelligence is in bad taste.

The work commonly referred to as *Anson's Voyage* is an elaborate literary account compiled by Richard Walter, the Chaplain of the "Centurion," from several journals published earlier and "papers and other materials" furnished by Lord Anson himself. This narrative was issued under the commander's own direction, and therefore probably contains only such facts as he wished the public to have. Walter's style is well represented by the following description:

This island of Staten-land far surpasses [Tierra del Fuego] in the wildness and horror of its appearance, it seeming to be entirely composed of inaccessible rocks, without the least mixture of earth or mold between them. The rocks terminate in a vast number of ragged points, which spire up to a prodigious height and are all of them covered with everlasting snow; the points themselves are on every side surrounded with frightful precipices, and often overhang in a most astonishing manner, and the hills which bear them are generally separated from each other by narrow clefts which appear as if the country had been frequently rent by earthquakes; for these chasms are nearly perpendicular, and extend through the substance of the main rocks, almost to their very bottoms; so that nothing can be imagined more savage and gloomy than the whole aspect of this coast.[17]

There are surprisingly few literary allusions or other attempts at adornment.

The three voyages of discovery of Captain James Cook are narrated respectively by Hawkesworth in his collection of 1773, by Cook himself in the same year, and by Captain King from Cook's notes in 1784. Hawkesworth was obviously inclined to the sentimental school of writing popularized by Richardson and his successors. Cook married a young lady

. . . whom he tenderly loved, and who had every claim to his warmest affection and esteem. It is said that Cook had been godfather to this lady, and that he declared at the time his wish for their future union. . . . His position in life . . . did not suffer him to enjoy matrimonial felicity without interruption; and like all officers of any worth, his first thoughts were turned to his profession.[18]

Of the sufferings of the slaves in Spanish mines, Hawkesworth says "Who can read this without emotion!" He also comments on Cook's humanity in shooting natives with small shot instead of ball.[19] All three accounts have the journals pretty well concealed in connected narratives and vivid details.

Despite, or perhaps because of, the increasing British naval activity up to and after Trafalgar, there were few important voyage narratives written between the Cook group in the 1770's and the story of Sir John Franklin's first expedition toward the North Pole (1818). Mavor's twenty-five volume collection (1796) is almost a *Recueil* to sing the glories of an age departed. Perhaps the neo-classical spirit was at last having its way with the English argonauts:

Sir, if you talk of [Hawkesworth's *Voyages*] as a subject of commerce, it will be gainful; if as a book that is to increase human knowledge, I believe there will not be much of that. Hawkesworth can tell only what the voyagers have told him; and they have found very little, only one new animal, I think.[20]

I told him that while I was with the Captain [Pringle], I catched the enthusiasm of curiosity and adventure, and felt a strong inclination to go with him on his next voyage. Johnson. "Why, Sir, a man *does* feel so, till he considers how very little he can learn from such voyages."[21]

At all events, about the time the voyage narratives ceased, maritime fiction left the imitation of them for the presentation of life in the Royal Navy; and it is in Wordsworth's *Prelude*, rather than in Davis's *Post Captain*, that one must look for the continuation of Dampier's influence.

That the condition of the mariners was little better in the Restoration than in the preceding period is indicated by Teonge. He makes numerous references to Black Monday, the day the boys are catted.

This day David Thomas and Marlin the cook and our Master's boy had their hand stretched out and with their backs to the rails, and the Master's boy with his back to the mainmast, all looking one upon the other, and in each of their mouths a marline spike, viz. an iron pin clapped close into their mouths, and tied behind their heads; and there they stood a whole hour, till their mouths were very bloody: an excellent cure for swearers.[22]

This day two seamen that had stolen a piece or two of beef were thus shamed: they had their hands tied behind them, and themselves tied to the mainmast, each of them a piece of raw beef tied about their necks in a cord, and the beef bobbing before them like the knot of a cravat; and the rest of the seamen came one by one, and rubbed them over the mouth with the raw beef; and in this posture they stood for two hours.[23]

. . . the last boiling of the beef that was bought at Cyprus was flung overboard, for the meat was so bad that they chose rather to eat bread dry than to eat that meat.[24]

A later entry refers casually to the pressing of six seamen from a merchantman. Many of the crew suffer from fever.

A seaman had twenty-nine lashes with a cat-o-nine-tails, and was then washed with salt water, for stealing our carpenter's mate's wife's ring.[25]

And as a fitting close to the list of unpleasant details: "I buried Francis Forrest, as 'tis said eaten to death with lice."[26]

Despite frequent references to punishments for infractions of rules, there·is little suggestion of serious disobedience among the sailors of the navy, even though so many of them were pressed against their will. It is true that the ship's company, officers and all, take part in a drinking debauch that results in severe punishment in certain cases, but no trace of attempted mutiny appears. Apparently there was wholesome fear of consequences in the king's service. Much reference is made to drinking, the worthy chaplain himself being overcome to the point where he sleeps with his head *under* the pillow. The traditional frailty of the sailor's wife is represented in the case of one Skinner, who is excused from being ducked three times from the yard arm for going ashore without leave, because he "having a wife a whore and a scold to injure him at home, ergo had the more need to be pitied abroad."[27]

Isaac Webb stood tied to the geares an hour, and had *speculum oris* placed in his mouth for saying to a seaman in the Captain's hearing: "Thou liest, like the son of a whore!"[28]

It is to be regretted that Teonge had no predecessor in Elizabethan times to record details of human interest.

The absence of any naval engagement and the comparatively good weather on these voyages allowed little opportunity for bravery. The captain having frightened a Dutch man of war into lowering her topsail to the English, as was the custom, laments:

I wish I could meet with one that would not vail his bonnet, so that I might make work for my brethren at White Hall [officers out of employment].[29]

The "Assistance" goes boldly to attack six other ships only to find that they are the rest of the fleet to which she belongs. On this occasion one of the captains comments: "These can be no other but the English, they come on so bravely."[30] Since the diarist was a clergyman, the constant pious exclamations are to be expected and probably are not significant as showing the attitude of the seamen of the time. Having shown how a parson viewed the English sailor, I shall try to indicate what a pirate thought of him. For whether "John Esquemeling," alias Alex. Olivier Oexmelin, was a Dutchman or a Frenchman and whether Basil Ringrose was a "Gent," or not, both were certainly buccaneers. Their two accounts were joined to form The *Buccaneers of America* (1685). Although several nationalities are dealt with in the former, the presentation can be made essentially English by limiting it to the account of Sir Henry Morgan, who probably represents the ideal pirate of later story. Unlike most of his profession, he had a facility for falling on his feet, and ended his career in a governor's chair instead of at Execution Dock. Leaving a comfortable home and assured future in Wales to seek his fortune on the sea, he finished his term as an indentured servant at Barbados, enlisted as a pirate, and within a few years was elected captain of the ship in which he had a share. In passing it may be mentioned that piracy as practiced in the West Indies at that time was a semi-respectable profession with a complicated organization and a carefully constructed code of rules. By using this organization to his advantage and violating most of the rules when occasion served, Morgan made a fortune, deserted with more than his share of the loot, and as Governor of Jamaica hanged his sworn companions. The various attempts to whitewash this desperado have failed to excuse his essential lack of honor as well as of honesty.

Perhaps because of the leader's ruthlessness, Morgan's band of cutthroats are disciplined in a way unusual among the gentlemen of fortune. There is no reference to the murmuring so common in other companies. Having stolen some marrowbones from a Frenchman, and then challenged him to a duel, an English pirate wounds his adversary treacherously in the back. Morgan stops the feud between the two nationalities by carrying the Englishman to Jamaica to be hanged. That this was simply a method of making peace temporarily with the auxiliaries is indicated by the fact that Morgan later invites the French officers to a council of war aboard "a great ship" and, on the thin pretext that they have taken provisions from an honest English merchantman, confines them in the cabin in order to take their ships for his own use. In celebrating a decision to await the Spanish treasure ships near Savona,

. . . they drank many healths, and discharged many guns, as the common sign of mirth among seamen used to be. Most of the men being drunk, by what accident is not known the ship suddenly was blown up into the air, with 350 Englishmen, besides the French prisoners above-mentioned that were in the hold. Of all which number there escaped only thirty men. . . .[31]

When he suspects any danger, however, Morgan is even able to keep his band sober, as evidenced by his strict enforcement of prohibition during the occupation of Panama.[32]

The outstanding element in this account, then, is not lack of discipline among the pirates, but the savage cruelty of everyone from the captain down.[33] Friars and nuns are used as a fire screen in the attack on Porto Bello; an imbecile is burned alive because he can not tell where the treasure is; prisoners by the dozens, both wounded and sound, are shut in the churches till they starve to death, or are blown up with powder; and the greatest mercy is the order usually issued before an attack, "No quarter!" Much of this material is too horrible to repeat.

Esquemeling seems to have morbid delight in dwelling on the wickedness of his erstwhile companions: "I myself was an eyewitness unto these things here related."[34] The following description is typical of life ashore under the great buccaneer:

. . . they fell to eating and drinking after their usual manner—that is to say, committing in both these things all manner of debauchery and excess. These two vices were immediately followed by many insolent actions of rape and adultery committed upon very honest women, as well married as virgins, who being threatened with the sword were constrained to submit their bodies to the violence of these lewd and wicked men.[35]

On the other hand, distinctly unusual is the attitude of the pirates who "compassionate" the sufferings of a virtuous Spanish lady carried with them as a hostage, until Morgan, having excused himself as best he can, finally releases her unconditionally.[36]

On the credit side should be mentioned the desperate courage cited somewhat illogically by Morgan's apologist as a proof of his virtue.[37] There is something very British in the sound of his speech before Porto Bello where he is reputed to have led the van in person:

If our number is small, our hearts are great. And the fewer persons we are, the more union and better shares we shall have in the spoil.[38]

His men follow him with "inimitable courage." They encourage each other in the face of bullets and cannon balls with the grim joke, "We must make one meal upon bitter things before we come to taste the sweetness of the sugar this place affords." A pirate, wounded by an arrow, pulls it out and fires it back from his own musket.

Esquemeling represents Morgan and his companions as entirely godless. He was obviously shocked at their failure to give any sort of burial to their dead companions and victims although they gathered up the bodies floating after the explosion in order to strip them of valuables. His own attitude is well expressed in his comment on that incident: "This unjust action of Captain Morgan was soon followed by divine punishment."[39]

While Morgan's expeditions were generally successful, those related by Ringrose, although carried on by some of the same men, were not, a situation that may account in part for the difference in discipline. Captain Coxon having become dissatisfied with the criticism made of his command in a recent engagement ("some sticked not to defame, or brand, him with the note of cowardice")[40] withdraws with seventy men, chiefly those who have been instrumental in his election. Captain Sawkins is chosen General. Although he proves a gallant leader,

. . . some of our men being drunk on shore, happened to set fire to one of the houses; which consumed twelve houses more before any could get ashore to quench it.[41]

He is killed in action leading a charge against breastworks at Puebla Nueva, and Captain Sharp succeeds, only to lose sixty-three of Captain Sawkins' followers by desertion. Ringrose is in his sympathies one of these, but decides fewer hardships are involved in staying with Sharp. Not long after the departure of these "mutineers" Captain Cook's crew refused to sail any longer under his command, whereupon "he quitted his vessel . . . determining to rule over such an unruly company no longer."[42] A New England Yankee, John Cox, who has convinced Sharp that he is a relative in order to further his own advancement, is given the command, which carries the Vice-Admiral's place with it, much to Ringrose's disgust, and we hear no more of this mutiny. After an attempt which meets with only medium success, apparently because of ignorance or slackness in carrying out Sawkins' plans, Sharp is deposed according to pirate rule (perhaps this represents good rather than poor discipline since no one is killed, but one wonders how Henry Morgan would have treated such an action), and Watling succeeds. He is killed at Arica and Sharp is restored to his old place; but Watling's followers remain disgruntled, and after a time forty-seven withdraw. In the same campaign the surgeons get so drunk during

the battle that they are of no service to the wounded.[43] At Sam-
ballas all the pirates get drunk, and Ringrose fights a duel with
the quartermaster.[44]

These pirates are not so savage as those under Morgan's command. Although there are a number of comments like, "We stood
out to sea, most of our men being fuddled," there is no suggestion
of torturing prisoners for amusement. Esquemeling is authority
for the statement that Watling caused the defeat at Arica because "he trifled away his time in giving quarter and taking
prisoners upon the breastworks." On the other hand, there is this
record:

> We placed some of these prisoners before the front of our men, when
> we assaulted the castle, just as Sir Henry Morgan did the nuns and friars
> at Porto Bello; but the Spaniards fired as well at them as at us.[45]

Under Coxon the Indian allies are instructed to murder the
prisoners, "for certain reasons which I could not dive into."[46]
Believing that he has been misinformed Watling orders an old
prisoner shot before the attack on Arica, but Sharp, having tried
in vain to prevent the action,

> . . . took water and washed his hands, saying: "Gentlemen, I am clear
> of the blood of this old man; and I will warrant you a hot day for
> this piece of cruelty, whenever we come to fight at Arica."[47]

Faithful prisoners are released, a man suspected of planning to
betray them to the Spanish is merely confined in irons, and
mutineers are ordinarily allowed to go about their business if
they will depart peaceably. There are no accounts of attacks on
women, nor any references to the pirates' relationships with
them. Ringrose comments on a lady found on a Spanish prize;
"In this vessel I saw the most beautiful woman that I ever saw
in all the South Sea;" but they detain only one prisoner, a man.[48]
The carelessness of the pirates about money is mentioned here
as in Esquemeling's account, but those who are always poor are

the ones who dice with their companions: this situation has a bearing on the whole conduct of the voyage since the losers always desire to continue the expedition and the winners are equally desirous of getting safely to some port.

Courage is not stressed so much either. Against the gallant Captains Sawkins and Watling are set the coward Coxon and the fact that the attacks made by the pirates are so frequently beaten off. Perhaps it is discipline rather than courage that is lacking, since the last view we have of Sharp shows him cutting out a French merchantman with a following of sixteen in a rowboat.[49]

There are some traces of piety in Ringrose. In addition to Sharp's melodramatic imitation of Pontius Pilate, the former is represented as believing that Watling's defeat and death are a judgment for the murder. A somewhat involved comment seems to mean that Sawkins threw the dice overboard when he found them in use on Sunday and had the day observed until his death, that then the custom ceased, but was revived at least once under Watling in honor of Sawkins' death.[50] The buccaneers have at least a military ceremony for their dead. Ringrose himself comments:

It was the great mercy of God, which had always attended us in this voyage.[51]

God directed us from following this resolution.[52]

I ought to bless and praise God Almighty for this deliverance.[53]

In general the picture of the men of the Royal Navy as given by Teonge and that of the lawless buccaneers as given by the two literary pirates are sufficiently similar to indicate that the British tar of the Restoration period is very like his Elizabethan predecessor.

Since William Dampier appears with Sawkins in Ringrose's account and again as pilot for Woodes Rogers after his own remarkable expeditions, I shall assume that the sailors he presents do not differ materially from those in the earlier and later works, and shall pass his narratives over rapidly despite their importance for geography and natural history. Some further reference to them will be made in connection with the discussion of Professor Secord's study of Defoe. That Dampier's sailors belong to the true breed is indicated by his references to lack of discipline and to carelessness. It will be remembered that he joined the buccaneers because the entire crew of the ship on which he was a passenger deserted. In another place he comments on Captain Swan's following:

The whole Crew were at this time under a general Disaffection . . . and all for want of Action . . . they grew Drunk and Quarrelsome.[54]

Of the pirates at Manila he says,

. . . near a third of our Men lived constantly ashore, with their Comrades and Pagallies, and some with Women Servants, whom they hired of their Masters for Concubines. . . . For many of them having more Money than they knew what to do with, eased themselves here of the trouble of telling it, spending it very lavishly . . . our Men were generous enough and would bestow half an Ounce of Gold at a time, in a Ring for their Pagallies, or in a Silver Wrist-band, or Hoop to come about their Arms, in hopes to get a Night's Lodging with them.[55]

Courage is indicated by half a hundred forlorn hopes, but there is little piety.

Johnson's pirates have most of the qualities found in Morgan's buccaneers. Low enjoys cutting off the ears and noses of his prisoners and occasionally torturing them to death. Rape is frequently mentioned, and Blackbeard marries fourteen wives. His last desperate fight and death with twenty-five wounds in his body will be considered with the discussion of Cross's pantomime.

Woodes Rogers' sailors are like the others, and those in charge of the expedition recognize it from the beginning by providing twice the usual number of officers to prevent mutinies and to allow for casualties.[56] Even with this foresight there are various murmurings and attempts at rebellion, particularly in connection with rules of which the mariners disapprove. The author stresses the fact that the English sailors are the mutinous ones. They compel a change in the provisions for dividing loot, have to be promised special consideration when ordered on shore duty, and plot almost continually. Captain Rogers admits that he is forced to wink at much, and pardons mutineers on promise of good behavior after a few lashes, given by those suspected of sympathy, and a period in irons.[57] Later he sees to it that the worst offenders are transferred to other ships. Attempted deserters are clapped in irons. Those who steal provisions are given a blow with the cat by every man in the watch. The careless attitude is indicated also:

Our people were very meanly stock'd with Clothes, and the Dutchess's Crew much worse; yet we are both forc'd to watch our Men very narrowly, and punish several of them, to prevent their selling what Clothes they have for Trifles to the Negroes.[58]

The liking for drink is mentioned frequently.

Clothes and Liquor were now excellent Commodity amongst our Ships Company.[59]

The Day was hot and two of our Men finding Liquors in the Houses, got drunk betimes.[60]

But after the capture of Guiaquil only one sailor drinks to excess, a record that Rogers feels is unusual. He generalizes: "Good Liquor to sailors is preferable to Clothing."[61] There is also some indication of amorous disposition. "Our Crew were continually marrying whilst we staid at Cork, tho they expected to sail immediately," but save for an Irish woman and a Dane, neither of whom could understand the other, they "drank their Cans of Flip till the last minute, concluded with a Health to

our good Voyage, and their happy Meeting, and then parted un-
concern'd."[62] He stresses the modesty of the sailors in searching
the Spanish ladies at Guiaquil,[63] insists that they are courteous to
all women prisoners, gives the impression that they leave the
female slaves severely alone, and then reports the death of a
sailor from scurvy and venereal disease.[64] Gambling reaches a
point where the officers have to interfere to prevent the sailors
from losing the necessities of life.[65] Several references are made
also to "abusive language."

Again there are dozens of occasions which must have required bravery, but the commander's comments are usually
grudging:

All the men in general behav'd themselves with great Courage, but like
Sailors could be kept under no Command as soon as the first Piece was
fired.[66]

The commander himself frequently inserts pious ejaculations,
and notes that he had prayers read morning and evening when
possible; but for all that the mariners are anxious to dig up
the burial place of the Spanish under the church floor in order
to secure more loot.[67]

George Shelvocke's *Voyage Round the World* is one long
lamentation at human frailty. Captain Clipperton fails to send
for his wine from Shelvocke's vessel at the convenient time.[68]
The base ingrates in the crew have the audacity to disapprove
of the commander's invention, a superior sort of pump.[69] An
officer, who tries to take comand after a mutiny is suppressed,
is a coward.[70] Shelvocke is in a "melancholy state" because his
ship is ordered around the Horn and is in no condition for the
voyage.[71] The gunner and chief mate become unruly and are
set ashore.[72] Captain Hatley fails to spend the money entrusted
to him for buying supplies to the approval of his superior.[73] Captain Hatley is a bribe taker or a thief! The crew are "indifferent

awkward sailors."[74] Perhaps because tired of nagging, the boat-swain raises a mutiny on the ground that he has not been treated with proper respect, but, says Shelvocke with the first trace of satisfaction so far displayed, "I soon drubb'd them into better manners."[75] The petition of the crew to have the spoils divided is denied, any they mutiny. The Captain of Marines protests against the food allowance at his table; Shelvocke increases it but confines the officer. Captain Hatley, who certainly must have had a glittering eye, believing that the black albatross brings tempestuous winds, shoots it.[76] The boat's crew are cowards. The officers are incompetent. The Marine captain resigns his command temporarily and is set ashore. The crew are discouraged, "damning the South Seas."[77] The crew again attempt to mutiny over division of the spoils. Captain Clipperton's actions are "grossly repugnant to his instructions." "This navigation [is] truly melancholy." The mournful record comes to a climax with the wreck on Juan Fernandez, after which Shelvocke, having seen his worst prophecies justified, cheers up considerably and becomes a gallant leader in a great emergency.

Despite the careless way in which the commander uses the word coward of his followers, they are obviously brave at times. The disgruntled leader himself records their melodramatic resolve "to stand by me and the Gentlemen in *England* with all fidelity . . . as long as they had a drop of blood in their veins"[78] Although they mutiny a few more times after the "Speedwell" is wrecked, and stop work arbitrarily, in the end they build a craft, trade forcibly with the Spaniards for a better one, and get home by way of California and China. The religious note is not struck.

The material on the sailor in the "Wager" cycle may be considered in one division, save that much of the Bulkeley and Cummins account is quoted elsewhere. The same details, are given by Byron and by the anonymous writer. In his preface the

Honorable John emphasizes the fact that although the mariners "appeared as mutineers, they were not actually such in the eye of the law; for . . . the pay of the ship's crew ceased immediately upon her wreck, and consequently the officers authority and command."[79] Captain Cheap says he will be the last to go ashore but cannot compel the drunken boatswain and his party to go, and is at length prevailed upon. Meanwhile, according to the anonymous version, the lieutenant and mate remain ashore against orders. Byron reports that the boatswain and his crew broke open the brandy casks and would not leave the ship "so long as there was any liquor to be got at." Some of them he adds had been "on their knees praying for mercy" a short time before.

It was scarce possible to refrain from laughter at the whimsical appearance these fellows made, who, having rifled the chests of the officers best suits had put them on over their greasy trousers and dirty checked shirts. They were soon stripped of their finery as they had been obliged to resign their arms [as soon as they were sober].[80]

While drunk they kill one of their number and fire a gun at those ashore. As soon as the boatswain reports for duty, the captain knocks him down with his cane.

Whether more blame attaches to the unfortunate Cozens or to Captain Cheap in the episode leading to the former's death and to the latter's deposition, can probably never be determined since all accounts to some extent blame both. The whole disgraceful business reveals how poor discipline was, for surely any properly trained midshipman would have supported his superior regardless of technicalities or competence. Between Bulkeley and the anonymous writer a fairly detailed story is given. Cozens, it seems, is rolling a heavy cask of peas up a steep part of the beach and becomes discouraged; whereat Captain Cheap accuses him of being drunk. "With what should I get drunk, unless it be with Water?" "You Scoundrel, get more Hands, and rowl the Cask up."[81] When no hands come to the call, the captain strikes the midshipman with his cane and orders him confined in the store tent for drunkenness. The commander later visits the prisoner, who complains, "Tho' Shelvocke was a rogue, he was not a Fool; and, by G—d, you are both." The trusty cane is again swung, but the sentry prevents the blow. Cozens is released because he has discovered the brandy in the store tent. He next has a quarrel with the Purser, who bawls out "Mutiny!" and discharges his pistol.[82] The captain, hearing the shot and seeing his enemy, apparently assumes that Cozens has fired at the Purser, and shoots the practically unarmed man through the cheek. One version has it that he leaves the midshipman on the ground to die a lingering death without medical attention, a not impossible action for an officer who considers six hundred lashes too light a sentence.[83] In another, the captain orders the injured man carried to the sick tent, but the surgeon will give no attention to a man known to be his enemy, lest it be said that he has hastened his end.[84] At all events, the victim dies and the murder serves as an excuse for deposing the captain. The whole impression given is that of demoralization in all ranks.

The anonymous version has some vivid bits of dialogue also. Says one of the sailors concerning those who remain behind:

Sink their Body's my Boys, if the silly Sons of Bitches will run to the Devil, what's that to any one?
Aye, by G--d, Jack, your'e [sic] in the Right.[85]

And the steward answers a request about provisions, "G--d d-mn you, now the Commodore is gone, you shall find the Difference."[86] The author comments on the clear day that dawns after the wreck:

You will perhaps imagine it was not without a mixture of Devotion, of Prayers for Safety, or Thanksgiving for Deliverance from Death. Some few Expressions in the Strain indeed were uttered; but our Crew were not void of the infernal Disposition which seems almost connatural with Sailors—so that Oaths and Execrations greatly prevailed.[87]

He also comments on a funeral: "There were no Tears shed . . . for those distil but rarely from the Eyes of Sailors."

In the various accounts there are also evidences of individual courage. All who survive do so after undergoing terrific privations. As Bulkeley says grimly, never before was the Purser of a King's ship known to starve to death.[88] Isaac Morris tells how his group again and again set out across the country after being driven back by need of provisions and bad weather. Reduced to four, with all their arms lost to the Indians, they march sixty miles to secure a rusty musket barrel in order to make a hatchet out of it.[89] And there is something admirable too about that stickler for military etiquette who tells the angry captain he shall not strike prisoner of his.[90] The Honorable John, according to Bulkeley, refuses a hat offered by a servant, with the statement that he thinks he can endure hardships with the rest.[91] Although discipline is bad, there is no suggestion of cowardice.

The comments already made indicate that the mariners are an irreligious lot, and Byron, respresenting the upper class, also reveals no sense of a miraculous preservation. Bulkeley, apparently religious himself, confirms the general godlessness:

At Night Lieutenant Beans Surpriz'd us with a new kind of proposal we little dreamt of, which was, to have a proper Place of Devotion to perform Divine Service in every Sabbath-Day; for this Sacred Office our Tent was judg'd the most commodious Place. The Duty of publick Prayer had been entirely neglected on board, though every Seaman pays Fourpence per Month towards the Support of a Minister; yet Devotion, in so solemn a Manner, is so rarely perform'd that I know but one Instance of it during the many Years I have belong'd to the Navy. We believe Religion to have the least Share in this Proposal of the Lieutenant.[92]

Instead they suspect a plot to deprive them of their arms. Bulkeley, however, later reports that

We call this Harbour the *Port of God's Mercy,* esteeming our preservation
this Day to be a Miracle. The most abandon'd among us no longer doubt
of an Almighty Being, and have promis'd to reform their Lives.[93]

He is a bit kinder to his fellow sailors when he contrasts them
favorably with the Portuguese who give up working their ship
in a storm to vow gifts to saints and call for intercession:

This Sort of Proceeding in time of Extremity is a thing unkown to our
English Seamen; in those Emergencies all hands are employ'd for Preser-
vation of the Ship and the People, and, if any of them fall upon their
Knees, 'tis after the Danger is over. The Carpenter and I . . . begg'd the
People for God's sake to go to the Pumps. . . .[94]

Walter's account of Anson's voyage around the world is a
highly literary production, and many of the details have therefore probably been softened in the interests of dignity. Presumably the crew of the ill-fated "Wager" are not too unlike the
others in the squadron to give a fair picture. The first chapter
complains, in a manner suggesting Shelvocke, of the inefficiency
of the Admiralty in preparing the ships. Supplies and equipment
are inadequate. The whole expedition is delayed until the enemy
knows about it. Instead of the complement of three hundred
able seamen, one hundred and seventy actually report and thirty-
seven of these are in sick bay. A land force of five hundred
amounts to only half that number for, although all are pen-
sioners of Chelsea and therefore invalids, those who can walk
immediately desert.[95] The squadron is held up at Madeira by
contrary winds, whereat there is much grumbling. Then they
are ravaged by the plague, and one of the ships is damaged
by an explosion caused by a spark from a forge. Storms and
scurvy follow. Off the Horn they lose the topman who inspires
Cowper's *The Castaway.*[96] In general one gets a vivid presentation of England's awful way of doing business.

There is no suggestion of poor discipline on board the "Cen-

turion" except occasional grumbling. During a period of short
allowance, a mariner hides the dead body of his brother in a
hammock so that he can draw the latter's share of food.[97] In
the attack on Payta there is considerable looting, but the commodore is able to compel the men to turn over their booty for
proper distribution. In the account of the same campaign appears a certain amount of sailor characterization:

In this march (though performed with tolerable regularity) the shouts
and clamours of three score sailors, who had been confined so long on
shipboard, and were now for the first time on shore in an enemy's country, joyous as they always are when on land, and animated besides in
the present case with the hopes of an immense pillage—the huzzas, I say
of this spirited detachment, joined with the noise of their drums, and
favoured by the night, had augmented their numbers in the opinion of
the enemy, to at least three hundred. . . .[98]

And again, after the town was taken,

. . . the sailors . . . could not be prevented from entering houses which
lay near them in search of private pillage: where the first things which
occurred to them being the cloaths that the Spaniards in their flight
had left behind . . . our people eagerly seized these glittering habits, and
put them on over their own dirty trousers and jackets, not forgetting,
at the same time, the tye or bag-wig and laced hat which were generally
found with the cloaths . . . but those who came latest into the fashion
not finding men's cloaths sufficient to equip themselves, were obliged to
take up with women's gowns and petticoats, which (provided there was
finery enough) they made no scruple of putting on and blending with
their own greasy dress.[99]

Finally it should be remembered that this expedition was essentially a buccaneering one, and that it was marked by ruthless
destruction of lives and property.

Surely a bull-dog courage animates the commander in this
undertaking. Despite his brutality, perhaps an evidence of the
spirit which later abandons Byng to his fate, one must admire

the persistence that drives a crew of invalids around the world, through land fight and sea fight, to the attainment of a satisfactory amount of plunder. Although there is no specific comment on the officers and men, the fact that they could be so driven is a tribute to their spirit. Quite appropriately, although he softens unpleasant details, Chaplain Walter does not picture either himself or his companions as inspired by God to rob and slay the Spaniards. Public opinion was changing; the burning of Payta met with disapproval in England; and, when Anson died in 1762, this last of the buccaneers had outlived the time in which his deeds could be praised unconditionally.

And with the end of the old piratical spirit pretty well came the end of the voyage narrative as a type. Somehow Cook's expedition "undertaken chiefly with a view to observing the transit of Venus over the Sun's disk"[100] strikes a new note. The sailors however continue much as they were pictured earlier. One recognizes the mariner who shoots a native on impulse, contrary to orders,[101] the boatswain's mate who dies of a bottle of rum although it is his usual amount, and the septuagenarian sailmaker who remains constantly drunk at Batavia and is the only member of the crew to escape the plague.[102]

The English tars, whose want of foresight and defiance of danger is notorious, seemed not to entertain the least idea that even sickness would attack a set of men so hardened as they were by different climates.[103]

To introduce any new article of food among seamen, let it be ever so much for their good, requires both the example and the authority of a commander. . . .[104]

Beginning by cheating the Indians, they become so gullible themselves that the natives offer sticks and stones in exchange. Captain Cook entertains the natives with bagpipes and dancing by the seamen. And, as usual,

The sailors . . . like true British seamen, would have cheerfully gone, as they ever have and ever will, wherever they are led.[105]

On that note the discussion of the sailor in the voyage narratives may well end. For over two hundred years the tar appears in the literature of fact as much the same: lawless, amorous, and brave. The following chapters will try to show how this character is modified in literary presentation by the conventions of different ages.

CHAPTER III

THE SAILOR IN FICTION AND DRAMA

1550-1600

In the creative literature of the last half of the sixteenth century nautical incidents increase in frequency. Fiction contains a considerable body of such material, and there is some in drama and poetry. Strangely enough, however, contemporary accounts of voyages contribute almost nothing to what is presumably another manifestation of the same spirit which sends the sea knights out to discover countries, and the increasing interest in maritime matters is expressed in terms going back to the Greek pastoral romances of Heliodorus, Longus, and Achilles Tatius in the fourth century A.D.

Although an extended discussion of these works is outside the field of this study, a few of the generally accepted facts concerning them may be worth recalling. It will be remembered that the term *pastoral* often applied to them is somewhat inappropriate. It is true that they contain idealized shepherds against a background of equally idealized rural life; but in addition they present all sorts of amazing adventures contrary to the spirit of Theocritus and his successors. Historians of Greek literature believe that a good part of this material derives from Greek New Comedy, the lost plays of Menander and Philemon, and, as far as the nautical incidents are concerned, the view is supported by the fact that similar romantic adventures occur in Plautus. Every Latin student remembers how Pyrgopolinices in the *Miles Gloriosus* kidnaps the beautiful courtesan aboard ship and makes love to her while she is in his power. In the first act of *Rudens* Palaestra and Ampelisca try to get ashore from their wrecked vessel in a boat; the former is dashed out but succeeds in making land; and, as each despairs of the other, there is great rejoicing at the reunion. In the Greek romances these and other melodramatic incidents occur: kidnapping aboard ship; shipwreck and miraculous rescue; capture of the ship by pirates; change of identity by the heroine; remarkable reunion; railing at love or marriage followed by love at first sight; and attack by an amorous captain on the heroine. Of course some of these situations are not essentially nautical: from Helen of Troy to the Mann Act, and from Tramtrist to Kipling's "William Parsons that used to be Edward Clay," kidnapping and shifts in identity have been material for literature; but they do occur here against the background of the sea.

Kidnapping aboard ship, which may be a reflection of the ancient Mediterranean custom of indiscriminate capture to maintain the slave trade, can be illustrated by the following incident from Achilles Tatius' *Clitophon and Leucippe.* Callisthenes, having fallen in love at first sight with Calligone, whom he mistakes for Leucippe, sends a boat's crew of men disguised as women ashore to take part in a sacrifice. When the pyre is raised, the sailors give a shout, draw their swords, and attack the worshippers unexpectedly, scattering them easily. The kidnappers seize Calligone and carry her off in their boat.[1] In similar fashion Daphnis and Chloe are separated by Methymnaean pirates and are reunited only by the intervention of Pan.[2]

What I shall call the formula storm may not be a formula at all, but a series of coincidences. It happens that a whole group of tempests in English creative literature parallel to a surprising extent the famous storm in the *Aeneid,*[3] that the storm in *Clitophon and Leucippe*[4] also parallels to some extent the Virgilian one, and that almost none of the actual storms described in the literature of fact resemble the literary ones.[5] The chief elements are (1) good weather; (2) sudden wind and mountainous waves; (3) darkness and a figure of speech suggesting a struggle; (4) deafening noise; (5) fright of the sailors; (6) destruction of rigging, mast, or oars; (7) wreck of the ship. These do not always appear in the same order but are nearly always found together.

Aeneid	*Clitophon and Leucippe*
(1) in altum vela dabant laeti, et spumas salis aere ruebant	the perfect calm we had hitherto experienced
(2) Incubuere mari totumque a sedibus imis/una Eurusque Notusque ruunt et terras turbine perflant	a wind blew upwards from the sea full in the ship's face . . . the billows were now like mountains
(3) Eripiunt subito nubes caelumque diemque Teucrorum ex oculis; ponto nox incubat atra	suddenly overcast by dark clouds and the daylight disappeared
(4) Insequitur clamorque virum stridorque rudentem . . . Intonuere poli	the heaven bellowed with thunder. . . . A confused noise of all kinds arose—roaring of waves, whistling of wind, shrieking of women, the calling of sailors' orders;
(5) Extemplo Aeneae solvuntur frigore membra	arose a great wailing . . . all was full of wailing and lamentation
(6) Franguntur remi	broken planks of the ship
(7) in saxa latentia torquet	drove unexpectedly on to a rock hidden under water, and was utterly broken in pieces

In the examples cited above the formula storm overlaps with the shipwreck and miraculous rescue. The shipwreck itself, as distinct from the storm on the one hand and the rescue on the other, is difficult to discuss because of its universal character; but the presence of the miraculous rescue, and more particularly of the spar rescue, pretty well identifies a given shipwreck with the material from the Greek romances. The spar element is probably derived from the story of Arion and the dolphins, surely an early example of miraculous rescue. The notable thing about it is that the mariner is usually represented as getting ashore *astride* a piece of wreckage. Sometimes he merely clings to it. Sometimes he reaches safety by a tremendous feat of swimming. And sometimes he vanquishes fate in a highly original fashion. Achilles Tatius has an example of the pure spar rescue. After the shipwreck described above, some favouring deity preserves part of the prow, on which Clitophon and Leucippe seat themselves astride. Several of their companions cling to spars but are carried away from them by the waves. The lovers land safely at Pelusium, believing that their friends have been destroyed, and this situation prepares the way for a remarkable union.[6] At the other extreme, a highly original rescue is presented by Longus. When pirates carry off cattle and kidnap Daphnis, Chloe pipes a well known cattle call, the herd rushes to the bulwark, thus capsizing the boat, and Daphnis swims ashore holding to the horns of two cows, while the pirates are drowned by their heavy armor.[7] In most cases some sort of remarkable reunion results from the miraculous rescue, as, for example, the coming together of Clitophon and Clinias after and many adventures following the shipwreck.[8] This incident is part of the stock in trade of the Greek romances.

Sometimes the separation that prepares for the remarkable reunion involves a change in identity, as Daphnis and Chloe are supposedly humble in birth, or as Leucippe calls herself Lacaena during her time as a miserable slave.[9] In the Greek romances, there is usually the motive of ignorance, or desire to be unrecognized, but the reasoning becomes more obscure in later works until characters change their names in Restoration drama for the express purpose of causing confusion.

Whether railing at love or marriage followed by love at first sight belongs to the group of sea incidents is doubtful. In the Greek romances this is represented as taking place on land. Clitophon expresses himself as opposed to love and unsympathetic toward lovers until he meets Leucippe.[10] Theagenes has the same attitude until he mets Chlariclea.[11] Both heroes are landsmen at the time, but in English literature sailors frequently have similar experiences.

Most persistent of all is the episode of the amorous captain. In the *Aethiopica* of Heliodorus, the Phoenician captain of the ship on which the lovers are escaping falls violently in love with Chlariclea and endeavors to force his attentions upon her. A conventional pirate attack prevents matters from coming to an issue.[12] This frustrated love affair is one of the commonest sea incidents of later times.

In his general conclusion that "the influence of Greek romance is variously felt by the chief writers of Elizabethan prose fiction,"[13] Professor Wolff cites some of the incidents referred to above, but naturally does not emphasize their maritime side. The general importance of the subject will be realized when it is noted that as late as the *Post Captain* (1802), which purports to give a realistic picture of "naval society and manners," an English sea novel contains a mildly amorous captain, the remnant of a kidnapping by ship—the lady goes willingly, changes her mind, and, after a pause to frighten her, is duly returned to her husband's ship—three first sight love affairs, and one remarkable reunion.

In analyzing the generalization cited above, Professor Wolff provides us with a method of securing corroboratory evidence that the sea material in Elizabethan fiction is derived from the Greek romances. He states that the various writers feel the influence in different degrees. "Lyly feels it as a tradition of certain conventions of form adapted to the treatment of the theme of Two Friends. . . . Lodge scarcely feels it; Nash feels it not at all. Greene gets from it a quantity of ornament and tinsel, and an abortive impulse toward structure. Only in Sidney does Greek Romance find a talent both receptive and constructive." An examination of the sea material shows that, on the basis of this statement, the amount of such material to be found in any Elizabethan novel is almost directly proportionate to the amount of Greek romance influence.

The third indication that the sea material in Elizabethan fiction comes from the Greek romances is the dangerous one of negative evidence: the absence from the voyage literature of the characteristic Greek sea episodes, and the presence there of suitable incidents that are not used in the novels. This must of course be considered with a great deal of caution.

The usual discussion of Elizabethan fiction recognizes three works as representing separate impulses: Sidney's *Arcadia*, very definitely influenced by the Greek romances; Lyly's *Euphues*, more interested in style, structure, and moralization than in its story; Nash's *Jack Wilton*, realistic and picaresque. As this is not primarily a discussion of the general subject, no attempt will be made to deal with cross influences and conflicting theories. It is enough that there exists a body of prose showing every shade of attitude from extreme romanticism to almost as extreme realism.

Arcadia (*c.* 1580) probably contains the best collection of Elizabethan sea incidents. Kidnapping by pirates, a formula storm, a shipwreck and spar rescue, capture of the ship, a change in identity, a remarkable reunion, and railing at love followed by love, are all to be found here. Pyrocles, having been captured by pirates, is made a prisoner "under board," is armed in an emergency and given a promise of liberty for "well fighting." After a scrimmage with mutineers, he leaps into the sea from the burning ship and is compelled by wounds and weakness to take refuge on the floating mast. He finds his sword caught in the rigging, and kills the pirate captain, after which he is rescued, through a remarkable coincidence, by his friends: "Upon the mast they saw a young man . . . who sat (as on horse back). . . ."[14] This suggests the figure used by Homer in describing the spar rescue of Ulysses after his raft is dashed to pieces. Pyrocles tells the story of his adventures on the mast in vivid but impossible detail:

There I found my sword among some shrouds, wishing I must confess, if I died, to be found with that in my hand, and withal waving it about my head, that sailors might have a better glimpse of me. [He discovers on the mast] the captain, who had been a pirate from youth, and often blooded in it [and who had earlier sworn] with a loud voice . . . that if Plexirtus bade him, he would not stick to kill God himself. "Villain," said I, "dost thou think to over-live so many honest men whom thy falsehood hath brought to destruction?" with that bestriding the mast, I got by little and little toward him after such a manner as boys are wont if ever you saw the sport, when they ride the wild mare. And he perceiving my intention, like a fellow of much more courage than honesty, set himself to resist: but I had in short space gotten within him, and giving him a sound blow, sent him to the fishes.[15]

The formula storm occurs on the journey of Musidorus and Pyrocles.[16] After calm weather a tempest suddenly arises, the sea (1-2) "making mountains of itself, over which the tossed and tottering ship should climb, to be straight carried down again to a pit of hellish darkness . . . cruel blows." (3) "So ugly a darkness . . . usurped the days right." (4) "accompanied sometimes with thunder, always with horrible noises." (6) "shrouds tore . . . with a gastful noise." (5) As morning dawns,

"some sat upon the top of the poop weeping and waling . . .
some prayed: and there wanted not of them which cursed
. . . a monstrous cry begotten of many roaring voices . . ." (7)
The ship begins to go to pieces.
Railing at love, following by love at first sight, is represented
by the affair of Musidorus and Erona.[17]
The same incidents frequently occur in other novels of the
romantic type. Greene uses practically all of them. He represents
the hero of his *Alcida* (1588) as caught in a formula storm on
the way from Tripoli to Alexandria:[18]

(1) . . . when the calme was smoothest, the sea without storme, the skie
without clouds; (2) then *Neptune,* to show he was God of the seas,
and *Aeolus* master of the windes, either of them severally and both of
them coniointly, so conspired, that the first (3) drew a foggie vale over
Phoebus face, that the heavens appeared all gloomie, (2) [continued]
the Trytons daunced, as foreshewing a rough sea : and Aeolus setting his
winds at libertie, hurled such a gale into the Ocean that every surge
was ready to overtake our ship, and the barke ready to founder with
every wave: (4) [missing] such and so miserable was our estate that
we shooke all our Sailes, weighed our Ankers, and let the ship hull at
winde and weather, (5) from our handy labours falling to heartie praiers.
(6) [combined with (7) when after five days the ship is wrecked on the
coast of Taprobane] an Iland situated far South under the pole Antar-
ticke, where *Canapus* [sic] the fairre starre gladdeth the hearts of the
inhabitants : there wee suffered shipwracke, all perishing in the sea, except [miraculous rescue] my infortunate selfe. . . .

It should be added that he has some interesting adventures
with the enchanted Alcida before she is turned into a fountain
at his rescue by an Alexandrian vessel.

In Greene's *Perimedes* (1588) Mariana is shipwrecked and
rescued; later her infant children, having been placed aboard
ship, are captured by pirates. The family is afterward brought together by a remarkable reunion. The desperate Constance drifts
ashore in her open boat to be united with the husband she has
supposed dead. In *Menaphon* (1589) Pleusidippus is kidnapped

by pirates.[19] The king's daughter and her husband are restored to the kingdom as the result of a shipwreck. In *Philomela* (1592) occurs the episode of the amorous captain, who "after his blunt fashion" tries to comfort the sea-sick heroine. Repulsed, he threatens to assault her, but is charmed by her music. He promises to help her, and lodges her with his wife at Palermo until her child is born.[20]

Riche's *Apolonius and Silla* (1581) contains a romantic change of identity in which the heroine dresses in humble garb and seeks to pass for the sister of Pedro, the loyal servant who accompanies her aboard ship. As a result of this descent in the social scale, the captain

. . . beganne to breake with her, after the sea fashion, desiryng her to use his owne cabin for her better ease, and duryng the tyme that she remained at sea, she should not want a bedde; and then, whispering softly in her eare, he saied that, for want of a bedfellow, he hym self would supplie that rome.

When she even refuses marriage, he responds that

. . . from henceforthe I will use the office of my authoritie: you shall knowe that I am the captaine of this shippe, and have power to commaunde and dispose of thynges at my pleasure; and seying you have so scornfully rejected me to be your loiall housbande, I will now take you by force, and use you at my will. . . .

She fools him into thinking she will admit him that night and plans to commit suicide in the meantime; but in the midst of her prayer

. . . there sodainely fell a wonderfull storme [not a formula one, by the way—to occupy the mariner's mind for a day and a night] . . . thei . . . were driven uppon the maine shore, where the gallie brake all to peeces: there was every man providying to save his own life; some got upon hatches, boordes, and casks, and were driven with the waves to and fro; but the greatest nomber were drouned, amongst the whiche Pedro was one; but Silla her self lying in the caben, as you have heard, tooke holde of a cheste that was the captaines, the whiche, by the onely providence of God, brought her safe to the shore.

In the chest she finds money and the captain's clothes. She changes her identity again by dressing as a man and taking service with Apolonius under her brother's name.[21]

Lyly's *Euphues and his England* (1580) is of course less directly affected by the Greek romances than the group of novels belonging primarily to the Arcadian school, but cannot be called realistic. The sea element here is hurried over as if the author resented the convention that bound him.

Thus for the space of eight weeks Euphues and Philautus sailed on the seas, from their first shipping. . . . What tempests they endured, what strange sights in the element, what monstrous fishes were seen, how often they were in danger of drowning, in fear of boarding, how weary, how sick, how angry, it were tedious to write: for that whosoever hath either read of travelling, or himself used it, can sufficiently guess what is to be said. And this I leave to the judgment of those that in the like journey have spent their time from Naples to England; for if I should feign more than others have tried I might be thought too poetical, if less, partial. Therefore I omit the wonders, the rocks, the marks, the gulfs, and whatsoever they passed or saw, lest I should trouble divers with things they know or may shame myself with things I know not. Let this suffice, that they are within a ken of Dover.[22]

Lodge, who according to Professor Wolff "scarcely feels" the influence of the Greek romances, produces two romantic novels with no sea material in them, although *Roselynde* (1590) was written by his own account "in the ocean where every line was wet with a surge, and every human passion counterchecked with a storm," and the *Margarite of America* (1596), in the Straits of Magellan "under hope rather the fish should eate both me writing, and my paper written, then fame should know me." This ironical situation also tends to indicate that sea material did come from the Greek novels and did not come from contemporary experiences.

The absence of nautical incidents from the realistic novels of
Nash, Dekker, and Deloney also indicates that such incidents
are not derived from the voyages of the time. Although the
forerunner of one type of sea novel, and although the work of
men who obviously knew something of maritime matters, this
sort of fiction limits its nautical contribution to a few figures
of speech and an occasional character. The hero of *Jack Wilton*,
despite the opportunities offered by this story for sea adventure,
contents himself with comparing his safety with that of a ship
in harbor, his fall into the cellar of the Jew's house with that of
a man falling "from the oreloope into the hold,"[23] the pitch
soaked garments of John of Leyden's followers with those of
sailors,[24] the feather in his cap with a flag in the fore-top,[25] and
cider at sea with *aqua caelestis*.[26] *Pierce Penilesse* (1592) describes a young waster as going to sea to mend his fortunes, only
to get scurvy and live on dogs, cats, poor John, and Haberdine "without mustard." He tells an anecdote of a mariner who
in a storm vows not to eat haberdine again, and then adds as the
waves die, "not without Mustard, good Lord, not without Mustard!"[27] Variations of this story occur in characterizations of
the sailor through the years.

In Greene's *Notable Discovery of Coosnage* (1591) is an
incident involving Jack ashore.[28] One Mal B. picks up the master
of a ship in Bishopsgate Street and takes him to a tavern where
she and her friends make him tipsy. From there she leads him
to her home, and puts him to bed with a girl. Mal's husband
comes by arrangement (this is of course an Elizabethan example of the well known "badger game") and threatens to call
the constable. In the meantime the victim has been robbed of
his purse, and three links have been broken from the chain of
his whistle—a realistic touch. Frightened at the husband's
threats, the captain goes with him to the tavern, and there pawns
his whistle for more money. He is now allowed to sleep in peace.

He wakes sober, and realizing that he has been fooled, announces
that he serves a great nobleman and will have the rogues punished unless they return all they have stolen. In great fear
they do so, whereupon the captain departs, quoting somewhat
unrealistically, "Fallere fallentem non est fraus."

It will be noticed of course that the sea material in the realistic
fiction is not only less in quantity than that in the romantic
but quite dissimilar to it. If there is any development in the
period 1550-1600, it is to be found in the lessening of nautical
material in fiction with the shift from romantic to realistic, and
the increase of such material in the drama.

Another indication that the sea incidents in Elizabethan romantic fiction are not derived from contemporary experiences
lies in the fact that parallels are not found in the literature of
fact. For example, if the carrying off of some natives of both
sexes be excluded, Hakluyt's only account of the kidnapping
of a woman is that of Macham's discovery of Madeira while
eloping, a story taken from the annals of the King of Arragon.
Equally exotic is Purchas' reference to the witches carried by the
Turks. Among all their gales and shipwrecks, Hakluyt and Purchas together provide only one formula storm, Strachey's *Reportory,* which will be discussed below in connection with Shakespeare's *Tempest.* Even the spar rescue is distinctly hard to find:
it is true that perhaps a half dozen crews either plan to escape
destruction in some such fashion as the sailors of Frobisher's
Anne Francis who "hoped to save themselves on chestes, and
some determined to tie the Hatches of the ships togither . . .
and so be towed with the ship-bote"; or actually attempt it.
The author explains that Frobisher's men would either have
starved or have been eaten by cannibals had they reached shore.[29]
Those who set out ordinarily drown or have to return to the
ship. In no narrative is there a mariner who violates naval training and laws of physics by riding astride a spar. The one actu-

ally successful spar rescue in Hakluyt is effected by twelve men out of fifty carried overboard with a falling mast, who "partly by swimming and other meanes of chestes gote on shore." There is no change of identity, no railing at love, no amorous captain. In short, it is clear that the stock incidents of romantic fiction have nothing to do with actual contemporary sea life as recorded by the voyagers.

The question may be raised whether the literature of fact does not ignore all incidents suitable for romantic story. It surely misses many opportunities for interest, but contains enough material to indicate that some, at least, of the other episodes would have been recorded if they had been at all usual in occurrence. As has been suggested, there are numerous wrecks sans spar, frequent explosions (the fire in *Arcadia* is about the only parallel to this in the romantic fiction, possibly because the material is drawn from a pre-gunpowder age), and rescues more marvellous than anything except the original dolphin story:

For the gally wherein he was, being either dashed against the rockes, or shaken with mighty stormes, and so cast away, after he had saved himselfe a long while by swimming, when his strength failed him, his armes & hands being faint and weary, with great difficulty laying hold with his teeth on a cable, which was cast out of the next gally, not without breaking and losse of certaine of his teeth, at length recovered himselfe, and returned home into his country in safety.[30]

There is even a romantic love story that just misses falling into one of the Greek romance formulas. John Oxnam becomes enamoured of a Spanish lady on a captured ship, and at her pleading frees his prisoners. Or, to pick another example at random, there is the pathetic account of Cornelius Martenson of Schiedam, who, as the ship is about to break up, tells his son

. . . not to take care for him, but seeke to save himselfe; for (sayde he) sonne thou art yong, & mayest have some hope to save thy life, but as for me it is no great matter (I am olde) what become of me. . . .[31]

The father perishes and the son is saved.

Enough has surely been said to indicate that the sea material
in Elizabethan prose fiction 1550-1600 is to be found chiefly
in the Arcadian novels, and is derived generally from the Greek
romances. The few nautical details in the drama of the period
may well come from the same source.

One exception however must be mentioned at once. A thin
trickle of realistic satirical influence deriving ultimately from
Brandt's *Narrenschiff* (1494) through Barclay's *Ship of Fools*
(1509) and possibly affected by Skelton's *Bowge of Court*
(1509) is slowly disappearing. Whether this has any effect on
later sea drama is a question difficult to answer. Hyckescorner
in the morality of that name (a. 1534) makes the sort of entrance later to be identified with the *Tempest* group of plays:
"A-le the helme! a-le! vere! vere! shot of! vera!" whereupon
Frewyll, presumably lest the audience fail to understand, comments, "Cockes body! herke, he is in a shyppe on the see!"
Later Hycke explains that he has been a bawd on a ship of
rogues and has encountered a navy of virtues setting out for
Ireland.[32] The humorous threat of Ralph Simnell, the king's
jester in *Friar Bacon and Friar Bungay* (1589), that he will
transmute Oxford into a ship of fools "like Barclay's Ship," and
carry it off to the Bankside,[33] needs not further comment. Says
Dulcimel in Marston's *Fawn* (1605):

There's a ship of fools going out! Shall I prefer thee, Nymphadoro?
Thou mayest be master's mate. My father hath made Dondolo, captain,
else thou shouldest have his place.[34]

Perhaps Ben Jonson is influenced by this tradition twenty
years later when he speaks of

—a colony of cooks
To be set ashore on the coast of America
For the conversion of the cannibals,
And making them good eating Christians.[35]

At all events there is nothing especially significant in these
scattered references.

In general the drama before 1600 contains little reflection of sea life. Damon and Pythias in the play of that name (1565) are costumed as mariners, but show no other signs of their occupation. There is surely nothing realistic about a master who stops his ship to set a sea-sick passenger ashore and a boatswain as polite as the one who lands Clyomon in *Clyomon and Clamydes* (1570):

Here let them make a noise as though they were Mariners; and after, Clyomon, knight of the G.S., come in with one.
Clyo. (within) Ah set me to shore, sirs, in what country soever we be!
Master. (within) Well, hale out the cock-boat, seeing so sick we do him see.

. . . .

Clyo. Ah, boatswain, gramercies for thy setting me to shore!
Boat. Truly, gentleman, we were never in the like tempests before.[36]

The mariner in Lyly's *Galathea* (1584-88) actually says less about the sea than the three ignoramuses he is trying to instruct. He fears the sea "no more than a dish of water" and uses some technical terms, but does not roar or use nautical oaths. His patience with Raffe, Robin, and Dicke classifies him with the gentle boastwain described above. The pirates of *2 Henry VI* are bloodthirsty and grasping but not individualized as .sailors. Walter Whitmore, the noble pirate, and Petruchio, the heart of oak, will be discussed under another topic.

The Comedy of Errors (1591) contains the spar rescue and remarkable reunion, although it will be remembered that in *Menaechmi* the twins are lost in the crowd at a fair. The shipwreck contains part at least of a formula storm: calm, sudden wind, darkness, and fear. Greene's *Looking Glass for London and England* (*c.* 1594) contains a formula storm also:

> (1) The faire Triones with their glimmering light
>   Smil'd at the foote of cleare Bootes wain,
>   And in the north, distinguishing the houres,
>   The Load-starre of our course dispearst his cleare

When to the seas with blithfull westerne blasts
We saild amain, and let the bowling flie.
(3) Scarce had we gone ten leagues from sight of land,
But, lo, an hoast of blacke and sable cloudes
Gan to eclipse Lucinas silver face;
(2) And, with a hurling noys from foorth the South,
A gust of winde did reare the billowes up.
         . . . [They take in sail]
For, loe, the waves incense them more and more,
(4) Mounting with hideous roarings from the depth
Our Barke is battered by incountring stormes,
And welny stemd by breaking of the flouds.

.   .   .   .

(6) Till all at once (a mortall tale to tell)
Our sailes were split by Bisas bitter blast,
Our rudder broke, and we bereft of hope
(5) There might you see, with pale and gastly lookes,
The dead in thought, and dolefull merchants lift
Their eyes and hands unto their Countries Gods.[37]

Since the ship finally makes port in miserable condition, element 7, the wreck of the ship on a rock, is of course absent from this.

Marston's *Antonio and Mellida* (1599) contains a similar storm in the author's own idiom. Antonio tells how, after a calm departure from port (1):

(2) . . . lo! the sea grew mad
His bowels rumbling with wind-passion;
(3) Straight swarthey darkness popp'd out Phoebus' eye.
And blurr'd the jocund face of bright-cheek'd day;
Whilst crudled fogs masked even darkness' brow:
Heaven bad's good night, (4) and the rocks groan'd
At the intestine uproar of the main.
(6) Now gusty flaws strook up the very heels
Of our mainmast, whilst the keen lightning shot
Through the black bowels of the quaking air;
(7) Straight chops a wave and in his sliftred paunch
Down falls our ship, and there he breaks his neck;
Which in an instant up was belkt again. . . .[38]

Unless hidden in the last involved locution, the fear of the mariners (5) is lacking.

Although this study contemplates discussing in detail only fiction and drama, the meager contribution of Elizabethan poetry may be summarized as part of the background for the present chapter. There are few enough references to the sea and sailors. Those in the historical poems, moreover, have been dealt with so exhaustively by Professor Cawley that any detailed examination is unnecessary. And the sea ballads, the chanteys, of the sailors themselves await a salt-water Dr. Child with a profound knowledge of that special field. What little interest in maritime affairs is expressed, appears in the form of a few panegyrics, some matter of fact records in the historical poems, and comparatively numerous figures of speech. An occasional chantey preserved in a later form, and not recorded until long after the period was over, appears in splendid isolation from the general course of Elizabethan literature.

Two early poems by John Donne, *The Storm* and *The Calm* (*c.* 1597) probably deserve the most attention. Donne was a gentleman volunteer with Essex, and these poems presumably represent the former's actual experience with typical incidents on a long voyage. *The Storm,* however, seems to be influenced by the formula:

> [After calm weather (1)]
> (2) Sooner than you read this line, did the gale,
> Like shot, not fear'd till felt, our sails assail;
> And what at first was call'd a gust, the same
> Hath now a storm's, anon a tempest's name.
> . . . [The next day]
> (3) . . . when I waked, I saw that I saw not;
> I, and the sun, which should teach me, had forgot
> East, west, day, night; and I could only say,
> If th' world had lasted, now it had been day.
> [The figure of speech suggesting struggle between
> sea and sky is missing.]

(4) Thousands our noises were, yet we 'mongst all
     Could none by his right name, but thunder, call

· · · · · · · · · · · · · · ·

(5) . . . some forth their cabins peep,
     And trembling ask, "What news?"
(6) . . . and all our tacklings
     Snapping, like too-too-high-stretched treble strings.
                    [There is no wreck. (7)]

The Calm gives a vivid description, but the sincerity of the presentation is rather weakened by the use of conceits:

> As steady as I could wish my thoughts were,
> Smooth as thy mistress' glass, or what shines there,
> The sea is now. . . .
> As water did in storms, now pitch runs out;
> As lead, when a fired church becomes one spout.
> And all our beauty and our trim decays,
> Like courts removing, or like ended plays.
> . . . in one place lay
> Feathers and dust, to-day and yesterday.

Neither gives any characterization of the sailor.

George Gascoigne, while praising Captain Bourcher of the "Leeland" expedition for demanding his sword as he lay dying, does not even indicate that Bourcher was a naval hero (1575). It is true that at the sight of Cyprus the master's mate "lepte for joye and thanked God,"[39] but the high flown speeches that precede the battle with the Turks have no salt water tang. In *Dulce Bellum Inexpertis* (a somewhat ironical title under the circumstances) Gascoigne reveals the soldier's hostility to the mariner. He complains that the "backward saylers" ran the ship aground so that he missed his share of the spoil.

> Againe at Sea the Souldiour forward still,
> When Mariners had little lust to fight.
>
> · · · · · · · · · · · · · ·
>
> Where boldest bloudes are forced to recule,
> By Simme the boteswayne when he list to frowne,
> Where Captaynes crouch, and fishers weare the Crowne.[40]

In *The Steele Glas* (1576) he ignores the sailor while characterizing nearly every other important walk of life. His Prefatory Epistle to *A Discourse,* etc., by Sir Humphrey Gilbert, and his *Prophetical sonnet on the same subject* are conventional panegyrics lauding Gilbert to the skies as a fifth Neptune in succession to Columbus, Vespucci, and Magellan, without concrete reference to the naval exploits of any of them.

Of the same type is Gervase Markham's dull and wordy *Tragedy of Sir Richard Grinvile* (1595), horribly stuffed with epic similes, allegorical figures, and quotations from Cicero. The author does try somewhat unfortunately, to be historically accurate:

> His fights set up; and all things fit prepar'd
> Low on the ballast did he couch his sick,
> Being fourescore ten, in Death's pale mantle snar'd,
> Whose want to war did most their strong hearts prick.[41]

Fitzgeoffrey's poem on Drake (1596) is so similar that the reference to a poet having "royalized" Grinvile's acts may indicate that the other was the model.

> Great God of prowess, thunderbolt of war,
> Bellona's darling, Mars of chivalrie,
> Bloody Enye's champion, foe-men's feare,
> Fames stately Pharus, map of dignitie,
> Joves pearle, pearles pride, prides foe, foes enemie:
> Spaine-shaking fever, regent of wars thunder,
> Undaunted DRAKE, a name importing wonder.[42]

Despite "a thousand hel-mouth'd cannon" and an equal number of "ratling muskets" in a hyperbolic anticlimax, little real information is conveyed concerning the naval career of the hero. The author's enthusiasm reaches its greatest height at the thought of the treasure brought home "maugre all their beards."

The list of other great seamen from Edward III to Clifford,

although followed by an equally imposing roll of soldiers, may serve as a transition to the next section of the discussion, the historical poems. Even in Drayton there is almost complete lack of interest in the sailor and sea life. An occasional naval battle is recorded, like the one in Deloney's ballad, with the emphasis on the spoil:

> Like lion's fierce they forward went,
>   to quite this injurie
> And bourding them with strong and mightie hand:
> They kild the men until their Arke
>   did sinke in Callice sand.[43]

Long lists of captains and countries make dull reading. In most cases they represent Hakluyt and his contemporaries abridged until what little human interest appeared in the original is lost entirely.

That the fairly numerous figures of speech derived from the sea have any significance for this study may be doubted. Most of them are conventional: Renaissance poetry in all languages is full of them. And Professor Cawley's study indicates that most figures derived from the English voyagers actually deal with the new countries rather than with the sea. Moreover Lois Whitney's *Spenser's use of the Literature of Travel in the Faerie Queene*,[44] despite the implication of the first part of the generalization that "there are scattering and fragmentary references throughout the Faerie Queene to the voyages of the sixteenth century seamen, to the countries new found by them, and to curious and interesting facts about the inhabitants," goes on to show that the large majority of those references could have come from the medieval fabulous voyages as well. There are of course some well known exceptions, e.g. "fruitfullest Virginia."

The chanteys await a thorough study by a scholar trained in that field. The various collections of sea songs are usually edited from a topical point of view with no attempt to show development.[45] *Sir Patrick Spens, The Wreck of the Hesperus,* Stephano's song of "The Master, the swabber, the boatswain, and I," and *Rule, Britannia* are likely to be presented as if examples of very much the same thing. Furthermore, the true chanteys are usually discussed in terms of the sort of activity they were intended to aid, as hoisting, pumping, furling sails, etc. Almost unintelligible to the landsman, these poems did not influence literature ashore until the development of the musical sea play two hundred years later. Like the other poetry, they are not significant in the Elizabethan period.

The characterization of the sailor in the Greek romances is generally unfavorable. He is represented either as a pirate of the most bloodthirsty sort, or as a coward. In the former rôle he probably comes from the rovers who infested the Mediterranean as far back as Homer, who played a considerable part in the life and death of Greek city-states, who cut off the Roman grain supply, and who were thereupon suppressed by Cneius Pompey. In the latter rôle he is probably influenced by the slaves who were used as mariners in Greek and Roman times. Sometimes the two personalities are combined, as in the ruthless fight over the boats in *Clitophon and Leucippe*. Obviously these characterizations are carried over into Elizabethan fiction with the incidents, so that the noble pastoral hero, who is only incidentally a sailor, appears against a background of brutal, lustful, and sometimes cowardly mariners, as in *Arcadia* and *Perimedes*. The crew who abandon the ship in the *Comedy of Errors* are of the same stripe.

Traces of two other characterizations appear in this period: one is the noble pirate, true ancestor of Byron's mildest mannered man; and the other, the heart of oak. The former perhaps grows from the combination of the pastoral hero with the

Elizabethan sea knight; and the latter, from actual acquaintance
with the robust virtues of the real old salt. Walter Whitmore
in *2 Henry VI*, although he has Suffolk beheaded and the body
left in a most barbarous fashion without burial, claims gentility
and policy as reasons for his procedure:

> I lost mine eye in laying the prize aboard,
> And therefore to revenge it thou shalt die;
> And so should these, if I might have my will.

Suffolk having proclaimed himself a gentleman, Whitmore continues:

> And so am I; my name is Walter Whitmore.
>
> .   .   .   .
>
> Never yet did base dishonour blur our name,
> But with our sword we wip'd away the blot;
> Therefore, when merchant-like I sell revenge,
> Broke be my sword, my arms torn and defac'd
> And I proclaim'd a coward through the world.[46]

He leaves to his lieutenant the actual dirty work of the execution. The "Marriners in sea-gownes and sea-caps" of *King Leir*
(*c.* 1594) are such cheerful rascals in the assertion, "a good
sheeps russet sea-gowne, will bide more stresse I warrant, then
two of his royal cloaks," that one cannot refrain from liking
them. At the suggestion of trading back, one of the sailors vir-
tuously insists that a bargain is a bargain: "Nay, if I do, would
I might ne'er eate powderd beefe and mustard more, nor drink
Can of good liquor whilst I live."[47]

And Petruchio, who like so many of the Elizabethan universal geniuses, has obviously been a sailor, is the nearest to a heart
of oak before 1600. Of course he is acting a part, but where
could he have learned it save on the sea? His general characterization at once suggests the sailor:

> HORATIO   . . . What happy gale
> Blows you to old Verona?

PETRUCHIO   .   .   .   .
    Have I not in my time heard lions roar?
    Have I not heard the sea, puff'd up with winds
    Rage like an angry boar chafed with sweat?
    Have I not heard great ordnance in the field
    And heaven's artillery thunder in the skies?[48]

.   .   .   .

KATHARINE   .   .   .   .
    A madcap ruffian and a swearing Jack [not nautical]
    That thinks with oaths to face the matter out
.   .   .   .
                                        [49]

Furthermore the description of his conduct at the wedding tallies pretty well with the usual conception of the bluff old salt ashore:

GREMIO   . . . when the priest
    Should ask, if Katharina should be his wife,
    "Ay, by gogs-wouns!" quoth he; and swore so loud,
    That, all amaz'd, the priest let fall the book

    .   .   .   .

    But after many ceremonies done
    He calls for wine; "A health!" quoth he; as if
    He had been aboard, carousing with his mates
    After a storm; quaffed off the muscadel
    And threw the sops all in the sextons face

    .   .   .   .

    This done, he took the bride around the neck
    And kiss'd her lips with such a clamorous smack
    That at the parting all the church did echo:
    .   .   .   .
                                        [50]

The conclusions based on this examination of the sea material in the creative literature of the period from 1550 to 1600, are that most of the incidents in fiction are derived from the Greek romances, that the same thing is true to a lesser extent in the drama, and that what material there is in the poetry belongs to a special study outside the scope of the discussion. Moreover the characterization of the sailor in fiction and drama is probably derived from the Greek romances also, although one or two examples of the noble pirate and the heart of oak can be found.

Chapter IV

THE SAILOR IN THE DRAMA

1600-1642

From the turn of the century to the closing of the theaters
the sailor appears chiefly in the drama. Part of the nautical material continues the Greek romance tradition and part of it is
derived from the voyage narratives or from actual mariners encountered by the playwrights. For example, it is usually assumed, on the basis of source studies, that *Twelfth Night* goes
back to the Greek novels through *Apolonius and Silla* and other
Elizabethan romances; but the same conclusion might surely
be arrived at on the basis of the shipwreck story alone:

> . . . after our ship did split,
> When you and those poor number saved with you
> Hung on our driving boat, I saw your brother
> Most provident in peril, bind himself
> Courage and hope both teaching him the practice,
> To a strong mast that liv'd upon the sea;
> Where, like Arion on the dolphin's back,
> I saw him hold acquaintance with the waves
> So long as I could see.[1]

The remarkable reunion following Viola's change of identity indicates that Shakespeare never derived this shipwreck from an
old sailor. On the other hand, it will be remembered that Mal-
volio smiles his face into more lines than the new map of the
world "with the augmentation of the Indies," an almost certain
reference to the 1600 edition of Hakluyt.

The convenient method of discussing the sea drama of this

period seems to be to divide it somewhat arbitrarily into a group
of plays presenting at least one scene at sea, and a group containing only a sailor or sailors ashore. Since most of the first
division have similarities to each other and to Shakespeare's
Tempest, I shall call it the *Tempest* school; and since most of
those of the second division use the methods of Ben Jonson in
characterizing the sailor, I shall call that group the humours
school. Neither of these terms, however, necessarily implies borrowing among the members of the respective groups. The continuation of the Greek romance influence is almost entirely in the
former.

Shakespeare's *Pericles* presumably derives ultimately from
the lost third or fourth century Greek novel that is supposed to
be the source of the *Gesta Romanorum* story.[2] Twyne's translation of the latter presents the shipwreck of Pericles at Pentap-
olis as containing a formula storm and a spar rescue. The play
contains a miraculous rescue and remarkable reunion besides
a fragment of formula storm in the surges that "wash both
heaven and hell." But the romantic throwing overboard of the
supposedly dead queen in deference to nautical superstition
is combined with some traces of the real Elizabethan sailor:

1 SAILOR Slack the bolins there! Thou wilt not, wilt thou?
          Blow, and split thyself.
2 SAILOR But sea-room, an the brine and cloudy billow kiss
          the moon, I care not.
1 SAILOR Sir, your queen must overboard. The sea works high,
          the wind is loud, and will not lie till the ship be clear'd
          of the dead.
PERICLES That's your superstition.
1 SAILOR Pardon us, sir; with us at sea it hath been still
          observed; and we are strong in custom. Therefore briefly
          yield her; for she must overboard straight.[3]

This is a scene actually at sea with at least one technical command, reckless courage, and a gruff attitude toward landsmen.

Roughly contemporary with *Pericles* is Heywood's *Fortune by Land and Sea* (*c*. 1607) which is placed here not because of any indebtedness to the Greek romances, but because it makes use of actual voyage material, and shows a scene on shipboard as does *The Tempest*. The play is based on a pamphlet dealing with the piracies of Clinton and Purser.[4] Act IV opens aboard the pirate ship, which has just taken a prize. In rather awkward exposition, Clinton commands his men to make merry with the spoil, explains that he attacks English ships only because he has been proclaimed an outlaw, and defends himself in good Falstaffian fashion:

> We know we're pirates and profess to rob;
> And would'st not have us freely use our trade?

Scene 2 is aboard a privateer where Young Forest, a landsman, has been chosen captain on the death of the former captain, although he protests that he has had too little naval experience. There is a suggestive scene of technical language conflicting with blank verse:

> YOUNG F. Climb to the main-top, boy [.] See what you ken there!
> BOY I shall, I shall, sir.
>
> .   .   .   .
>
> BOY (above) Ho there!
> MARINER Eh, boy?
> BOY A Sail
> MARINER Whence is she?
> BOY That I cannot ken. She appears to me out of our hemisphere
>   no bigger than a crow.
>
> .   .   .   .
>
> BOY Boatswain, ho!
> 1 MARINER Whence comes thy ken
> BOY She makes from south to west.
> 2 MARINER How bears she?
> BOY To the leeward.
> YOUNG F. Clap on more sail, and quickly fetch her up.
>   What colours bears her maintop?

BOY She's not so near in ken.
YOUNG F. Discover her more amply.
          Now my mates,
          Prepare yourselves; for it may be some prize.
     You master Gunner, load your ordnance well,
     And look well to your cartridges and fire:
     See that your gunner room be clear and free,
     Your matches bear good coals, your priming powder
     Pounded, not dank. Next charge your murderers
     For fear of boarding. Steersman, Port the helm. . . .
          And, Master, you
     Heed well your compass. Boatswain, with your whistle
     Command the sailors to the upper deck,
     To know their quarters and to hear their charge.

The preparations of the other ship are described in great detail by Young Forest. During the action the scene shifts back and forth between the two vessels. When Clinton complains of his gunner's marksmanship in shooting high with his upper tier of guns, the latter replies that he pierced them with the "chace piece." The privateersmen capture the pirate ship by boarding. There follows a philosophical and moralizing discussion on the fate of the pirates and the division of the spoils. The part taken from the captured merchantman is restored to him when it develops that he is the brother of Young Forest's sweetheart (remarkable reunion). The last scene shows the pirates at Execution Dock, resolving to die as befits brave seamen. They joke with the hangman about the rope, and express a sense of their own superiority. They prophecy that many other noble captains will die at Execution Dock.

In the thick of the fight, Young Forest makes a comment that is similar to one in *The Tempest* and that is to appear in one form or another in many following plays. Whether this had some influence on Shakespeare's boatswain and thence on the others, or whether all of the group of speeches are derived from the superstition mentioned by Overbury and Ward, is hard to say.

> 1 MARINER Where is the gunner, captain?
> YOUNG F. Where he should not be.
>   At his pray'rs, I think.
>   Is this a time to pray, when the sea's mouth
>   Seems to spit fire; and all the billows burn?[5]

The chief justification for including *Fortune by Land and Sea* in this group of plays lies in the fact that it does very poorly what *The Tempest* does well.

Daborne's *Christian Turn'd Turk*, published the year after *The Tempest* is thought to have been written, and possibly produced later than the latter, is based on some pamphlets dated 1609 and some undated ballads of about the same time. These, it should be mentioned, do not account for all the incidents in the play, even allowing for such elaborations as the evolution of Ward's going through the ceremony of becoming a Mohammedan from the figurative statement, "Christians are turned Turks." This play is a long rambling production of the early Elizabethan type, with suggestions of Marlowe in the brimstone rant of the superhumanly wicked Ward and in the character of the Jew. The elements of the *Tempest* school are present.

In the story of Alizia's disguising herself as a sailor when she attempts to escape the pirates (change of identity), and perhaps also in her death when she discovers that her lover has been killed, is surely a trace of the Greek romance influence. Gismond, like Clinton, is a noble pirate:

> How dare I sir? [Advocate mercy to the captives]
>   I am a Gentleman
> Equall unto your selfe.[6]

There are a number of scenes aboard ship, but the most vivid is the one in which Gismond sights the French vessel.

> GISM. *Hoy*, of whence your ship, and whither are you bound?
> DAVI. We are of *Marcelles*, bound for *Normandy*.
>   Of whence are you?

GISM. We are of the Sea.
SAIL. The Divel land you.
GISM. Bring your maister a boord, or wee'l give you a broad side.

. . . .

GISM. The curs are asleepe, wee'le waken 'em,
  Gunner give fire.
LEMOT. In their owne language answere them.
GISM. Zounds do they beginne to prate, have with you, lace the netting,
  let downe the fights [sic!], make ready the small shot, gunner,
  give them a broadside, wee'le prate with 'em, A starre board there.[7]

There is just a suggestion of the heart of oak in Gismond's
elegiac comment,

. . . S'foot we shall share the more sir,
I alwaies thought Fortune had markt him out to dye by the French.
He had so much of the English spirit in him.

Ward uses a special ceremony in drinking to the dead pirates,
suggestive of Claudius in *Hamlet:*

. . . and every draught
The Cannon makes report off, a Frenchman
Shall over-board, who to our friends may tell,
We drank a rowse to them.[8]

The bibliography of articles dealing with *The Tempest* is
surely long enough without any repetition of matters already
discussed and rediscussed. In general, the conclusion expressed
by Professor Cawley, that Strachey's *Reportory* and some other
voyage accounts are the chief sources for the shipwreck and
landing, are entirely acceptable.[9] On the other hand, if this play
is to be considered as a type of nautical drama, some analysis
should be made with that purpose in view. In the first place, no
one can doubt that, owing to Shakespeare's commanding position through a large part of the time since his death, *The Tempest* has had considerable influence, whether recognized or not,
on practically every author of romantic sea drama. When then
did it have to contribute? Probably the most noticeable element

is the one derived from the Greek romance tradition: a ship is
wrecked by a formula storm; the company are scattered and
saved miraculously; the survivors are reunited on a desert island.
All this might well have been taken from Achilles Tatius. Then
there are a series of realistic details borrowed from the voyagers,
but carried through such a sea change that they are almost un-
identifiable. Last, there is the scene on the doomed ship that,
when all is said and done, cannot be derived in the form in
which it appears from Strachey. Each of these elements will be
considered in turn.

In the claim that the shipwreck, rescue, and reunion follow
the Greek romance episodes, too much must not be asserted.
It is true that Strachey's *Reportory* indicates that the incidents
actually took place in connection with the Gates wreck. The
first three parallels that Professor Cawley quotes immediately
suggest the formula storm: (1) *Figure of contest between sea
and sky;* (2) *Desperation of crew and passengers;* (3) *Condition of ship.* (4) *Personnel, and relations between classes on
board* contains a realistic rather than a romantic note. (5) *Ariel
and St. Elmo's fire* is not far from the lightning so frequently
present in the formula storm as contrast with the blackness of
heaven. (6) *Prospero and safe landing* is compared with the
praise to the Almighty in Strachey's account, and surely with
equal appropriateness may be compared with the miraculous
rescue in the Greek romance. The last three elements, *Harbour,
Sounding,* and *Miscellaneous* are probably realistic. Considerably over half the material in the *Reportory* therefore conforms
to this romantic tradition despite the fact that scarcely any
other storm in the voyage narratives does so, not even the variation of the same one. The implication is fairly obvious. "William Strachy, Esq.," a gentleman of education, after what was
probably one of the great events of his life, sat him down to
do justice to it in what Purchas calls "a pathetical and retorical

description;"[10] that he was writing at ease with attention to literary effect is indicated by his long philosopical commentary on how much worse death appears at sea than on land; and that he had the classics in mind is shown by the quotation with which he ends this discussion:

> Hostium uxores, puerique caecos
> Sentiant motus orientis Haedi, &
> Aequoris nigri fremitum & trementes
> Verbere ripas.

What is more natural then than that he should call on the details of the formula storm, with which he must have been familiar in Virgil and the various Elizabethan romances, for the verbiage to deck out a story already sufficiently similar to suggest that procedure? Professor Cawley's comment[11] that the figure of a struggle between sea and sky does not occur in the other accounts, but appears in this and frequently in Shakespeare, merely indicates that Strachey and Shakespeare were familiar with the formula storm. It is reasonable to assume then that, while the storm in *The Tempest* did come from the voyage, the voyage from which it came is one owing a great deal to the Greek romance tradition. This hypothesis would account for the attempts to derive the shipwreck in *The Tempest* from *Pericles*, from Spanish romantic stories, from Erasmus' *Colloquia*,[12] and from many other sources, all indebted to a considerable extent to the formula storm.

Shakespeare's version, as is to be expected since he was not limited by actual facts, conforms even more closely to the Greek romance tradition. Practically all the elements of the formula storm are present.

1. [The calm or good weather is implied in Prospero's claim that he caused the storm by magic.]
2. the sea, mounting to the welkin's cheek,
3. Dashes the fire out.

4. A plague upon this howling. They are louder than the weather or
our office.
5. All lost! To prayers, to prayers! All lost!
6. We split, we split!
7. A brave vessel. . . .
Dash'd all to pieces![13]

Following this, we have a fairly conventional scattering of the
ship's crew and passengers, and a miraculous rescue through the
intervention of Prospero. An indication that Shakespeare here
had in mind the romantic formula rather than Strachey's
account, is that a butt of sack thrown over merely to lighten
ship in the latter, becomes the means of a spar rescue for
Stephano.[14] On the desert island, a remarkable reunion takes
place with great rejoicing. In the search for specific sources,
the influence of a general tradition has, I believe, been neglected.

What happens to the realistic details mentioned in the intro-
ductory paragraph is indicated by the use made of the butt of
sack. Bits of language and incident are passed through the
magic synthesis of the master and appear as part of the general convincing effect of the fairy story. Mr. Cawley has sur-
veyed the field of these parallels with great thoroughness. How
far Shakespeare's successors of lesser genius were able to use
the method, is doubtful: further discussion is therefore unnecessary.

The realistic presentation of action aboard ship, with which
the play opens, is still a field for source study; and, since this
scene becomes an essential part of later romantic sea drama, is
an important one. As presented here, the scene has some interesting parallels to the one in *Pericles:* (1) technical nautical commands; (2) reckless courage, in this case expressed partly in resentment that praying should interfere with the working of the
ship, although later, when all is lost, there is a call to prayers;
(3) insistence on the sea custom that the mariners on duty
outrank the highest landsmen; (4) a suggestion that all sailors

are drunkards, and that the boatswain at least is a pirate: all this on board a ship in a storm. The outstanding figure is the old sea dog that Professor Thorndike has christened "the swearing boatswain." If the *Pericles* elements are subtracted from this longer scene, it is chiefly the boatswain that is left, and he has most of the characteristics of the other mariners individualized. It looks almost as if Shakespeare has taken what he was beginning to regard as the normal naval scene, and has intensified it by adding a realistic figure—sprung full tarred from the master's head. The analysis may, therefore, be made in two parts: the scene aboard ship; and the swearing boatswain.

A careful examination has revealed no scene prior to *Pericles*, except *Hyckescorner*, opening with technical commands, although there is some indication that sea terms are an outstanding element in any landsman's conception of the mariner, as, for example, in the comments made in Overbury, *Galathea*, and *Westward Ho*. From Smith's *Accidence for Young Seamen* (1626-1627), Boteler's *Six Dialogues about Sea Service* (*c.* 1634), and the occasional term appearing in creative literature, not to mention the fact that many nautical words of today are obviously of ancient derivation, it is clear that there was a technical vocabulary among Elizabethan sailors; surely any landsman making a sea voyage or listening to a sea tale must have been impressed by it. For want of other evidence the credit for popularizing it on the stage goes to Shakespeare. (Incidentally it should be noticed that too much must not be made of this introduction of naval commands: Shakespeare does not represent his boatswain as using sea language figuratively in his cursing the landsmen; i.e., this worthy mariner is not necessarily the prototype of the "shiver-my-timbers" tar.) The commands concern an emergency, an attempt to keep the vessel off a rocky shore in the face of a terrific storm: the suggestions for this scene in Strachey are quite general and do not contain the essential nautical touch. "Prayers . . . [are] drowned in the outcries of the Officers,"[15] but the orders are not described; the Governor and the Admiral help with the pumps when a leak is discovered (why does Shakespeare omit this intensifying detail?), but the commands or entreaties are not recorded; the most vivid technical detail, that six or eight men are required to hold the tiller if the ship carries "only a Hollocke," or half forecourse, is not used by Shakespeare. The reference to the "drunkards," Mr. Cawley thinks, may have come from May's *Briefe Note*,[16] as the suggestion that the sailors are intoxicated does not appear in Strachey. I am inclined to suggest another possibility. Early in *Damon and Pithias* the two friends come in "like mariners," Pithias complains of seasickness due to the unusually contrary winds, and a servant named Stephano grumbles:

> Not far hence! A pox take these mariner knaves!
> Not one would help me carry this stuff.
> Such drunken slaves
> I think be accursed of the gods' own mouths.[17]

At all events whether derived from Strachey, from a sea tale, from a lost sea grammar, from an earlier play, or from a magic synthesis of many sources, this scene aboard a vessel at sea becomes a frequently present element in romantic sea drama after *The Tempest*.

The swearing boatswain has been praised as the perfect type of old sea dog, heart of oak, old salt, etc. Surely his characteristics are worthy of examination. The only suggestion of his appearance is that he has a hanging face. He resents praying that drowns out the orders. He has little respect for land authority. He does not fear the tempest. By one interpretation, he resents praying even at the point of death. As has been pointed out above, he does not use the nautical profanity later to be typical of the stage tar. Of this sturdy figure there is no trace in Strachey; there is just a bit of him in *Pericles;* if Stephano in *Damon and Pithias* is of any significance, the gruffness of that worthy may have contributed. A careful investigation has brought up no entirely similar figure in the voyage narratives. Yet, after reading dozens of them, I have the feeling that he is there in the actual sea life, obscured by lack of interest in his occupation, scattered a detail at a time many accounts apart, but still recognizable. On that basis I am forced to conclude that this figure probably represents an actual type familiar to Shakespeare, here individualized by the hand of the master dramatist.

The *Custom of the Country* (1619?) continues the Greek romance kind of story without presenting a vivid scene at sea. Leopold and his pirates capture Zenocia after a hard fight in the harbor, all this described in pre-*Tempest* fashion by an eyewitness. Some of the sailors escape by swimming, waving their swords like Pyrocles.[18] Later, as usual, everyone is safely reunited. None of the characters is sufficiently nautical to make further study worth while.

Fletcher's *Sea Voyage* (c. 1622) shows considerable influence of *The Tempest*, exaggerated almost to burlesque. G. A. Jacobi has pointed out that the plot comes from Chapter LII cf William Warner's *Pan his Syrinx*, which in turn, through Ariosto, goes back to the classical story of Hypsipyle of Lemnos: this history accounts well enough for the presence of Greek romance elements in Fletcher's plot.[19] Herr Jacobi also summarizes the attempts of other critics, notably Dryden and Dyce in England, to show the extent of the influence of the storm scene in *The Tempest*. The question of whether Fletcher's island comes from Warner or Shakespeare is of no great importance to a discussion of the growth of the naval play: the significant thing is that *The Sea Voyage* is a later play making use of essentially the same dramatic elements as *The Tempest*, and therefore presumably carrying on the same school. The opening storm has suggestions of the formula:

> . . . the Sea grows dangerous,
> How it spits against the clouds, how it capers,
> And how the fiery element frights it back,
> There be Devils dancing in the air I think
> I saw a Dolphin hang i'th horns o'th'moon
> Shot from a wave. . . .
> See, what a clap of Thunder, there is,
> What a face of heaven, how dreadfully it looks![20]

It later develops that the ship has five leaks, that her rudder is almost gone, and that her ribs are broken. In desperation the ship's company jettison the entire lading, much against the will of some of the passengers. Then they land on the desert island where they find two maroons and much treasure. The two unfortunates, wiser than Ben Gunn of glorious memory, use the gold to start a squabble among the sailors and passengers, and escape with the ship. When food runs out, the surgeon and passengers plan to eat Aminta, the heroine, whose presence they believe has caused the storm; Albert, the pirate leader, defends her and, although he has kidnapped her in good Greek romance fashion, wins her love in the end. The two maroons come back with Raymond, Aminta's brother, with whom of course she has a remarkable reunion. When all have sold their liberty to the Amazons for food, Aminta attempts to pass as Albert's sister since the queen loves him. And there is the inevitable happy ending.

Along with this Greek romance plot are details that indicate the *Tempest* influence. In the first place several echoes occur here that are not essential and are not found in later plays of the same group. The greeting of the maroons by the newcomers is similar to that of Caliban by Stephano,[21] and the former say that they must seem "monsters." The constant squabbles among the various parties ashore also suggest the divided counsels of Prospero's island. Sebastian's description of the island, although the details differ, is not too far removed in spirit from Caliban's account of how he greeted Prospero.[22] Tibalt refers to the passengers who wish to devour Aminta as "damn'd Canibals."[23] Her awakening in the nick of time is like that of Alonzo.[24] The "Horrid Musicke" suggests the beautiful music that surprised Stephano and his followers.[25] All this is of no importance save to show how much influence the earlier play had on the later one.

A comparison of the two storm scenes makes any doubt that the latter comes from the former hypercritical. Act I, Scene 1, opens with the stage direction, "A Tempest, Thunder and Lightning Enter Master and two Sailors." Omitting the formula storm quoted above, we have left:

> Lay her aloof . . .
> How she kicks and yerks!
> Down with the Main Mast, lay her at hull,
> Farle up her Linnens and let her ride it out.

A mariner complains that, "She'll never brook it Master," and another comments unfavorably on the look of the sky. At once the master turns on him with language copied from the boatswain:

> Thou rascal, thou fearful rogue, thou hast been praying;
> I see't in thy face, thou hast been mumbling,
> When we are split you slave; is that a time,
> To discourage our friends with your cold orizons?

A rather colorless boatswain is introduced apparently for the purpose of realism: he does assert the importance of seamen on duty by directing the jettison of the cargo. But it is the master who continues to show the qualities identified with the lower office in *The Tempest*:

> . . . Peace woman,
> We ha storms enough already; no more howling.
> . . . Clap this woman under hatches.

To her appeal for a promise of safety, he replies, "Am I a God?" and to Tibalt's suggestion that a boat be launched he responds, "You are too hasty, Monsieur." He threatens to resign his direction of the ship if Albert will not carry Aminta below: his gruffness to her at this time grows from his belief, suggestive of the sailors in *Pericles*, that the "sweet sin-breeder" causes the storm by her presence aboard. The boatswain however has some sympathy for the damsel in distress: "Yet save some little Bisket for the Lady. . . ." Since the whole crew are pirates, there is no significance to the master's being one. No reference to drunkenness is made in the first part of the play and, as in *The Tempest*, the mariners rather fade out after the beginning. However, their rough and ready qualities are passed over to a Petruchio-like roaring blade, Tibalt du Pont, who becomes the life of the party thereafter. Toward the end there is the stress on drinking so usual in nautical plays. Says Tibalt to the master:

> Hast thou liv'd at Sea
> The most part of thy life, where to be sober
> While we have Wine aboard, is capital Treason;
> And dost preach sobriety?[26]

In addition to the qualities suggesting the Shakespearean mariner, one or two other characteristics belonging to the sailor of the time are stressed: the master is old but loves "the game," and is so tough that he plans to live on "Tarts of Tarr" when provisions run out.

Fletcher's use of the *Tempest* formula then was to adopt a still more complicated and romantic story, to heighten all the details as much as possible, and still to stay close enough to his model so that point after point may be recognized. His perhaps slightly earlier *The Double Marriage* (1620?) shows what may be a transition form. Act II, Scene 1, is on board a ship, this time not in a storm. A boatswain and that other chief petty

officer, a gunner, enter, and the former, amid a rather poorly
described setting, shouts some commands:

> Lay her before the wind; up with your Canvase,
> And let her work. . . .
>
> . . . .
>   Ho, below there:
> Ho, ho, within.
> Lay her North-east, and thrust her missen out. . . .

The boatswain gives high praise to the pirate captain (an
exiled duke; Prospero become an enemy of society?) "so fear-
less, and so fortunate"; and the gunner praises the warlike Martia for manning the guns. The boatswain explains:

> . . . cheerily, cheerily boys,
> The ship runs merrily, my Captain's melancolly,
> And nothing cures that in him but a Sea-fight:
> I hope to meet a sail boy, and a right one.
>
> . . . .
> To th' Main top, Boy.
> And thou kenst a ship that defies us,
> Here's Gold.

The gunner also shows reckless courage:

> Let the worst come,
> I can unbreech a Cannon, and without much help
> Turn her into the Keel; and when she has split it,
> Every man knows his way, his own prayers,
> And so good night I think.

Instead of storm and shipwreck there is an attempt to present
a sea fight with the technical commands for firing a broadside
and capturing the enemy by boarding. This is much less successful than the nautical scenes in the *Sea Voyage*. Again, the
whole crew are pirates, so that there is no special point in the
stress on their lack of scruples. But the boatswain's attempt to
cure a swimming in the head by "a thousand pils of Sack, a

thousand; a thousand pottle Pills"[27] sounds natural. After the sailors get ashore in their attempt to avenge the duke, they become somewhat ridiculous, almost in the Jonsonian fashion, as additional fun for the audience. The romantic elements here are not important: there is a suggestion of change of identity in the duke's becoming a pirate, love at first sight between Martia and the prisoner (and Martia is no lover of love before), and a suggestion of kidnapping aboard ship in their elopment together in the long boat. But the more conventional details are missing.

Killigrew's *The Prisoners* (1640) continues the *Tempest* school in the direct line. The story is long and complicated. Cecilia, sister of the king, is kidnapped aboard the galley of Gallipus who loves her (kidnapping aboard ship). Pausanes and Hiparchus, "the prisoners," followers of the pirate, help rescue her when the latter threatens force (amorous captain); Pausanes falls in love with her at first sight. After various incidents of a melodramatic nature, Gallipus performs another kidnapping aboard ship, this time on Lucanthe, the king's love. In a storm he attempt to ravish her (an almost perfect amorous captain!), but shipwreck saves her. Meanwhile, Cecilia has gone searching for Pausanes in boy's clothes (change of identity) and is also wrecked. All the characters are cast ashore near each other (remarkable rescue and reunion), the pirate is killed, and all ends happily.

The technical commands to meet the storm situation are chiefly put in the mouth of Zenon, who seems to be the actual captain under Gallipus since he gives orders to the master:

> ... Veere more theare!
> Hale tacke aboard; who's at helme? Maister!
> Set a yare man to the helme, thus, thus
> HEL. Done 'tis.
> ZENON Lower your maine saile, 'twas your fault we lac'd our bonnet
>   too; full.
> HEL. Done 'tis.

MAST. Strike our foresaile, heer's a gust will beare
        Our Mast by the board else.
GALLIPUS How now Master is she tight?
MAST. No a pox upon her for a whore she leakes
        But we have girt her; port, port hard
HELME Done, done 'tis.
ZENON Who keepes the lead there?
                    Within
        O dem a deepe fifteene fathome and a halfe O,
GALL. Where's the wind?
ZEN. North-East.
MAST. What ground ha' yee?
                    Within
        Corrall.
MAST. Hell and confusion! Corrall? Luff, luff hard
        Veare tacke and hale your sheate abord, Boatswaine;
        Brace your Foresaile, bring her ith wind,
        Be yare mates, clap helme a lee, Bring her   *Whistles*
        Upon her stayes: Hell and confusion!
        We are upon the rockes of Asuara.
.   .   .   . *Groaning within*[28]

Meanwhile Hiparchus and Pausanes are fighting their ship
through the same tempest with similar commands and ejaculations. Here however a boatswain takes final command:

        Whose at the Helme, slave woo't bring our sailes
        Into the wind, veare more sheate there,
        For heavens sake Gentlemen to your Cabbins and pray
        Now mates stand to your Sailes, in with the leade there
        Hoh the Cunnerey dew, west, [sic] steere dew-west.

A few minutes later the ship goes aground:

        KING She strikes Oh! We'are lost, she strikes Oh.
                    Within, Oh, oh, oh.
        PAUSANES Man the Long-boate, not a man enters
                Till the King and Queene be in. . . .[29]

Surely the similarities to the storm scene in *The Tempest* are
too obvious to require recapitulation.

While all the mariners represented have some of the characteristics of Shakespeare's boatswain, Gallipus and the master of his galley divide chief honors. Both are brave to recklessness: in the middle of the storm the former makes a long ranting speech about his former experiences, incidentally bringing in traces of the formula storm, and shouts at the praying slaves:

> Hence yee dogges leave your howlings, death!
> Have we liv'd as if we hop'd for mercy or
> Expected protection from our prayers, be gone
> And endeavor. . . .
> . . . why stay yee? who plyes the pump now?
> .   .   .   .
> Villaine thou shalt not dye by water, Ile be thy fate.
>> He *stabs the Slave*
> And yours if yee stay.[30]

The only suggestion of the superiority of sailors, when on duty, to landsmen lies in the boatswain's request to the "Prisoners" above, and the latter apparently have knowledge enough of the sea to give some orders and to complain bitterly of their "cranksided" craft that will not answer the helm. There is no suggestion of drunkenness. Gallipus and his master are of course pirates, and the former is a precious rascal with more than a touch of the Machiavellian. Save for his courage in the face of the storm, he has no admirable qualities: in fighting he is distinctly cautious.

In general the mariner of the *Tempest* school is much like the one pictured in the contemporary narratives of voyages, a somewhat reckless piratical sea dog, much inclined to drink and no respecter of persons, but brave in emergency. With him is likely to appear as commander or officer a noble pirate such as Antonio in *Twelfth Night*.

With the humours school may be grouped the general presentation of the mariner in drama, since the latter is usually unfavorable in attitude also. In the *Tempest* school even the sailor's

faults may be subjects for admiration; in the humours school
his virtues are likely to receive contempt. The reason for the
second attitude is not hard to find. The attempts of the voyage
writers to defend their pet discoveries show that there was no
great enthusiasm for the expeditions among those not interested
professionally. Unfavorable or satirical comments in the plays
indicate the same thing. Grausis in *The Broken Heart* may be
expressing a feminine view when she bursts out:

> Island! prison;
> A prison is as gaysome: we'll no islands
> Marry, out upon 'em! whom shall we see there?
> Sea-gulls, and porpoises, and water-rats,
> And crabs, and mews, and dog-fish; goodly gear
> For a young lady's dealing—or for an old one's!
> On no terms islands; I'll be stewed first.[31]

But Rosalinde is obviously making an ironic generalization when
she says, "A traveller! By my faith, you have great reason to be
sad."[32] Glister in the *Family of Love* also refers flippantly to the
aim of maritime exploration: "the wind of my rage has blown
him [Gerardine] to discover countries; and let the sea purge his
love away and him together—I care not. . . ."[33]

FIRST GALLANT Whence is your ship—from the Bermoothes?
REGINALD Worse, I think from Hell:
>   We are all lost, split, shipwrecked, and undone. . . .[34]

SIR MAURICE . . . I will undertake
>   To find the north passage to the Indies sooner
>   Than plow with your proud heifer.[35]

LAZARILLO . . . Bright and unclipt angels, if I were to make a
>   discovery of any new-found land, as Virginia or so, to
>   ladies and courtiers, my speech should hoist up sails fit
>   to bear up such lofty and well rigged vessels . . .[36]

No one knows exactly what Sir Andrew Aguecheek means by his
compliment to Sir Toby Belch, but "the equinoctial of Queubus"

is surely nothing to the fame of'the gentle craft of discovery. There are a dozen other hostile or flippant remarks in Shakespeare alone. If this is the attitude toward the discoveries, which to most Elizabethans formed the essential part of marine activity, it is not surprising that the sailor and sea life proper are also represented unfavorably. When to this is added the fact that the humours school is satirical in general purpose anyway, it is safe to assume that the presentation of the seaman is distinctly unfair.

The chief stress in the passing references is laid on the bad qualities.

> Lovers' oaths are like mariners' prayers, uttered in extremity;
> but when the tempest is o'er, and that the vessel leaves tumbling,
> they fall from protesting to drinking. . . .[37]

Hastings refers to the drunken sailor on the mast as if that were a common circumstance, and Gremio's comment on Petruchio has already been noted. Says Camillo of his disposition:

> Marry, my lord! o' the Captain's humour right;
> I am resolved to be drunk this night.[38]

Water-Camlet is reproached by his wife on the ground that, "item, I lent money to a sea-Captain on his bare Confound him he would pay me again next morning."[39] The amorous experiences of the mariner and the proverbial frailty of his wife are mentioned also:

A painted Lady best fits a Captain; for so both may fight under their colours.[40]

Troth, and I never had any sea-captain boarded at my house. [i.e. her maid is chaste.][41]

> A seaman's wife may ask relief from her neighbor
> When her husband's bound to the Indies, and not be
> blamed for't.[42]

> . . . How can the merchant
> Or the mariner absent whole years from wives
> Experienced in the satisfaction of
> Desire, promise themselves to find their sheets
> Unspotted with adultery at their
> Return.[43]

Two other works scarcely to be classed as fiction indicate that the general conception of the sailor is more unfavorable than the facts presented in the voyage narratives warrant. Middleton describes what is almost certainly a sea lieutenant in sufficiently unfavorable terms:

> Then another door [of Pict-Hatch] opening rearward, there came puffing out of the next room a villainous lieutenant, without a band, as if he had been new cut down, like one at Wapping, with his cruel garters about his neck, which fitly resembled two of Derrick's necklaces. He had a head of hair like one of my devils in *Doctor Faustus* . . . his brow was made of coarse bran . . . his eyebrows jetted out like the round casement of an alderman's dining-room . . . his nostrils were cousin-germans to coral . . . his crow-black muchatoes [sic] were almost half an ell from one end to the other . . . a down countenance he had, as if he would have looked thirty mile into hell . . . he began . . . first to fray me with the bugbears of his rough-cast beard, and then to sound base in mine ears like the bear garden drum. . . .[44]

And Overbury's "character" of *A Sailor,* while stressing the peculiar belief suggested in *The Tempest* and referred to definitely in *The Sea Voyage,* gives few of the favorable details that are in the plays

> . . . a fair wind is his creed and fresh water the burden of his prayers . . . nothing but hunger and hard rocks can convert him. . . . In a storm 'tis disputable whether the noise be more his or the elements, and which will first leave scolding? on which side of the ship he may be saved best? whether his faith be starboard faith or larboard, or the helm at that time not all his hope of heaven? his keel is the emblem of his conscience, till it be split he never repents . . . he can pray, but 'tis by rote, not faith, and when he wou'd he dares not, for his brackish

belief hath made that ominous. . . . His language is a new confusion . . . his body and his ship are both of one burthen, nor is it known
who stows most wine or rowls most. . . . A rock or a quicksand pluck
him before he be ripe, else he is gathered to his friends at Wapping.[45]

The bits of evidence from the voyages themselves indicate
then that, like the generalizations in drama and prose, the presentation given in the humours school of drama reflects an unfavorable conception of the Elizabethan sailor. The earliest detailed characterization is probably that of the Captain—he has
no other name, but, as the other characters have names that are
labels, e.g., Castiza, this is probably thought of as one—in *The
Phoenix* (1603-1604). He is an amazing scoundrel. Desirous of
returning to piracy, he resents the bonds of matrimony and tries
to sell his wife. He fears to go to sea unless he does lest the
storms be thought of his raising on account of the cuckold's
horns. His discussion of marriage with his companions is typical:

FIRST SOLDIER Of a man that has tasted salt water to commit
          such a fresh trick!
CAPTAIN Why, 'tis abominable! I grant you, now I see it.
FIRST SOLDIER Had there been fewer women—
CAPTAIN And I to play the artificer and marry, to have my wife
          dance at home, and my ship at sea, and both take in
          salt water together! O lieutenant, thou'rt happy!
          thou keepest a wench.
FIRST SOLDIER I hope I am happier than so, captain, for a my
          troth, she keeps me.
                    (Exeunt all but captain)
CAPTAIN What lustful passion came aboard of me, that I should
          marry? was I drunk? yet that cannot altogether hold, for
          it was four a' clock i' th' morning; had it been five,
          I would ha' sworn it. . . . O that a captain should yet live
          to be married! . . .[46]

His principal oaths are "Pox on't," " 'Sfoot," " 'Slife," and he
shows no trace of what Overbury calls the new confusion, i.e.,
nautical technicalities. He shows no religious influence, unless

his claim that he had "sworn all heaven over and over" that he would not marry, is one. In reply to a question he insists that a captain is "of no occupation," and is insulted at the suggestion that he write his name:

'Sfoot, dost take me for a penman? I protest I could ne'er write more than ABC, those letters, in my life.[47]

Foiled in all his plans, he declares his intention of going to sea and becoming a scourge.

Captain Seagull in *Eastward Ho* (1605) is overshadowed by Sir Petronel Flash, the admiral of this ill-fated Virginian voyage, but, since the latter is a sea knight in intention only, discussing him with the others of this group is scarcely legitimate. Seagull, however, rattles off the geography that puts the authors in jail, expresses complete confidence in his ability to sail anywhere on the seven seas, is most gallant to Winifred, and carries out to the letter his promise to get drunk. Although this company does not get to sea, it is wrecked in the Thames. The incident may well be a burlesque of the romantic shipwreck of the novels, with the cuckold's horns in place of Aeolus or some other storm provoking divinity, a small boat in place of the ship, the river in place of the ocean, rescue on the Isle of Dogs instead of a desert island Arcadia, and separation and reunion as usual. There is some "humours" characterization in Touchstone's sarcastic soliloquy on Sir Petronel:

Ha, sirah! thinkes my knight adventurer we can no point of our compasse? Doe wee not knowe north-north-east and by east, east and by north, nor plaine eastward? Ha! have we never heard of Virginia, nor of Cavallaria, nor the Colonaria. Can we discover no discoveries? Well, mine errant Sir Flash, and my runnagate Quicksilver, you may drinke dronke, crack cannes, hurle away a browne dozen of Monmouth capps or so, in sea-ceremonie to your *boon voyage;* but for reaching any coast save the coast of Kent or Essex, with this tide, or with this fleete, Ile be your warrant for a Gravesend tost. . . .[48]

Captain Otter in the *Silent Women* (1609) has some education since he interlards his speech with Latin tags, and is eloquently polite to his "princess," as he calls his wife. Perhaps this circumstance results from his being both a land and sea captain, although apparently not actively engaged in either profession. His wife is a shrew, whom he has agreed to obey as princess in the home. She supports him, allows him a half crown a day, and provides bands and cuffs, "when I can get you to where them." By his interest in bear baiting, evidenced in the names of his cups, "bull," "bear," and "horse," he turns every day, when courtiers or "collegiates" come to his home, into a Shrove Tuesday. His opinions on matrimony are much like those of the captain in the *Phoenix:*

> Wife! buz? titivilitium! There's no such thing in nature. I confess, gentlemen, I have a cook, a laundress, a house-drudge, that serves my necessary turns, and goes under that title; but he's an ass that will be so uxorious to tie his affections to one circle. Come, the name dulls appetite. Here, replenish again; another bout. (Fills cups again.) Wives are nasty, sluttish animals. . . . A wife is a scurvy clogdogo, an unlucky thing, a very foresaid bear-whelp, without any good fashion or breeding, *mala bestia.* . . . A pox!—I married with six thousand pound, I. I was in love with that. I have not kissed my Fury these forty weeks.[49]

He elaborates his description of her shortcomings while she listens behind him; and, when she can stand it no longer, she falls upon him and beats him. He immediately becomes meek again "under correction." It should be noticed also that in intention she is not a particularly faithful wife.

Captain Shunfield in the *Staple of News* (1625), Jonson's other contribution to sea types, is also amphibious, practicing jeering as his land profession. Actually, he is less scurrilous than his unnautical companions. The chief flavor of the sea lies in the occasional maritime figures of speech used by him or, more often, applied to him: "Well pump'd, i' faith, old sailor," "We'll give him a broadside first." Pennyboy senior holds up his nose at

Shunfield's odor of tar and pitch, and says he cares not for "pickled security."[50]

Meanwhile Middleton's *The World Tost at Tennis* (*c*.1620) presents a fire-eater in the same satirical light. After an entrance suggestive of the rival school, he demands the world from the land captain:

> SEA-CAPTAIN Peace
> > Purser, no more; I'm vex'd, I'm kindled.—You,
> > Land-Captain, quick deliver.
> LAND-CAPTAIN Proud salt-rover,
> > Thou has the salutation of a thief.
> SEA-CAPTAIN Deliver, or I'll thunder thee to pices,
> > Make night within this hour, e'en at high noon
> > Belch'd from the cannon: dar'st expostulate
> > With me? my fury? what's thy merit, land worm,
> > That mine not centuples?
>
> .   .   .   .
>
> > When we go to't and our fell ordnance play,
> > 'Tis like the figure of a latter day:
> > Let me but give the word, night begins now,
> > Thy breath and prize both beaten from thy body:
> > How dar'st be so slow? not yet? then—
> LAND-CAPTAIN Hold! (*Gives orb*)[51]

Later the sea captain explains that "the Indies load us" whereas the land captain has only his pay. He accuses his purser of throwing wounded men overboard in battle and calls him "coward and cozener." He shouts:

> Leave me, and speedily; I'll have thee ramm'd
> Into a culverin else. . . .

His sailors, anticipating a convention of the next century, come in dancing and singing a song with "pipe and can":

> Hey, the world's ours, we have got the time by chance
> Let us carouse and sing, for the very house doth skip
> > and dance
> That we now do live in:

We have the merriest lives,
We have the fruitfull'st wives
    Of all men;
We never yet came home,
But the first hour we come
We find them all with child agen.[52]

Gaffer Compass in *A Cure for a Cuckold*[53] differs somewhat
from the other mariners in this group, and perhaps belongs over
with the hearts of oak. The impression given is that his method
of eradicating his horns is worthy of emulation, since no sailor
can hope to have a faithful wife. Still, there is condescension in
this view, and something of the "humours" method in his characterization. After four years at sea Compass returns to find his
wife still, as he thinks, unfertile: "lank still! Will't never be full
sea at our wharf." Later he finds that he is the titular father
of a three months old child. He explains the long period of ges-
tation as the result of sail, horizon, and clime: "these things
you'll understand when you go to sea." He insists in the face of
all argument that the child is his, browbeats his wife and the
actual father, and divorces and remarries his wife so that there
may be no legal question. His good humour and tenacity of purpose are engaging, but, save his rough and ready attitude, there
is little salt flavor in his speech.

Shunfield, Seagull, Otter, Compass, and the two anonymous
captains, regardless of differences in detail, indicate that one
method of amusing an Elizabethan audience in the years following 1600 was to present a mariner ashore rather unfavorably as
a subject for ridicule.

One other play should be mentioned as belonging to the humours school, although in this case the attitude of the author toward his seamen is favorable rather than otherwise. Davenant's
News from Plymouth, originally set in Portsmouth, (1635), has
a title and plot suggestive of the group of comic operas so popular toward the end of the next century. Captain Seawit is the

hero, a fine gentleman with little of the sailor about him; Topsail is young and extravagant with a sweetheart in every port; Cable is an old salt, rough and ready, with more than a suggestion of the heart of oak about him. They are held in the harbor by a south wind, and the towns-people have overcharged them until Cable is down to his whistle. He constantly rails at marriage, but has an eye to the main chance.

CABLE Your honest women are still unfortunate
    To me, they talk of marriage . . . [he cannot pay a jointure]

Or again:

No, no, I love churches. I mean to turn
Pirate, rob my country-men and build one.

. . . .

But for marriage, do not think on't. It is
A most excellent receipt to make cuckolds.[54]

There is a boatswain who talks blank verse and shows no particular realism. It is chiefly Cable who justifies the inclusion of this play in the humours group.

From 1600 to 1642 then one must look in the drama for most of the presentation of the mariner, and particularly in the *Tempest* school, where he appears among elements impossibly romantic, for anything like a fair picture of him. In the humours school he is presented with his bad qualities heightened and with individual absurdities added.[55]

CHAPTER V

THE SAILOR IN FICTION

1660-1760

English prose fiction pretty well leaves the sea with the decline of the Elizabethan novel based on the Greek romance. The pamphleteers were not interested; the Civil War discouraged production; and the picaresque tradition had not yet acquired a nautical background. It was not until the Restoration that the conception of a maritime fiction was definitely established. Whether Kirkman and Head's *English Rogue* is the landmark, or rather sea mark, that it has been thought to be is doubtful on the basis of Professor Secord's investigations;[1] but the fact remains that, with the writing of that book, the mariner again appeared as a hero in prose.

In his discussion of the sea tale in French literature, Professor Atkinson recognizes the following possible types: pastoral, adventurous, burlesque, philosophic works of the *Utopia* sort, fantastic imaginary voyages to other planets or to non-existent countries, and, the one in which he is especially interested, the extraordinary voyage.[2] After defining the last rather carefully, he states that "the realistic setting . . . was based almost entirely on French accounts of travel. After 1720 there was naturally much conscious imitation of Defoe's *Robinson Crusoe.*"[3] Although I do not believe it possible to distinguish the types very carefully in English, the generalization, mutatis mutandis, will hold: the chief source for the maritime novel in English during the century following the Restoration was the voyage literature.

Most of the novels purport to be accounts of actual voyages and borrow the obvious elements of technique. They actually include many details having nothing to do with the main story, such as Van Sloetten's cryptic references to his correspondent's old acquaintance Petrus Ramazina and "those concerns of which I wrote to you in *April* last."[4] They are usually told in the first person from the point of view of the officer class. They usually contain many dull details of ship's position, flora and fauna, natives, climate, and products. They usually obscure the central adventure with interesting incidents in the supposed author's earlier or later experiences, such as the Yarmouth storm in *Robinson Crusoe*. The fact that some of the supposed originals were themselves forgeries, e. g., *The Voyage of François Leguat*,[5] only goes to show how far the imitation was carried. Without the narratives of actual voyages, this development of fiction could hardly have taken place.

Yet certain elements remain. The heroes are kidnapped much more often than in the true accounts; they are frequently cast away and rescued miraculously, and are almost as frequently reunited with their loved ones by a series of coincidences; beautiful maidens fall into the clutches of amorous captains and are saved by storms or other accidents more often than real life can possibly justify. The episodic structure, so noticeable in most of the sea stories, may be from the Greek romance tradition as well as from the real voyages. And the desert island may be from Arcadia as well as from Juan Fernandez.

As suggested above, the statement of W. L. Cross that "Kirkman and Head sent their hero on a voyage to the East, and thus began the transformation of the rogue story into the story of adventure as it was soon to appear in Defoe,"[6] represents the common view held concerning the picaresque influence until recently. Professor Bernbaum has shown in connection with his study of the *Mary Carleton Narratives*, however, that there was a school of imitation biography, whether terrestrial or maritime, owing little or nothing to the picaresque; and Professor Secord asserts that the "weakest assumption . . . identifies Defoe's fictions with the picaresque tradition of which the adventures of that 'witty extravagant,' Meriton Latroon, was the chief seventeenth century example in English.'"[7] The rogue story may have contributed the episodic structure—if the other elements did not. It may have suggested the villain-hero. It may have contributed rapidity of incident: one has only to compare a real voyage, such as Shelvocke's or Cooke's, with an imitation, such as *Robinson Crusoe* or *The Honourable Captain Boyle*,[8] to realize that fiction usually requires a more careful selection of details than truth. But the episodic structure, etc., can have come from somewhere else.

From the accounts of actual voyages, from the Greek romance tradition, and perhaps from the literature of roguery, the English sea novel from 1660 to 1760 is derived. As will be shown in a later chapter, the last source has a special development toward the end of the period, under the influence of Fielding and Smollett; and it is there that one must look for stress on sailor characterization. Since, however, the very first novel to be discussed belongs to the picaresque group and does have some emphasis on character, the attempt to distinguish between the types may well be left until later.

The English Rogue cannot be dated accurately because it is known to have been circulated in manuscript prior to its publication in 1665. Since it was regarded as obscene, the printed version is probably bowdlerized. Professor Secord contends that the picaresque story had little influence on Defoe, and by implication at least, cites *The English Rogue* as an example of what *Robinson Crusoe* is not. Yet the latter is, by his own showing, an imitation voyage, deriving from Dampier, Woodes Rogers, Pitman, and many similar sources; and the nautical part of the former, the part that is referred to by Cross, is an imitation voyage, deriving from Linshoten. As practically the first of a long line of English novels of the sort, the *Rogue* deserves attention.

After over two hundred pages of closely printed land adventures that belong unquestionably to the picaresque school, Latroon is sentenced to transportation:

The ship that was to transport me lay at Woolwich, about the latter end of Aug. 1650. . . . I was conveyed aboard . . . and was instantly clapped under hatches; but I knew they would quickly call me aloft if there was any fighting work; as such a thing might easily be, since the sea was nowhere free from such as would make a prize of what vessels were too weak to contend with them.[9]

When the ship springs a leak, Latroon escapes in a boat with some others and is picked up by another vessel bound for the Canaries. This ship in turn is caught in a storm, of which few details are given beyond the loss of bowsprit and mizzen, and the cutting away of other masts. Driven before the wind for four days,

. . . our ship struck so violently against a rock that the horrid noise thereof would have even made a dead man startle: to which, add the hideous cries of the seamen, bearing a part with the whistling winds and roaring sea; all which together, seemed to me to be the truest representation of the Day of Judgment.[10]

By something of a miracle Latroon and his companions crawl out on a rock and are saved. Latroon goes to sea with a Spaniard of Perimbana, near which they were wrecked, and is captured by Turkish pirates who sell him to a Jew who in turn sells him to a Greek. Setting out with his new master for the East Indies, he is again captured by pirates, and after many adventures escapes during a storm. He joins an English ship at Swalley Road, sees a good bit of the far East, and at Bantam marries a "black Indian" for her fortune. With Latroon's decision to settle down in the colony, Head's volume closes.

In general, the realistic details of sea life are ignored or presented in a hazy, unconvincing fashion, although there is one passage bitterly satirizing the sailor much as the Elizabethans did:

I was so like a seaman in this short time that none could distinguish me from one that received his first rocking in a ship. I carried about me as deep a hue of tarpawlin as the best of them, and there was no term of art belonging to any part of the ship or tackling but what I understood. [He is surely chary of using them!] I could drink water that stunk . . . as well as any of them, and eat beef and pork (that stirred as if it had received a second life . . .) I say, I could devour it with as much greediness . . . as if it had been but nine hours, instead of nine months, in salt. And to make me more complete, I had forgot to wash either hands or face, or what the use of a comb or shirt was, neither did I know how to undress myself or if wet to the skin, to make use of any other means than my natural heat to dry myself. I never looked on a hat or band, but as prodigies.[11]

That *The English Rogue* may be classed with the other imitation voyages is shown by its borrowings from John Huyghen Van Linschoten's [sic] *Voyage to the East Indies* (1598). Head's method is to boil down the traveller's account, at the same time making specific application of the latter's generalizations. The following passages may well be compared: the italics are mine.

They [the Indian women generally] *have ringes through their noses, about their legs, toes, neckes, and armes, and upon each hand seven or eight ringes or bracelettes, some of silver or gilt.* . . . When the Bramenes die, all their friends assemble together, and make a hole in the ground, wherein they throw much wood and other things: and if a man be of any accompt (they cast in) sweet Sanders, and other spices, with Rice, Corne, and such like, and much oyle, because the fire should burne stronger. Which done they lay the dead Bramenes in it: *then cometh his wife with Musicke and (many of) her neerest friends,* all singing certain prayers in commendation of her husbands life, putting her in comfort and encouraging her to follow her husband, and goe with him into the other world. Then she taketh (al) her Jewels, and parteth them among her friends, *and so with a cheereful countenance, she leapeth into the fire, and is presently covered with wood and oyle: so she is quickly dead, and with her husbands bodie burned to ashes: and if it chance, as not very often it doth, that any (woman) refuseth to be burnt with her husband, then they cut the haire cleane off (from her head): and while she liveth* . . . *she is dispised, and accounted for a dishonest woman.*—Linschoten

The husband was carried before the combustible pile; *his most dearly loving wife closely following after, attended by her parents and children; musicke (such as they have, which I cannot compare to that of the spheres) playing before, behind and on each side of her.* She was dressed both neatly and sumptuously, to the height of the rudeness of their art; *her head, neck and arms (not counting her nose, legs, and toes) each bedecked and charged wih bracelets of silver, with jewels everywhere about her distributed.* She carried flowers in her hands which she disposed of to those she met. . . . The Bramin all along inculcating to her thoughts the sense-ravishing and affable joys she shall posses after her decease. . . . We followed them till they came to the fire, which was made of sweet odoriferous wood. As soon as her dead husband was committed to the flames, *she voluntarily leapt in after him, incorporating herself with the fire and his ashes.* . . . *Such as refuse to burn in this manner, are immediately shaven, and are hourly in danger to be murdered* by their own issue or kindred, *looking upon them as strumpets:* . . . —Head[12]

Likewise when any *gentleman or nobleman* will marrie with a maide, hee goeth to seeke (one of his friendes or) a *straunger* (and entreateth him to lie with) *his bride the first night* of their marriage, and to take her *maydenhead* from her, which he esteemeth as a great pleasure and honour (done unto him) . . . —Linschoten

They have a strange custom in their marriages, observed among them by *the highest to the lowest:* whoso marrieth is not to have the *first night's embraces with his bride,* but is very well contented to bestow her *maidenhead* on the Bramini, or priests, who do not always enjoy it, being glutted with such frequent offerings, and therefore will many times sell them to *strangers.* [Latroon goes on to tell how he personally took advantage of this situation.]—Head[13]

The Peguans have *a costome, that when any stranger* commeth into their land to deale and traffique (with them) of *what nation soever he bee:* they ask him how long he meaneth to stay there, and having tolde them, they bring him *many maids,* that of them he may *take his choice,* and make contract (and agree) with the parentes of the maid that liketh him best, (for the use of her) during his continuance there: which done he bringeth her to his *lodging,* and *she serveth him about all (his affaires both) by day and by night,* like his slave or his wife, *but hee must take heede that (in the meane time) hee keepeth not company with other women, for thereby he may incurre great daunger, and stand in perill of his life.* When the time of his residence is ended, *he payeth the friendes or parents (of the maid) as much as he agreed for (with them which done) he departeth* quietly away, and *the maid returneth with credits* home againe unto her friendes, and is as well esteemed of as ever.—Linschoten.

So soon as we arrived (which is *a custom they use to all strangers, of what country soever*) we had presented us *choice of many virgins;* our boat-swain choosing one he fancied for a small price, she guided him to a *lodging,* where if he would have stayed so long, *she would have performed his domestic duties as well at board as bed,* discharging her duty very punctually. *But he that undertakes any such thing must be very wary that he be not venereally familiar with any other woman, lest that she* with whom he hath contracted himself for such a time, *doth recompense his inconstancy with mortal poison. At his departure, her wages must be paid to her parents; she returns then with much joy,* and they receive her with as *much credit* and ostentation.—Head[14]

Besides parallel passages, of which there are several others, a good many details in Linschoten may have been suggestive to Head. The former talks of the "Baneanem" and of "Iewes," of "a hill of Brimstone that burneth continually," and of "Pagodes, cut (and formed) most ugly, and like monstrous Devils." Latroon cheats a Banian and is sold to a Jew, climbs a "burning mountain" and sees idols in "monstrous shapes," one of which he later likens to the Devil. Both accounts contain references to the women worshipping the moon, although Head is ribald as would be expected, both describe the juggernaut car, and both comment on the slashing of faces and bodies as a method of beautifying. Head's descriptions of the fruits and animals of Mauritius, although not parallel, could easily have been evolved from the similar material in Volume II of the Dutchman's work. Kirkman's continuation of the fortunes of the "witty extravagant" has so few nautical details that a careful examination of it does not seem worth while, but perhaps the story of the escape of the Englishmen from Ormuz by leaving a shop full of goods derives from incidents in Volume II of Linschoten. At all events, it is clear that the first sea story of the Restoration owes not a little to an actual voyage.

The Isle of Pines, which was almost a best seller in 1668, has received careful discussion *(q.v.)* in the privately printed edition of Worthington C. Ford. He refers to the suggestion pencilled on a German version that the whole thing is a glorious burlesque, the joke lying in the phenomenally rapid population of the island, a transposition of the name Pines, and a pun on the word "slut" in Van Sloetten. If this view is correct, a dozen opportunities for broad Restoration humour have been missed and, in building up a matter of fact background, a great deal of space has been wasted. I am inclined to believe that Mr. Ford's other suggestion is correct, that this is intended as a comment on institutions, humanity, etc.—in short, that this is what Professor Atkinson would call an "extraordinary voyage . . . distinguished . . . because of its realistic setting in a far-off country and because of its didactic content."[15] It differs from the contemporary French school of Vairasse and Foigny in its brevity and in the method of presentation in two different accounts. It agrees in having a traveller discover a strange land and people after being blown far south out of his course.

First published was the account written by Pines of his discovery and colonization of the island; then followed Van Sloetten's story of how he found Pines' descendents living on the island; these were so popular that they were combined and printed as one work during the same year. It is the combined version that Mr. Ford has reëdited. Van Sloetten sets out from Amsterdam in a ship of the same name, April 26, 1667. The

matter of fact details of the voyage occupy a page or two until,
as the vessel is leaving Madagascar, she is blown off her course
for a fortnight in a storm. Many hands sicken and some die. Ten
days of good weather are followed by sixteen more days of
storm, "the Weather being so dark all the while, and the Sea so
rough, that we knew not in what place we were. . . ."[16] When
the sky clears suddenly, they see a fire, and discover the island.
They are hospitably entertained by the inhabitants. Van Sloetten describes them and their government, social conditions, etc.,
in considerable detail. The Prince brings out "two sheets of
paper fairly written in *English*,"[17] the manuscript account of the
colonization of the island. In 1569 Pines sets out as bookkeeper
for his master, who is to be a factor somewhere in the East Indies, on a voyage "to the South of *Affrick*." The details of the
early part of the voyage are given as usual. Almost within sight
of Madagascar, the fleet is dispersed by a storm that continues
many days, and, about the first of October, he and his master's
daughter, two maids, and a negro girl, are carried ashore on the
bowsprit. There follows the usual desert island story of adjust-
ment to primitive environment. Pines and his concubines rapidly
populate the country, marrying the children to their half brothers and sisters, until in his eightieth year and fifty-ninth on the
island the census is 1789.[18]

Van Sloetten continues his account of the people, manners and
customs, and products of the island. Then he tells how his company set out for home, how they are almost lost in another
storm, how the ship is almost fired by the negligence of the
ship's boy, how they are chased by a pirate, and how they put
in safely at Madagascar. Frightened from there by an earthquake and unfriendly natives, they go to Saint Helena, where
the Dutchman meets Petrus Ramazina and takes care of "those
concerns of which I wrote to you in *April* last;"[19] surely this
detail gives verisimilitude to the pretended letter. He gets home

May 26, 1668. He adds a postscript on the enjoyment of bag-pipes by the islanders. The fact that the story, despite its brevity, devotes so much space to details irrelevant to the account of the island, shows the influence of the voyage literature to be great, although I have not succeeded in finding a specific source.

Realistic as this tale is in almost every detail, there is one episode suggestive of the Greek romance tradition, namely, the miraculous spar rescue of Pines and his women folk when the ship is wrecked on the island.

The Captain, my Master, and some others got into the long Boat, thinking by that means to save their lives, and presently after all the Seamen cast themselves overboard, thinking to save their lives by swimming, onely myself, my Masters Daughters [sic], the two Maids, and the *Negro* were left on board for we could not swim; but those that left us, might as well have tarried with us, for we saw them, or most of them, perish, our selves now ready to follow their fortune, but God was pleased to spare our lives, as it were by a miracle, though to further sorrow; for when we came against the Rocks, our ship having endured two or three blows against the Rocks (being now broken and quite foundred in the Waters), we having with much ado gotten our selves on the Bowspright, which being broken off, was driven by the waves into a small Creek . . . so that we had opportunity to land ourselves. . . .[20]

As an example of the real burlesque voyage, the sort of thing *The Isle of Pines* is charged with being by the anonymous German, Head's *The Floating Island* (1673) may be noticed. The author is apparently the same Richard Head who wrote the first part of *The English Rogue,* but here he abandons seriousness altogether and produces a biting satire in the *Ship of Fools* tradition. A ship of debtors called the "Paynaught" is fitted out under Captain Owe-much with two other vessels. The Captain tells the story much as Dampier or Shelvocke might have done, the fun lying in the absurd details. The "Paynaught" finds the admiral by means of "a *Leek* that was placed in her Stern, in place of the Lanthorn."

The next morning about ten a clock, my *Pylot* . . . descryed a Sail making towards us; coming up we vilely suspected him by his flag to be the *Water Cannibal* of *Troy-novant*.

Whereupon I called a Council aboard, to consider what was to be done in the imminent extremity. Some advised, that it was most fit to make to Land, if any knew where to touch without hazard: Others of more undaunted Spirits, and higher resolution, advised to run the risk of an engagement, and to draw our number out of sight into the Hold, the more to encourage the Enemy to a nearer approach; which opinion was generally approved of and allowed.[21]

The supposed enemy luckily proves to be a friendly ship bound from the Canaries to "Fox-hall." The "Excuse" is stranded, and the whole squadron has to await another tide.

. . . in two Watches we discerned *Firme land,* lying upon the Savoyans Eastward from Lambethana . . . a spacious *Continent,* fit for *Plantation* at foure degrees Westward from *Terra del Templo.*

Having sailed due south from Cape Verde, they come upon Scoti-Moria or Summer Island, around which they sail in twenty-four hours.

. . . it is much larger than it is broad, but how many leagues the length may be, I cannot tell, for I took not its dimension; it lies in the midst of *Golpho de Thame-Isis:* The *Christian-shore* lying to the *Norward,* and the *Turkish-shore* to the *Southward,* bounded to the *Eastward* with *Pont Troy novant,* but to the *Westward* thereof you may sail up the *Streights* till you go as far as Maiden-head, and farther, crossing the Equinoctial-line, [presumably that of Queubus!][22]

This is of course a satirical allegory on contemporary London, with perhaps a dash of the picaresque in the rascally crew and the obscene humour. Unless the reference to the Amazons be so considered, there is no suggestion of the Greek romance tradition.

Defoe's tales of adventure should be discussed in this place, but Professor Secord has dealt with them so thoroughly that little remains to be done. His chief purpose is to indicate Defoe's narrative method and to show that *Captain Singleton* and *Robinson Crusoe* are not a continuation of the picaresque tradition. As has been suggested in connection with the discussion of *The English Rogue*, there is not much point to the latter conclusion as far as the nautical elements are concerned (it is of course highly important in the general study of fiction) since Head did exactly what Defoe did in adapting actual voyage material to his ends, except that he did not do it so well. The whole study indicates that Defoe, like most of his predecessors and successors in fiction dealing with the sea, used the general technique of the actual voyage.

Professor Secord believes *Captain Singleton* to be a reworking of Defoe's own *King of the Pirates* (Captain Avery) (1719), which contains much of the legendary material that had appeared in Johnson's play, and of various other supposedly true narratives, such as Knox's *Historical Relation of Ceylon*. The study goes into great detail in tracing bits of characterization (e.g., Knox, the pious slaver who cheats a native out of a Bible, has much in common with William, the Quaker pirate),[23] tricks of expression, geographical details, etc. There are even some reminiscences of *Robinson Crusoe*, e.g., in the palisaded camp. The story summarizes the early life of the hero and tells how, involved in a mutiny, he sets up as a pirate, and later becomes commander of a pirate ship. It recounts his adventures in Madagascar, the old haunt of Avery (and that pirate's capture of the Mogul's daughter is mentioned in passing),[24] in Africa, and at sea, with his return to England a man of wealth, his reformation, and his marriage to William's sister.

Robinson Crusoe, the first two parts of which preceded *Captain Singleton*, while the last appeared some months later, is so well known that a summary of the story is scarcely necessary. I shall content myself by reproducing Professor Secord's table[25] of chief sources, although it should be remembered that he cites illustrative material in great detail, so that his results are more convincing than a list can indicate.

PART I

Portion of story	Certain sources	Probable	Possible
C's roving disposition		Esquemeling	
Yarmouth storm	Defoe's *Storm*		
Sallee slavery		Ogilby's *Africa*	
Island story	Published accounts of Selkirk Knox's *Ceylon* Dampier Leguat's *Voyage* Pitman's *Relation*	Knox's MS.	Peter Serrano *Simplicissimus* *Krinke Kesmes*

PART II

Voyage Bengal to China	Dampier
	Le Comte's *China*
Adventures in China	Ide's *Travels*
Peking to Archangel	

It will be noted that no reference is made to *The Isle of Pines*, although it is mentioned in passing as a possible source for Grimmellhausen's *Simplicissimus*. Yet elsewhere the statement is made that "Knox's experience is the only one of the kind [presumably that of a man imprisoned in some way on a *distant* island, since this account is in no sense a *desert* island story] which approaches Crusoe's in the matter of time covered."[26] In another place Professor Secord says, "I know of no narrative other than *Robinson Crusoe* of a man cast away by shipwreck and later delivered by pirates, with a long period intervening between the catastrophe and the deliverance."[27] He adds that he believes Henry Pitman's *Relation* to be the source for the rescue by pirates.

These comments, however, incline me to agree with Wackwitz²⁸ that, despite its absence from the known lists of Defoe's reading, *The Isle of Pines* deserves consideration as a possible source. It seems to me that the shipwreck method of getting the hero ashore is just as important as the desert island element. Here is a mariner shipwrecked on an island after being blown off his course. He and his four women companions (of whom one is a negro) secure much wreckage from the ship. It is three generations before another vessel comes to the island, and although there is no desire to be taken off and hence no deliverance, pirates are mentioned in the last part of the story. The Bible is the only book. The title used by the head of the clan is "king and governor." After the death of Henry Pines, there is much the same confusion as that which follows Crusoe's departure from the island. Many minor details are similar, e.g., a superfluous earthquake and the relation of part of the history at second hand.

The technique of *Robinson Crusoe* is of course that derived from Defoe's sources, the actual voyages. It will be remembered that the unfortunate mariner gives an interesting account of his early life and adventures, too frequently skipped, I fear, by boys desirous of reaching the shipwreck, that he uses the journal method to describe his first days on the island, and that in the second part he tells at great length of his visit to China and Russia, with only an incidental return to the island. He fills in with much detail concerning climate, flora and fauna, and nautical information. Defoe took the name Will Atkins from *Strange News from Plymouth* (1684) and that sailor's characterization from Pitman's *Relation,* a Bible and miscegenation from Knox or *The Isle of Pines,* a footprint and a route around the world from Dampier, and of the whole made the masterpiece of all imitation voyages; but still a work not differing in conception from others of its kind.

The Voyages, Dangerous Adventures and Imminent Escapes

of Captain Richard Falconer (1720), ascribed with no great certainty to Chetwood, is an example of the imitation voyage with no further purpose than that of entertainment, the sort of thing Leguat's *Voyage* and *Robinson Crusoe* obviously are, and the sort of thing Vairasse's *L'Historie des Sévarambes* and *Gulliver's Travels* obviously are not.

After an account of Falconer's parentage and youth, the story tells how his father, a tax collector, having fallen on difficulties, sends his son to sea with a friend. The usual disconnected incidents follow, until the hero, reading aboard a boat in tow, is caught by a storm and left behind. Partly by swimming, he gets ashore on a low, sandy island, still retaining the Elzevir *Ovid* which he was reading when the storm broke. His attempts to get a living are described in detail. After some time, four other men are wrecked on the island; and one of them, Thomas Randall, tells a long story of an earlier wreck in which he spent the summer on a barren rock and finally escaped to the coast of Denmark in a drifting boat. The five companions refit the wrecked ship, but Randall dies before they can leave. The night before their departure, they get drunk in celebration. Falconer, who sleeps aboard, wakes to find that the vessel has been blown out to sea. Believing that this is punishment for drunkenness, Falconer resolves, as he has done at least once before, to lead a better life. He lands safely at Yucatan and secures a rescue ship of which he acts as captain. He finds his companions about to eat Randall's body for food. Part of the crew of the rescue ship are pirates who revolt and threaten to send the honest men off in an open boat; but a pistol held at the head of a prisoner explodes and kills the pirate leader, whereupon the tables are turned. After many other adventures, Falconer by a series of coincidences gets back to his original ship just as they are about to declare him officially dead by selling his clothes. The next episode is his capture by Turks commanded by an English rene-

gade, who starves and poisons himself. When the prisoners re-
take the ship, Falconer gets lost ashore at Santo Domingo, is
captured by Indians, and marries an Indian wife. He violates a
taboo and is about to be burned at the stake after his wife is
killed in the melee, but is rescued by another tribe. He joins Benbow's fleet in time for the *Breda's* single-handed fight with Du
Casse's squadron (August, 1702) and the death of the Admiral.
After three more voyages he retires, concluding "with my Prayers and Thanks to Heaven for the many Mercies I have received. . . ."[29]

As has been suggested, this long narrative, although told, except for one lapse, in the third person, is obviously modelled on
actual voyages and imitations, with particular influence from the
newly established Defoe method. One of the principal sources
seems to be Esquemeling's *The Buccaneers of America* (1684-
1685). Early in the account of his voyage to Jamaica, Falconer
describes the ceremony of ducking at the crossing of the equa-
tor. The neophyte escapes only by paying "a bottle of rum and a
pound of sugar." Esquemeling describes a similar ceremony on
the coast of Brittany "that being ended, every one of the bap-
tized is obliged to give a bottle of brandy for his offering. . . ."[30]
After a pirate encounter off Barbados not unlike some of those
in the *Buccaneers*, an old sailor tells of his adventures as a buccaneer and logwood cutter at Campeachy; he also recounts the
sinking of a Spanish man-of-war, another favorite incident in
Esquemeling.[31] Cast on his island, Falconer finds it low, sandy,
and destitute of food and water. He later finds eggs and kills
boobies. The other work describes many islands of all sorts, tells
of the casting away of a man on Juan Fernandez and of the
marooning of the Mosquito Indian, again and again stresses
hardships from lack of food and water, mentions the finding of
eggs, and discusses the booby in detail.[32]

Falconer describes how he and his companions get drunk to

celebrate their approaching departure from the island; that
night the cable pulls up the tree to which it is fastened, and
allows the ship to drift out to sea. Ringrose tells how the slaves
nearly rebel while the buccaneers are "all in drink," and a few
pages later reports: "About midnight the wind came to north
with such great fury that the tree to which our cable was fastened on shore gave way and came up by the roots."[33] The exposure of the slave plot is not unlike the exposure of that of
Falconer's pirates, and the method which the latter adopt in
disposing of their prisoners is used again and again in Esquemeling. Falconer cuts a considerable epitaph to Randall on a
tree. Ringrose refers twice to cutting inscriptions on trees.[34]
Randall when cast away is forced to eat puppies. Ringrose reports: "Captain Sharp, bought the dog, with intention to eat him,
in case we did not see land very soon."[35] The three survivors dig
up Randall's body for food, whereas the buccaneers hope to meet
some Spaniards "intending to devour some of them rather than
perish."[36] When Falconer asks a sailor his opinion of the women
of Jamaica, " 'Why truly,' says Tarr very bluntly, 'if there's one
honest Woman shou'd happen to tumble down, I believe there's
never another to take her up.' " Esquemeling reports of the
same favored island, "they find more women than they can make
use of." A privateersman tells Falconer concerning his share of
spoil,

Psha! (says he) that, and five times as much is gone since then. And
this is no wonder, for sailors are such Fools, that what they get with
the utmost danger, they spend as the meanest Trifles.

Esquemeling may almost be said to harp on the licentiousness
and prodigality of the buccaneers:

Such of these Pirates are found who will spend 2 or 3 thousand pieces-
of-eight in one night, not leaving themselves peradventure a good shirt
to wear on their backs in the morning.

Or again,

> Being arrived, they passed here [Jamaica] some time in all sorts of
> vices and debauchery, according to their common manner of doing, spend-
> ing with huge prodigality what others had gained with no small labour
> and toil.[37]

A number of other similar details may be found in both. That
the attitude of extreme piety, while characteristic of the imitation voyage in general, may also have been suggested in this
case by the source is indicated by the index reference in the
Buccaneers: "God Almighty, etc., Thanks given to: 53, 109,
116, 117, 395, 411, 447-8, 461."

Finally there is an amusing parallel arising from the fallacy
of cause and effect. Ringrose tells of an unfortunate accident:

> In this pond, as I was washing myself and standing under a mancanilla
> tree, a small shower of rain happened to fall on the tree, and thence
> dropped on my skin. These drops caused me to break out all over
> my body into red spots, of which I was not well for the space of a week
> after. Here I ate very large oysters. . .[38]

The mançanilla is highly poisonous (and Ringrose knew it to be
so), but for all that I am inclined to accept Mr. Stallybrass's
suggestion that the " 'red spots' were more probably due to the
oysters than to the rain!"[39] Falconer has been swimming when
a shower comes up.

> I went under a Tree to save my Cloaths from being wet, and in placing
> them together in a Cavity of the Shore, the Drops of Rain fell on a
> Mangineel Tree, and so on my Back, but in less than half an Hour
> my Flesh burn'd very hot, and white Blisters appear'd upon my skin . . .
> the Spots remain'd upon my Skin several Years afterwards. . . .[40]

In general it is safe to say that the *Falconer* novel owes a great
deal to Esquemeling and Ringrose.

Yet one must admit that probably the arrival of Falconer at
his old ship just in the nick of time after months of adventure,

the interposition of Providence in the form of a faulty pistol,
and the assortment of captures and disasters, all just at the
right moment, continue the tradition of the Greek romances.
Furthermore, Randall's first shipwreck involves an almost perfect spar rescue, of which there is no suggestion in the *Buccaneers:*

I by good Fortune laid hold of the Rigging that hung to the Mast; so
once more *got on stride it,* [Italics mine] but with little Hopes of Life. . . .
At last, after being tossed about for two or three Hours more, the End
of the Mast rush'd with such Violence against a Rock (as I suppos'd)
that with the Shock I was thrown off; but laid hold of some of the
Cordage again, and held fast till it fix'd it self in some of the craggy
Cliffs of the Rock.[41]

In 1725 a Yankee minister, John Barnard, published at "Boston N.E." a tract called *Ashton's Memorial* that is of no special
importance in the development of the English sea romance, but
constitutes almost the only American contribution to the desert
island literature of the century. This short account pretends to
be the story of a real adventure and, although catalogued as
fiction, must have a considerable element of truth since it was
used in a comparatively small community as an illustration of
the workings of Providence.

The "infamous Ned Low" captures Ashton's finishing boat by
a trick, and gives the youth a chance to sign article since he is
unmarried: married men, says Low, make poor pirates. When
Ashton refuses, he is confined and abused, although the married
men are allowed to go home in a boat. After several incidents
almost too interesting to be true, Ashton gets an opportunity to
go ashore on an island in the Gulf of Honduras,[42] escapes, and
lives a Crusoe existence for nearly a year. He is totally without
equipment and has a hard time. A Scotchman, who has lived
with the Spaniards for twenty-two years, comes to the island
but is lost in a storm three days later. After a total of nearly

sixteen months from home, Ashton is rescued. All through the story he is in a state of continuous shock at the depravity of mankind and spends much time on the island in meditating on his sins (although there is nothing to indicate that he is anything but the perfect hero).

This narrative is either actual experience or an imitation belonging to the Defoe school. As suggested earlier, it shows rather too interesting choice of incident to be unsuspected; yet, as Ashton is not a sailor and does not keep a journal, his recollections written as the "memorial" would naturally omit the duller details, especially those of latitude, soundings, and climate. Johnson's *History of the Pirates,* the lost first edition of which seems to have appeared the year before, shows that Low was in New England waters about the time represented, that he frequently captured fishing boats and treated their crews as described, and that he may well have sent an expedition ashore in the Gulf of Honduras. Low's sadism, suggested in the *Memorial,* is confirmed by Johnson's account of the pirate's amusement in cutting off the ears and slitting the lips and noses of his victims. But the sending ashore of the captured Frenchmen to demand a medical chest sounds like an episode connected with Avery in the *History.* A bit of evidence against the imitation voyage hypothesis is the absence of the earlier and later life of the hero, but it must be remembered that the Reverend Mr. Barnard is telling a thrifty rather than a murie tale. In general the *Memorial* sounds rather like a record of the facts, or the working over of some other source, rather than like a narrative derived from Johnson. There are no events just in the nick of time or other suggestions of the Greek romance tradition.

At this point it is necessary to digress from the main development of the imitation voyage group to notice what Professor Atkinson calls the "fantastic voyage," a type to which *Gulliver's Travels* (1726) belongs. Th. Borkowsky, whose article *Quellen zu Swift's "Gulliver,"*[43] written in 1893, is still cited as authoritative, lists a variety of sources; and W. A. Eddy, whose *Critical Study* (1923) makes a somewhat different classification of voyages from that of Professor Atkinson, surveys what he calls the "philosophic voyage" in great detail as it affects the *Travels.*[44] Some of the chief influences are Cyrano de Bergerac's *Voyage to the Moon and Sun*, Rabelais, Vairasse's *Sévarambes*, Foigny's *Jacques Sadeur*, Godwin's *Voyage of Domingo Gonzales to the World of the Moon*, Joshua Barnes' *Gerania: a New Discovery of a little Sort of People*, More's *Utopia*, and Lucian's *Icaromenippus*. Since these studies are chiefly concerned with the fantastic peoples rather than with the influence of actual voyages, and especially since many of the sources do not contain sea voyages at all, I shall omit even summaries of them.

For the purpose of this discussion, the important point is that Swift's stories follow the technique of the voyage narrative rather more closely than the concentration of scholarly interest on the queer inhabitants and the contemporary references has indicated. Gulliver tells his tales in the first person. The voyage to Lilliput opens with an account of his parentage and early life; and he is the sole survivor at that island of the crew of a small boat caught in a storm. At Brobdingnag he is captured while ashore for water. Taken by Dutch and Japanese pirates, he is set adrift in an open boat near Laputa. The voyage to the country of the Houyhnhnms opens with a series of ordinary nautical details such as speaking other ships. Part of the crew die of fever, and are replaced by recruits at Barbados. The latter mutiny with the intention of setting up as pirates, and, after confining Captain Gulliver for several months, put him ashore on the strange land. The pretended editor, Gulliver's cousin Richard Sympson, explains that:

This Volume would have been at least twice as large, if I had not made bold to strike out innumerable Passages relating to the Winds and Tides,

as well as to the Variations and Bearings in the several Voyages; together with the minute Descriptions of the Management of the Ship in
Storms, in the Style of Sailors; likewise the Account of the Longitudes
and Latitudes; wherein I have Reason to apprehend that Mr. *Gulliver*
may be a little dissatisfied.[45]

Sympson's apprehension is correct: Gulliver writes him that,
while he has authorized him to hire a young gentleman of either
university to put the "loose and uncorrect account" of his travels
in order, "as my cousin Dampier did by my advice in his book
called 'A Voyage round the World,' " he has not given him per-
mission to omit anything.[46] He elsewhere states that writing
voyages requires no talent "except a good Memory or an exact
Journal."

The sort of thing Master Sympson omits elsewhere may be
represented by the description of the storm off Brobdingnag,
which is paraphrased from Samuel Sturmy's *Mariner's Magazine*
(1679):

Finding it was like to overblow, we took in our Spritsail, and stood by
to hand the Fore-sail; but making foul Weather, we look'd the Guns
were all fast, and handed the Missen. The ship lay very broad off, so
we thought it better spooning before the Sea, than trying or hulling.
We reeft the Fore-sail and set him, we hawl'd aft the Fore-sheet; the
Helm was hard a Weather. The Ship wore bravely. We belay'd the Fore-
down-hall; but the Sail was split, and we hawl'd down the Yard, and got
the Sail into the Ship, and unbound all the things clear of it. It was a
very fierce Storm; the Sea broke strange and dangerous. . . . We got
the Star-board Tacks aboard, we cast off our Weather-braces and Lifts;
we set in the Lee-braces, and hawl'd forward by the Weatherbowlings,
and hawl'd them tight, and belay'd them, and hawl'd over the Missen
Tack to Windward, and kept her full and by as near as she could lye.[47]

Surely such a mass of technical terms would have indicated
voyage influence, even without the known source.

The anonymous *Voyages and Adventures of Captain Robert
Boyle* (1726), while based to a considerable extent on *Falconer,*
has more of the romantic element. It begins with the usual ac-

count of the early history of an orphan boy. After some picaresque incidents ashore, the hero is decoyed aboard ship by the
proverbial wicked uncle who wishes to retain his fortune, and is
carried toward America. In a fight with Barbary pirates he is
knocked overboard by the recoil of a gun, picked up by the cor-
sairs, and carried to Barbary. He falls in love with a beautiful
English captive, who aids him in escaping. She tells her story.
Decoyed aboard one of her own ships, she is carried off by the
captain, who makes violent love to her. She appeals to the crew,
and succeeds in getting the captain deposed and imprisoned; but
the ship is captured by the Barbary pirates. All the ship's company except the lady are allowed ransom. She and Boyle escape to
the French ambassador in the guise of two men, and there they
marry by formal declaration to each other. They board a ship;
but Boyle has to go ashore, and on his return finds that is wife has
been recaptured. He hears further that she has drowned herself to
escape the renegade captain of the pirates. Boyle decides in his
despair to take to the South Seas as a privateer. He falls in with
the renegade, defeats him, kills him, and shares the money with
his crew at the Canaries. At St. Catherines he has dinner with
Captain Dampier. After many adventures, he returns to England
wealthy, finds his uncle dead, and discovers a large estate await-
ing him in charge of an honest cousin. He is instrumental in saving the life of his own child without recognizing her, and is reunited with his wife, who has been miraculously preserved. He
finds that a young gentleman from Brazil is a woman in disguise,
who has followed him for love. She readily transfers her affection
to his loyal cousin, and all ends happily.

This story belongs in general to the imitation voyage type.
The slavery episode may have been suggested by Crusoe's experiences in Sallee. Some details are actually borrowed from *Falconer,* and the general outline of the story is the same. Each begins with land episodes and the going to sea of the hero as the

result of a special accident: (F) financial pressure, (B) kidnapping. Each contains a series of incidents leading up to capture by pirates, (F) after the desert island story which is the main event, (B) as the main event. Each provides an unusual marriage among foreigners, (F) to an Indian woman, (B) to an English prisoner among the Mohammedans. Each brings in, somewhat awkwardly, one historical character toward the end, (B) Benbow, (F) Dampier. Each provides a retirement to England in comfortable circumstances.

The following details may be compared to show that there is actual borrowing: it should be noticed of course that Boyle makes two different fights out of the original one.

The Fight continu'd half an Hour with all the Fierceness imaginable; at last the Spaniard prepar'd to board us with his Boats at the same Time, but were receiv'd so briskly, and so damag'd by our Hand-Granado's, that they were oblig'd to make to the Ship with Great Loss. The Hand-Granado's stood us in great stead, for we dispatch'd three or four of our Men into the Main-Top, who from thence discharg'd several Granado's, that by their own Report kill'd and wounded above thirty Men. . . . Broad-side . . . rack'd her fore and aft.—*Falconer*

The Fight continu'd half an Hour with the utmost Fury. The Rover prepar'd to board us. We had some Hand Granadoes on board. . . . He [the gunner] ordered several Men into our Main-Top with Granadoes . . . and fir'd our Guns upon him, which rak'd 'em fore and aft. . . . Our Gunner above in the Top threw in upon them with his Granadoes, which we could perceive put them into much confusion.—*Boyle*[48]

Knocked overboard while preparing to board, Falconer is captured by an English renegade captain of Turkish rovers, Lewis Gordon, alias Hamet. This worthy singles him out because the other prisoners say he is wealthy and "for being I was not in a Sailor's Habit, they thought I was something above the rest, and therefore hop'd to get a considerable Sum for my Ransom."

Knocked overboard by the recoil of a gun, Boyle is captured by an Irish renegade, Hamet, who singles him out for special treatment "for he took •me for more than a common Sailor, being I was not in a Sailor's Habit."⁴⁹

The long story of difficulties with the Indians in *Falconer* may well have suggested the briefer account in *Boyle*. On the other hand *Boyle* differs from *Falconer* on the realistic side in the attempt to characterize the common sailor very much in the fashion pursued in the drama. Says a merchant—

I wonder that you Seafaring Men will venture upon Wives. Why so? replied the Captain. Why so! return'd my Master, Because in my Opinion it should put you in Mind of *Cuckold's Point* as you went by Water: Your Absence gives 'em such Conveniency that I believe few let slip the Opportunity.⁵⁰

A certain irony is lent by the fact that the reader knows the speaker's own wife to be unfaithful. Again, a sailor on being offered the maid Susan by the heroine's usurping captain replies, "Damn it! I love a Woman well enough, but don't care to have her forc'd upon me. . . ."⁵¹ Boyle's men "soon dispos'd of their Money [chiefly for] Wine and Brandy."⁵² The captain praises them, "for tho' most Sailors are rough and blunt in Speech, yet they can in their way admire a generous Action as well as other Men."⁵³

With all its realistic detail, however, the Boyle narrative is largely a Greek romance expressed in contemporary terms, for after all the essential plot is the meeting under romantic conditions of two lovers who are then separated by a series of accidents and re-united by a series of coincidences. The hero is kidnapped aboard ship and captured, almost miraculously, by pirates. He and the heroine fall in love at first sight; it is true that he does not rail at love before the meeting, but at least he pretends to do so afterward to avoid suspicion. The heroine accompanies him in boys' clothes, (a form of change of identity repeated in the episode of the Brazilian lady near the end of the story; this is surely the romantic Fidelia episode so common in plays). His passion for her is so great that his health suffers. In the story of her earlier life there is a good example of the amorous captain: having decoyed her aboard the ship, he makes violent love to her; the maid who has first betrayed her now takes her place, but when the captain discovers the truth he plans immediate action; a storm, which the ladies claim is caused by outraged Divinity, prevents his attack; although the shipwreck does not follow, the ladies are evidently familiar with the tradition, for they greet the tempest with wishes for death, or to be "cast away upon some Shore, and receive assistance when we least expect it."[54] Boyle believes his wife to be dead, and rejoins her in a remarkable reunion. The Brazilian lady and his noble cousin fall in love with each other at first sight.

The shipwreck-desert island element is provided by another narrative, *The Voyage, Shipwreck, and Miraculous Preservation, of Richard Castelman, Gent.*, published in the same volume with *Boyle*. This is a short but vivid account of how the ship is driven on a sandbank at Ronoke [sic!], Virginia. Only a few of the ship's company save themselves before she goes to pieces, and they have a hard time for a day or two from lack of food and water. Then they are rescued. There is a distinctly snobbish note in the criticism of the sailors for saving themselves immediately after the officers (!) when the captain's sister and children remain aboard, although the hero is among the first to leap into a boat: Cassio's theology seems to have applied generally to the sea.

Longueville's (?) *The Hermit* is chiefly notable, as Professor Lowes has pointed out,[55] for its debt to Dampier. It also owes something to *Robinson Crusoe*. Book I consists of Edward Dorrington's account of his voyage from Mexico, with all the usual dull details of the imitation voyage school. The ship puts in at an island on the coast; and there they find a pious hermit who refuses to go back to wicked civilization with them, but gives them an account of his life. Book II contains Quarll's life as recorded in his memoirs down to his shipwreck on the island. The early part consists of picaresque land episodes, including his marriage to three wives, and a Macheathean prison scene. His comments on naval conditions, and especially on the treatment of sailors, are rather more bitter than those of Crusoe. He is duly cast away on the island. Book III tells of his life there, chiefly meditation, piety, dreams, visions, and the practical business of living. He is discovered by a boat's crew who plan to carry him off to put in a show, but are drowned by an act of Providence before they can carry out their nefarious plan; one boy survives who remains with him ten years, and then escapes to the wide world.

In the first book there are a number of details suggesting the Crusoe story: a wonderfully intelligent pet monkey; discussion of the baptism of negro women, with the name Atkins used;[56] the overhearing a plan to mutiny; and the desertion of the ship by the intended mutineers. The discovery of Quarll is much like the discovery of Crusoe. The hermit's account also contains many reminiscences of the other work. There are the series of earlier adventures, the ship blown off her course and wrecked, the miraculous rescue of the hero alone, his gathering supplies from the wreckage, his way of life and tendency to meditate on his fate, his debate over whether his life is good or evil, his fear at the arrival of the hostile boat's crew, his adoption of the boy survivor much as Crusoe adopts Friday, and his sudden loss of his companion. Many minor details also are obviously borrowed.

The critical tendency is noticeably in a different spirit from the few comments of the sort in *Robinson Crusoe*.

Being come to *Gravesend*, where the Ship lay, they found, according to Custom, the jolly Crew in an Ale-House, spending like Asses what they had earn'd like Horses even before they had received it. At the Ladies coming, the elevated Sailors, who had been sailing on salt Water for the

Space of three Years, and since set their Brains floating in strong Drink, for six Hours, had lost the Rudder of their Reason, so did run Headlong upon those quick Sands, where most lost all they had before they could get off. . . . By that Time, the absent revelling Crew were cloi'd with their Mistresses, and had dismiss'd them with rough Usage and ill Language, of which they generally are flush, when Money is scant.[57]

Or later,

The Ship being unladen, the Cargo prov'd damag'd, by the leaking of the Vessel, which is commonly made good by the Sailors; so that instead of three Years Wages, being due, the poor Men stood indebted to the Merchants.[58]

The chief interposition of Providence is the drowning of the boat's crew who wish to put Quarll in a show; but his rescue as compared with Crusoe's is surely miraculous.

. . . the Wind continuing two Days, encreas'd to a very great Storm, which held for one Day and two Nights more, during which time they perceiv'd themselves near some Rocks. The Storm rather increasing, and growing dark, they despair'd saving the Ship; and as the Main-yard could not lower, the Ship's Tackling being disorder'd by the Violence of the Storm, *Quarll*, being bold and active, took a Hatchet as tumbled about the Deck, and ran up the Shrowds, in order to cut down what stop'd the working of the Main-yard; but, by that time he was got up, there came a Sea which dash'd the Ship to Shatters against the Rock, and with the Violence of the Shock, flung *Quarll* who was astride upon the Main-yard, a Top of the Rock, and having the good Fortune to fall in a Clift, was hinder'd from being wash'd back again into the Sea, and drown'd as every body was that did belong to the Ship.[59]

It seems legitimate to call this a spar rescue.

Brunt's *A Voyage to Cacklogallinia,* published the same year, belongs unquestionably to the group which Professor Eddy calls the "fantastic voyage" and probably owes much to Vairasse and Foigny, with the moon element derived from Cyrano de Bergerac. The immediate impulse for writing such a yarn was probably *Gulliver's Travels,* published the year before. Since the derivation of the queer inhabitants does not belong primarily to the nautical influence, I have not attempted to make a special study of it, but, as an imitation voyage, this is much like the others. The author bows to convention by explaining that he will skip the story of his birth and parentage because such material is dull. A young orphan, he is apprenticed to the master of a merchantman. After several voyages as superfluous as the details he omits, he deserts his ship to avoid being pressed in the navy, and is captured by runaway slaves near Port Royal, Jamaica. Many adventures follow, including a brutal attack on the negroes by whites. The remnant escape in canoes, but the hero is captured by pirates in crossing from Hispaniola to Cuba. Although he refuses to sign articles, he is spared by the captain, a noble pirate, who almost single handed puts down a mutiny. This officer shows great piety. After various sea fights and captures, the pirates start from near Porto Bello, for "Campechy," and are caught in a storm which blows them south in darkness for ten days to be wrecked on the coast of Cacklogallinia. The hero is preserved alone and finds himself among a strange race of fowls endowed with human characteristics. (He later finds that some of his companions have saved themselves on wreckage, and have been picked up by Indians.) After passing some time among the feathered race, he constructs a flying machine with which he proceeds to the Moon; and from there, having an opportunity to get his bearings, returns to Jamaica. The fantastic elements do not begin until the shipwreck, and then increase in intensity until the return from the Moon.

The storm is practically a formula one:

The Thunder growl'd at a distance, and it began to blow hard; a smart Thunder-shower was succeeded by a Flash of Lightning, which shiver'd our Main-mast to the Step. A dreadful Peel of Thunder follow'd; the Sea began to run high, the Wind minutely encreased, and dark Clouds intercepted the Day; so that we had little more Light, than what the Flashes of Lightning afforded us . . . the Ship rang with Imprecations, and not a Word was uttered, not back'd with Oaths and Curses. . . . [But the captain prays.] On the Tenth Day, about Nine in the Morning, we struck upon a Rock with that Violence, that those who walk'd the Deck, were struck off their Legs . . . in less than ten Minutes, she struck again, and a Sea coming over us, I saw no more either of the Ship or of the Crew. I rose by the side of a large Timber, which I laid hold of, and got upon, heartily recommending myself to my Creator, and sincerely endeavoring to reconcile myself to my God, by an unfeigned Repentance of the Follies of my past Life [of which no record appears] and by making a very solemn Resolution, that, if his Mercy should preserve me from a Danger which none but his Omnipotence could draw me out of, to have for the future, a strict Guard upon all my Thoughts, Words, and Actions, and to shew my Gratitude, by the Purity and Uprightness of my future Life. . . . The Piece of Wreck which I was upon, was, after being toss'd some Hours, thrown ashore, and I got so far on Land, that the returning Surf did not reach me.[60]

He regards the destruction of the pirates as divine punishment for their evil deeds, an interposition such as is so common in the Greek romance.

Early in 1751 appeared Robert Paltock's *Peter Wilkins and the Flying Indians*, as the title is usually phrased today. Peter's early life is given in full in the first three chapters, and in the fourth he goes to sea. Taken by a French privateer, he and other prisoners are set adrift in a small boat with inadequate provisions. Some die, and the others eat one of the corpses. The survivors are picked up by a Portuguese bound for San Salvador, and work their passage. On a special expedition Wilkins escapes with a native slave and takes refuge with the latter's family. He plots with some English to sieze a Portuguese ship and escape. When they stop for water at a desert island, Wilkins and one Adams are blown to sea in a storm, and then against a great rock where Adams is lost. Wilkins lives for some time on the wreck: this really amounts to a desert island story. Then he tries to circumnavigate the rock, is drawn into a subterranean stream, and at length finds himself in a beautiful country by a large lake, within the circle of the rock. Here he lives another desert island existence for a chapter or two until Youwarkee, the flying Indian girl, falls on his roof. There follows his courtship and marriage; and later on his visit to her country, and their long life in that remarkable kingdom. In his old age, after the death of his wife, Wilkins becomes homesick to see England again, and sets out to fly in a machine constructed in imitation of the natural equipment with which his wife's people have been born. He falls into the sea and it is picked up by a passing ship. He spends his few declining years with the editor of his story.

Despite the suggestion of the *Monthly Review* that this story "seems to be the illegitimate offspring of no very natural conjunction, like *Gulliver's Travels* and *Robinson Crusoe*," it is of course a form well recognized by this time, a fantastic philosophic voyage. The editor of the *Review* did not realize that Swift's reducing of the realistic voyage elements to a few paragraphs was the real abnormality. This long narrative carries on the tradition of Foigny, Vairasse, and Brunt. It should be added that Wilkins is not essentially a sailor since he is on his first voyage, or, at most, the continuation of his first voyage, when he is wrecked. A specific source I have been unable to find: there are reminiscences of Robinson Crusoe in the domestic economy of the castaway, in his association with a native, and in his debate over his fate; but most of this could also have been derived from *The Hermit*.

The same year appeared *John Daniel*, another extraordinary voyage, called by W. T. Lowndes in his *Bibliographer's Manual of English Literature* an imitation of *Peter Wilkins*. This view is based on the fact that in both stories men land on desert islands and in both stories men fly. As a matter of fact the two narratives are quite dissimilar. After a brief summary of his early life and adventures, Daniel tells how he sets out with a Dutch skipper and has a prosperous voyage to Madagascar. Then a great storm blows them southeast for seventeen days. They strike a rock, the crew are washed overboard with the exception of the hero and two companions, and one of these is lost in an attempt to get ashore on the mast. After a time Daniel discovers that his companion is a girl in disguise. They marry by a self chosen ceremony, and live many years on the island. On the example of Adam, they marry their children to each other at the proper ages. The wreck of a ship provides them with supplies.

One of the sons develops a flying machine, a purely mechanical contrivance bearing no resemblance to the graundee of Youwarkee; and father and son set out to explore. They lose their bearings and are carried to the Moon. Then they visit an island inhabited by half human sea monsters, the issue of a union between the wife of a castaway and a sea beast. They visit Lapland, where one of the proverbial witches gives a seance in which they obtain news of their island home: Daniel's wife is dying of grief at losing him; the third generation is afflicted with dissension. The son, Jacob, is drowned by a whale in a casual fashion suggestive of the death of Friday. Daniel finally gets back to England, and dies at the age of ninety-seven.

As is suggested above, the flying machine bears no resemblance to that of Wilkins, which was an artificial adaptation of the physical equipment of the flying Indians. It rather recalls Cyrano de Bergerac's contrivance, and that fact, in connection with the lunar destination, indicates that this narrative is a continuation of the tradition of fantastic voyages represented by Cyrano, Godwin, and Brunt.

The source for the nautical incidents can be found, I believe, in the *Isle of Pines,* although the echoes are not so conclusive as one could wish. There are a number of general similarities.

The *Isle* is a brief pamphlet. *John Daniel* in a modern edition
occupies, in large type with generous margins, only 276 pages,
whereas *Peter Wilkins,* for example, consists of nearly six hundred closely printed pages. In each there is a shipwreck story
inside the main story. In each the Bible is the sole book. In
each a written relation "to whom it may concern" is left by
someone dead when the story opens. In each the history of the
island is given as far as the third generation. In each brothers
and sisters are married in order to continue the population of
the island. In each the island is south of Madagascar. In each
a miraculous spar rescue occurs.

There are also some parallel details. Soon after the survivors
get ashore (I) "we kindled a fire and dryed our selves;" (J)
"we hung our breeches, waistcoats, and shirts up to dry. . . ."⁶¹
(I) "When we were got upon the Rock we could perceive the
miserable Wrack to our great terrour. . . ." (J) "We looked
wistfully towards our ship, of which we could only now and
then see something blackish. . . ."⁶² (I) "We were at first
affraid that the wild people of the Countrey might find us out,
although we saw no footsteps of any . . . the Woods round
about being full of Briers and Brambles, we also stood in fear
of wild Beasts. . . ." (J) We saw . . . the skirts of some
large woods . . . we knew not by what men or beasts they
might be inhabited. . . ."⁶³ (I) On the morrow being well
refresht with sleep. . . ." (J) "We waked very reasonably re-
freshed. . . ."⁶⁴ And the spar rescues may well be compared.
(cf. the *Isle* above.) (J) Most of the crew having been washed
overboard,

we all three leaped upon the mast, and disjoining it from the vessel,
delivered up ourselves to the mercy of the wind and waves.
We clung to the mast till we were within half a mile of land; but the
billows broke so high over us, that we were immersed frequently for near

a minute wholly in water . . . [Rogers is lost through fear of landing
with the spar] . . . a prodigious surf . . . raised up the mast with us upon
it, and letting us furiously down upon the sand, almost beat the breath
from our bodies; (for we drew up our legs and lay flat upon it.)[65]

The parallel is not very close; yet there is a general similarity of method. Aside from the spar rescue with its miraculous outcome, and the suggestion of riding upon the mast contained in the last line of the quotation, there is no touch of the
Greek romance tradition in this.

David Price (1752) continues the imitation voyage school,
with a considerable romantic influence. After a few comments
on his early life the hero tells how, setting out in an English
merchantman, he is captured by a French privateer which is in
turn taken by an Algerine pirate. Arrived at Algiers, he assists
an English merchant's daughter, Cleone, to escape from the
Bassa. In the course of their wanderings they kill two robbers,
and Cleone dons the clothes of one. A traveller whom they rescue is discovered to be the pirate who captured Cleone, and who,
after an attempt to ravish her, sold her to the Bassa. He is
drowned crossing a stream. Price and his companion, after
many shore adventures, secure a ship from Aden to Coromandel; but he is washed overboard and picked up by another
ship. At the first port, he sets out to recover Cleone, whose vessel he finds wrecked on a desert island. He can discover no
survivors. He goes to sleep, has a nightmare, and wakes to find
that Cleone and others have come ashore in a boat. They beat
off an Indian attack and start for home. The Dutch skipper of
the rescue ship tries to kill Price and makes Cleone a prisoner,
at Rotterdam, in an effort to force her to marry him. Price
once more rescues her, and marries her. A sentimental reconciliation with the captain a few years later concludes the narrative.

The voyage elements are getting rather thin by this time. There are few details of climate and products, and the fight with the Indians and the plague of locusts are probably the most realistic incidents. There seems to be a general similarity to *Captain Boyle,* although the events are shuffled a bit and the style is quite different. Each hero falls into the clutches of Mohammedan pirates and is thereafter instrumental in rescuing an English merchant's daughter who disguises herself as a man. Boyle's renegade is called Hamet; Price's corsair, Hammel.[66] In each the heroine has suffered at the hands of an amorous captain[67] and is later separated from her lover by kidnapping. In each the hero loses a ship by being carried overboard.[68] In each there is a sentimental reconciliation at the end. By definition then this narrative is an imitation voyage because it imitates an imitation voyage, even though most of the incidents borrowed are from the Greek romance tradition: amorous captain, change of identity, remarkable reunion, love at first sight.

With the brief desert island story inserted in Volume II of *The Mother-in-Law* (1757) this chapter may close. A ship bound from Dabul to Malacca is blown south by a storm and captured by pirates. There is a realistic description of the rovers' legislative method of settling whether the captured crew shall be given the alternative of death or of marooning if they refuse to sign articles, much in the vein of the *History of the Pirates.* By a close vote the latter plan wins. The loyal seamen are set ashore, a few at a time, without equipment. They explore the country, and some of them are captured and eaten by cannibals. The survivors escape by sea and find a wreck. They help the crew of that vessel ashore, and from her secure provisions and equipment. They explore the country, build houses, and live in vast plenty until they can construct a pinnace

from the pieces of the wreck. They put to sea and are picked up
by a Portuguese. After various adventures of little nautical
flavor, the survivors get safely home to England. About the only
really vivid nautical details are those dealing with the pirates;
the others, like the rest of the story, are rather hazily romantic.
The personality of the sailor is not particularly stressed in
this group of novels: it is indicated by the adventures in which
the mariner involves himself, and by the way in which he re-
acts to them, rather than by direct comment on the part of
the author. On account of this, it is difficult to dissociate the
details bearing on the presentation of the sailor from the discussion of the narratives; but a few generalizations can be
made. As in the actual voyage accounts, the point of view is
in general that of the officer class: although he may have
"climbed in through the hawse holes rather than the cabin
window," as the sea expression has it, the supposed author
tends to be unsympathetic toward the foremast hand. He emphasizes the difference between the diligence, combined with
unusual ability, that enables him to rise, and the shiftlessness
of seamen in general. There are few scruples as to money
matters on the part either of the merchant and buccaneer captains or of their men, although there is much piety of the sort
that causes Singleton's pirates to be shocked at the treachery
of the Indians. Yet courage in danger, persistence in the face
of continued obstacles, and sound common sense in emergency,
combined in the case of the pretended author-captains with almost Yankee ingenuity, stand out as a general impression.
Heightened somewhat for literary purposes, the sailor of the
novels is still recognizable as brother to the one in the accounts
of actual voyages.

In this chapter I have tried to show that the maritime novel
of the hundred years following the Restoration, regardless of

minor variations such as *Cacklogallinia,* remained close to the
model set by the narratives of real voyages. That these did provide the standard is indicated not only by similarities of technique such as the journal method of telling the story, but in
most cases by the actual borrowing of details and phraseology.
With Fielding and Smollett came a different method of presentation, leading to more stress on character, and the inclusion
of a different kind of sailor.

CHAPTER VI

THE SAILOR IN THE DRAMA

1660-1760

Both the *Tempest* and humours schools of presenting the sailor on the stage persisted through the Restoration, and on into the eighteenth century. At the reopening of the theaters, *The Tempest* was one of the Shakespearean plays assigned to Davenant's company, and he, together with Dryden, who is often unjustly given most of the credit, made a revised version that was played at the Duke's House, Lincoln's Inn Fields, November 7, 1667. This version with minor changes, and Shadwell's opera based on it, held the stage until 1838 in competition with Shakespeare's own play, Duffet's shattering burlesque *The Mock Tempest, or the Enchanted Castle* (1675), and the revival of *The Sea Voyage* mentioned below. Most of the source work on this drama has been concentrated on the Hippolito-Dorinda[1] element, since the creation of a man who has never seen a woman to play opposite the woman who has never seen a man is the chief addition to Shakespeare; but I believe the expanding of the nautical scene is equally significant.

The first change is one that would occur to anyone contemplating economy of characters. Stephano, the drunken butler, becomes master of the ship; Trincalo (sic), the equally drunken jester, becomes the swearing boatswain:[2] it is surely illuminating as to the popular conception of these nautical figures, that the humble drunkards of Shakespeare should be considered suitable for the advance in rank. Next, the master is given a mate of the same stripe, Mustacho, and one of the mariners is named Ventoso; both make non-Shakespearean comments on the weather at the beginning of the play. The first forty or fifty lines are like Shakespeare's, save that the map-derived "blow till thou burst thy wind" becomes the contemporary nautical expression "blow the Devil's head off"; and that Stephano shows a trace of his old character in his command at the height of the storm, "Give the Pilot a Dram of the Bottle." But the boatswain's line or two of technical commands preceding, "A plague upon this howling!"[3] has become over a page of orders: with these the master tries to get his ship off to sea before the storm shall render it impossible:

STEPH. Let's weigh, Let's weigh, and off to Sea
        (Exit Steph.)
        (Enter two Mariners and pass over the Stage)
TRINC. Hands down! Man your Main-Capstorm.
        (Enter Mustacho and Ventoso at the other door)
MUST. Up aloft! And Man your seere-Capstorm.
VENT. My Lads, my hearts of Gold, get in your Capstorm-Bar.
        Hoa up, hoa up, &c.
        (Exeunt Mustacho and Ventoso)
        (Enter Stephano)
STEPH. Hold on well! Hold on well! Nip well; there; Quarter-Master,
        get's more Nippers.
        (Exit Stephano)
        (Enter two Mariners and pass over again)
TRINC. Turn out, turn out, all hands to Capstorm?
        You Dogs, is this a time to sleep?
        Heave together Lads.   *(Trincalo whistles)*
        (Exeunt Mustacho and Ventoso)
MUST. *(within)* Our Viall's broke.
VENT. *(within)* 'Tis but our Vial-block has given weigh. Come heave
        Lads! We are fix'd again. Heave together Bullyes.
        (Enter Stephano)
STEPH. Cut off the Hamocks! Cut off the Hamocks; come my Lads:
        Come *Bullys,* chear up! Heave lustily. The Anchor's a peek.
TRINC. Is the Anchor a peek?

STEPH. Is a weigh! Is a weigh!

TRINC. Up aloft my Lads upon the Fore-Castle! Cut the Anchor, cut him.

ALL WITHIN Haul Catt, Haul Catt, &c. Haul Catt, haul: Haul, Catt, haul. Below.

STEPH. Aft, Aft! And loose the Misen!

TRINC. Get the Misen-tack aboard. Haul Aft Misen-sheat!

(Enter Mustacho)

MUST. Loose the main Top sail!

STEPH. Furle him again, there's too much Wind.

TRINC. Loose foresail! Haul Aft both sheats!
  Trim her right afore the Wind.
  Aft! Aft! Lads, and hale up the Misen here.

MUST. A Mackrel-Gale, Master.

STEPH. *(within)* Port hard, port! The Wind grows scant, bring the Tack aboard, Port is. Star-board, star-board, a little steady: now steady, keep her thus, no neerer you cannot come.

(Enter Ventoso)

VENT. Some hands down: the Guns are loose

(Exit Must.)

TRINC. Try the Pump, try the Pump!

(Exit Vent.)

(Enter Mustacho at other door)

MUST. O Master! Six foot Water in Hold.

STEPH. Clap the Helm hard aboard! Flat, flat, flat in the Fore-sheat there.

TRINC. Over-haul your fore-boiling.

STEPH. Brace in the Lar-board.

TRINC. A Curse upon this howling, etc.[4]

Since even an amateur of naval command can make a fair degree of sense from this attempt to meet the series of crises growing from putting to sea in foul weather, the comment in the Furness *Variorum "Tempest"* that "amidst a wild and incoherent mass of nautical nonsense, orders are issued which, if obeyed, would drive the ship straight to destruction on the rocks," is an exaggeration. It is true that the attempt is unsuccessful: Bosun Trincalo miscalculates in luffing to avoid a rock on the starboard bow, which appears suddenly as they are trying to obey the master's order to run the leaking ship ashore. But it is also true that Shakespeare's seamen, for whom Furness has such admiration, fail to carry out their maneuver to avoid a lee-shore. The one or two commands that are absurd, e.g., "Cut the anchor!" are either misprints or attempts at phonetic spelling.

This amplification of technical material is certainly evidence that the audience considered it an essential of the nautical play. It indicates that the development in this direction, stopped by the closing of the theaters twenty years earlier, was ready to continue.

The swearing boatswain and the master are characterized much as in Shakespeare, by the simple method of using most of that author's lines. Trincalo is said to have a hanging face, and the whole crew are called drunkards, an accusation justified by the fact that they have the drinking parts originally given to the servants in the episode of Caliban. There is some sentimental talk about how their wives will weep at their loss; and their lustfulness is indicated by Trincalo's love affair with Caliban's sister, Sycorax.[5]

The Greek romance elements are much the same as in Shakespeare: the formula storm is still farther from the type, but contains the interesting statement that "the waves did heave him [the ship!] to the moon"; and a spar rescue is provided, as in the earlier play, by a butt of sack. A runlet of brandy also floats ashore to give additional refreshment in the new dukedom.[6] The offer of Sycorax to share the cabin with her love, probably reflects the actual conditions of the time, which permitted higher naval officers to carry their wives with them.[7]

A few months before the presentation of the revised *Tempest*, Fletcher's *Sea Voyage* was revived at the Theatre Royal and the two ran as counter attractions for some time. It was not until 1685 that Durfey's revision of the latter as the *Commonwealth of Women* was made; then this continued for half a century. The point to be noticed is that the two most important sea dramas of the Jacobean period held the stage in one form or another through the height of neo-classicism.

Meanwhile, the humours method of presentation was also making its contribution, much as in the preceding period, by showing Jack ashore; but in the later plays he is often given some admirable characteristics. He is usually a captain in rank, and is represented as rude, boisterous, amorous, and inclined to drink and fight on any occasion. Yet his very rudeness is regarded as superior to the hypocrisy and artificiality of manners on land. The figure which naturally comes to mind first is that of Captain Manly in Wycherley's *Plain Dealer* (1677). It is a commonplace that the inspiration for this character comes from Molière's *Misanthrope* and the Malcontents of the Elizabethan period, but it should be equally clear that Wycherley made his plain dealer a mariner because his conception of the typical mariner involved some of the characteristics of the misanthrope. To Sebastian at least, the swearing boatswain is a "bawling, blasphemous, incharitable dog," and it will be remembered that the Captain in *The Phoenix* plans to recover from his chagrin ashore by becoming a pirate at sea.

One of Manly's own sailors, a group that love him apparently for the oaths and kicks he gives them, says of him, "A pox! He's like the Bay of Biscay, rough and angry, let the wind blow where 'twill," and another reports that he was going "to settle himself somewhere in the Indies," if the ship had not been sunk in the Dutch War.[8] The nautical element in *The Plain Dealer*, then, is suggestive of both Pre-Restoration schools: the presentation of a sailor, especially a captain, ashore as a "hu-

mours" character comes from Jonson and his successors; his
rough and ready characteristics probably come from the swearing boatswain.

Since the plain dealer appears in many plays, this example is
worthy of additional analysis. Probably his most noticeable
quality is his frankness and discourtesy, of which he is inor-
dinately proud. The first lines of the play illustrate this:

Tell not me, my good Lord Plausible, of your *decorums,* supercilious
forms, and slavish ceremonies! your little tricks, which you, the spaniels
of the world, do daily over and over, for and to one another; not out
of love or duty, but your servile fear.[9]

After being deceived by Olivia, he rails at women:

Hell and the devil reward thee! . . . Well, there is yet this comfort by
losing one's money with one's mistress, a man is out of danger of getting
another; of being made prize again by love, who, like a pyrat, takes you
by spreading false colours: but when once you have run your ship
aground, the treacherous picaroon loofs; so by your ruine you save
your self from slavery at least.[10]

His sailors say they never saw him pleased except in a fight:

Dost thou remember after we had tug'd hard the old leaky long-boat to
save his life, when I welcom'd him ashore, he gave me a box on the
ear, and call'd me fawning water-dog?[11]

Angry at their allowing Lord Plausible to visit him, Manly calls
them "rascals," "dogs," (repeated several times) and "brandy
casks." Later he kicks them for joking, although his lieutenant
protests that they are entitled to their "forecastle jests"; that
they "cannot help 'em in a fight, scarce when a ship's sinking."
His pride and incontinence are both stressed in his refusal,
despite his desperate straits, to borrow from some of his mistresses. In her railing Olivia mentions his "brutal courage" and
"more brutal love," his desire to win a wooden leg, his failure
to remove his hat in her presence, his scenting her alcove with
tar and brandy ("Foh! I hate a lover that smells like Thames-

Street!"), his "weather beaten complexion," the "manly rough-
ness" of his voice, "that captain-like carelessness" in his dress,
and his narrow-mindedness and spirit of contradiction.[12] He
bristles on all occasions, hustles the fops about in an attempt to
get them to fight, and will, as his sailors say, receive no one but
the bearer of a challenge. His coarseness is indicated by his
his plan to seduce Olivia to avenge the insults she has heaped
on him. Truly, he is a person more to be feared than admired.

Mrs. Behn's Wilmore in *The Rover* (1677) has little sea
flavor. He uses no nautical language and little more profanity
than the other characters. He is stated to be a gentleman and
is inferior to the other cavaliers chiefly in his lack of delicacy
(evidenced, if nowhere else, in his failure to understand why
Belvile should resent an attack on Florinda since it does not
succeed) and the swashbuckling manners which sometimes em-
barrass the rest of the party. He rails at marriage: "Hold, hold,
no Bugg words Child, Priest and *Hymen,* prithee add a Hangman to 'em to make up the consort. . . ."[13] He uses at least
one nautical expression in commenting on his ill-success: "I was
never claw'd away with Broad-sides from any Female before."[14]
His courage is undoubted: "Faith Sir, I can boast of nothing
but a Sword, which does me right where e're I come."[15] With
Angelica's pistol at his breast, he says, "Whe then there's an
end of a proper handsome Fellow That might a liv'd and done
good service yet. . . . That's all I can say to't."[16] When the
Spanish Dons show signs of objecting to the various marriages,
he brings in an element belonging to the old Greek romance tradition, the kidnapping aboard ship, or, at least, the suggestion
for it:

. . . my Pow'rs greater in this house than yours; I have a damn'd surly
Crew here, that still [sic] you till the next Tide, and then clap you
on board my Prize; my ship lies but a League off the *Molo,* and we
shall show your Donship a damn'd *Tramontana* Rovers Trick.[17]

Somewhat different from the other nautical plays, but a development presumably of the humours method, is Otway's *Cheats of Scapin* (1680?). The villain-hero fools a merchant by reporting that his son has been decoyed aboard a Dutch privateer commanded by an English renegade. Later, having hidden his master in a bag supposedly to protect him from the sailors' attack, he belabors him with a club, at the same time taking the parts of the attackers with his voice. They are those of a Welsh sailor (thus anticipating Smollett in sending Fluellen to sea), an Irish sailor, a French sailor, a Lancashire sailor, and an English *(sic)* sailor. The latter is made to say: "Where is the Dog? I'll lay him on fore and aft, swinge him with a Cat o' nine tails, Keel hale, and then hang him at the Main Yard."[18] As soon as Gripe gets the courage to peep out of the bag, Scapin is exposed. I cannot see the point of the comment in the *British Tar* that Scapin's change of costume must be difficult to arrange: all that is involved is a change of voice.

Durfey's *Sir Barnaby Whigg* (1681) continues the plain dealer tradition. Among the dramatis personae are listed "Captain Porpuss—A blunt Tarpawlin Captain, and one that uses his Sea-phrases and terms upon all occasions, 'and' Livia—Wife to Porpuss, cunning and wanton, and in love with Townly." The plot involves the usual series of cross-purposes, in which the captain fails to win the Welsh girl, and is several times deceived by his wife, although he suspects her in the end. The title rôle is an attack on the puritan Whig as an unscrupulous turncoat and arrant coward.

And Porpuss is surely a plain dealer! He says he goes right to it "without parles." He courts his Welsh love, Winifred, by describing a broadside:

When wilt thou come to the *Tower*, and let me salute thee with the great Guns—hah? Bounce, bounce, bounce, thou shalt have Royal sport my girl.[19]

One is inclined to sympathize with Winifred's protest that "her has put a poor weak prains, and never can apide creat Guns, nor Pounce, pounce, pounce, her cannot apide pounces, look you." His comments on polite literature are also typical:

Why now a Storm, a Sea-fight or such a Song wou'd delight a man—Sbud, there's both Body and Soul in't; and a Pox on *Phillis* and Chloris, they were both Strumpets I warrant.[20]

He describes a hunt in nautical language:

Sailing a hunting this morning, we had not Cruzed above a League or two, but we found a Hare a-ground . . . we presently turned her adrift; and then she stood off and the Dogs stood after, and we stood after the Dogs; West Sou-West, Tail and End. . . .[21]

The climax of this experience occurs when the narrator tumbles "overboard." He rails at marriage even more emphatically than the Rover:

This [Livia's deception] comes of Matrimony. I had been an Admiral before now, if it had not been for a damn'd wife. . . . Oons I'le go home and flea her.

He also has Manly's desire to escape to his own element:

And I'le to Sea agen, I and my Jolly Crew . . . there will I Conquer some flourishing Island, where I will plant a Colony, live out the rest of my days merrily, and defie the Devil and Fortune.[22]

How brave this tar is supposed to be is not clear since he himself is the only one to mention his "notable service." He is sentimental: when he thinks of his old ship, "the pearly Dew falls from [his] Eyes." He is the least attractive plain dealer presented so far.

Sailor Ben (his rank is not made clear) in Congreve's *Love for Love* (1695) is also a true plain dealer:

Mess, I love to speak my mind— . . . Flesh, you don't think I'm false-hearted, like a land-man. A sailor will be honest, tho'f may-hap he has never a penny of mony in his pocket—

. . . it's but folly to lie: for to speak one thing, and to think just the
contrary way; is as it were, to look one way, and to row another. Now,
for my part d'ye see, I'm for carrying things above board, I'm not for
keeping any thing under hatches,—so that if you ben't as willing as I, say
so a God's name, there's no harm done. . . .[23]

Such is his proposal to the girl he has just met, scarcely an
indication of love at first sight. He has already expressed his
opinion of matrimony in no uncertain terms:

. . . now a man that is marry'd has as it were, d'ye see, his feet in
the bilboes, and may-hap mayn't get 'em out again when he wou'd. . . . A
man that is marry'd, d'ye see, is no more like another man, than a
gally-slave is like one of us free sailors, he is chain'd to an oar all his
life; and may-hap forc'd to tug a leaky vessel into the bargain.[24]

Miss Prue calls him an "ugly thing," "a sea-calf," and "a stink-
ing tar-barrel." He retorts,

. . . if you shou'd give such language at sea, you'd have a cat o' nine
tails laid cross your shoulders. . . . Sea-calf? I an't calf enough to lick
your chalk'd face, you cheese-curd you—[25]

After the sea song and the entertainment by his sailors (whom
he summons by whistle: he has already mentioned the author
of "Buxom Joan" as the boatswain, so that, if Ben is not the
captain of the ship, he is probably one of the principal officers),
he says, "For my part, I mean to toss a can, and remember my
sweet-heart, a-fore I turn in. . . ." There is a suggestion of
Caliban in Mrs. Frail's description of him:

. . . thou wert born amongst rocks, suck'd by whales, cradled in a tempest,
and whistled to by winds; and thou art come forth with fins and scales,
and three rows of teeth, a most outrageous fish of prey.[26]

Ravenscroft's *The Canterbury Guests* (1695) comes closer
to *The Rover* in its details. The words of Careless to Hilaria
parallel Willmore's so nearly that they must have been borrowed:

But let me give you this caution, be not deceived with the vain considerations of Virtue, Modesty, Chastity, Honour, Reputation and the like, these are Bugg-words, that aw'd Women in former Ages, and still fool a great many in this.[27]

Durzo is much like Willmore, but somewhat more unpolished. Careless describes him as

An honest Tarpaulin—The Son of an *English* Renegade: He was born a Ship-board, and never was ashore beyond a Sea Port Town—except up in the Countries amongst the *Indians* and *Spaniards* to Ravage, Burn and Plunder, for he has been a Buccanier from his Infancy.[28]

He says of himself,

I can't talk at your rate, but if you are for Ship shape language, downright drinking, or will come to grapling, I am for you.[29]

Careless continues,

Stout he is and brave—and that temper has inclin'd him to leave that hellish Crew and employ his Valour in the Service of his Father's Native Country . . . from Captains of Ships, and Governors of Plantations, the King has heard much of his Valour. . . .[30]

Durzo says of the ladies that they are

Three very snug Frigates, well Rigg'd; 'twere pity too but they were as well Man'd. . . . I like them all; I am for a whole Tier of them. . . . Why, a Woman's the finest thing I ever saw, except a *Cannon Mounted*, and a Ship under Sail. . . . Will you give her to me.

LOVELL If you can get her.

DURZO Why, I can take her up in my Arms and run away with her.

ARABELLA And whither wou'd you carry me?

DURZO Aboard—and he that dares come to take you from me there, had as good leap into a Blazing Fireship, or kiss Thunder.[31]

As in *The Rover*, the suggested kidnapping does not take place, this time because Captain Durzo is made to see that such action would not be sporting.

Hilaria says of him that, "he looks as ruff as a storm," Arabella that, "he looks as if fighting was his business," and Jacinta

that, "He's not very curious in his dress." He protests that he
cannot find his way on land. When Lovell asks him whether he
can read, he replies, "No, I am a Sea Captain, the Sea breeds
Soldiers, but no Schollars; 'tis out of my Element." When
Arabella pretends to jilt him, he rails at her:

Do you play with my Anger; am I so tame to be laugh'd at? sure I
have seem'd more terrible, when with this Sword, I have lop'd off Limbs,
strow'd Decks with Carcases, turn'd Fleets to floating Hospitals, sent
Navies to their Ports to cut down Masts, and hew the Timber of their
scatter'd Vessels into wooden Legs and Crutches, to under-prop the Crip-
ples they brought home.[32]

There is also a flavor of Captain Porpuss in his frightening
Arabella nearly out of her senses by his description of a sea
fight.

Shipwrecks and plain dealers continue on into the eighteenth
century. Such incidents as love at first sight after railing at love
and change of identity occur in most of the comedies of the
humours group; they can scarcely be regarded as significant,
but they are there anyway. An exception is Fidelia Grey, who
follows Manly disguised as a gentleman volunteer, and ultimately wins his love at first sight (as a woman): this episode is
almost certainly derived from *Twelfth Night,* and therefore from
the Greek romance tradition. When the incidents appear with
other romantic material, they are presumably a continuation of
the influence of Greek romance on Elizabethan drama. There
are plays with and without the scene at sea, and with and without the realistic nautical figures.

Motteux' *Beauty in Distress* (1698) tells how the heroine,
Placentia, is to be kidnapped aboard a brigantine with her own
consent, but the plot is foiled by premature discovery. When
the captain comes ashore to help his friends, a gang of pirates
in the pay of the villain cut out the vessel: but the loyal lieutenant and crew pretend to join the pirates, and later recapture

the brigantine. All ends happily, with no scene at sea. The captain, leaning on his stick as he defends the door despite his wound, is something of a heart of oak, but the play is not significant.

Farquhar's contribution to the naval tradition is almost buried in the concentration of his drama on the title rôle of Sir Harry Wildair (played 1701). Sir Harry pays too much attention to Colonel Standard's wife; and Standard's brother, Captain Fireball, the plain dealer, is brought in as a kind of warning chorus or *raisonneur*. He rails at marriage by implication in his warning to his brother:

But faith, brother, I had rather, turn skipper to an Indian canoe, than manage the vessel you're master of. . . . She'll run adrift with every wind that blows: she's all sail and no ballast. . . . We seamen speak plain, brother. . . . Hell! that a man who has stormed Namur should become the jest of a coffee-table!—The whole house was clearly taken up with two important questions, whether the colonel was a cuckold or Kid a pirate.[33]

Fireball is also a swashbuckler:

Brandy! you dog, abuse brandy! flat treason against the navy-royal!— Sirrah, I'll teach you to abuse the fleet!—Here, Shark!
Enter Shark
Get three or four of the ship's crew, and press this fellow aboard the Beelzebub.
SHARK Ay, master.
. . . Ay, ay, sir!—Avast, avast!"

Clincher has earlier commented on Fireball's religion:

Hi! hi! hi!—religion! . . . And to hear a sea-captain talk of religion! that's pleasant, faith![34]

Since he drinks the brandy, and is almost immediately paralyzed, they do not carry him aboard as threatened, but take him to Lady Lurewell's instead.

One other episode is worth calling attention to, since it probably gives its name to the last play of this series. After a session at cards the captain comes in swearing, "Blood and fire, I have lost six months pay!" and is only made happy by news that the King of Spain is dead, with a war sure to follow. At this he sings, "Tall dall de Rall!"[35]

The plain dealer of Dennis' *Gibraltar* (1705) is an old sea dog, Nick Porpus:

Why, look you, do you see . . . I am Honest for all I can't Compliment, I am no Wordy-Man, do you see—Wordy-Men are Knaves [This is probably satirical considering his long speech, and the fact that he surely is a knave in acting as pandar] and most on 'em Cowards to boot too; do you see, a Man of Words and not of Deeds, Words are but Wind, and some of our Bully Captains are all Wind. When they shou'd go to Loggerheads, then they call a Council, do you see, to ask one another, whether they shall run away or no, when, Godsbud, they have all resolv'd upon it aforehand. My name is *Nick Porpus,* do you see, and a Word and a Blow is the way of old Nick, old Nick, I' faith, Gentlemen,—I am sorry we were top heavy [drunk], when we shou'd have done your Business . . . and Zoo's, we'll face a Storm for you, now do you see, tho' it shou'd blow till it blew the Devil's head off.[36]

And elsewhere he says,

Bluff is the Word, I'll ply him Larboard, do you see. A Word and a Blow with old *Nick,* I' faith Gentlemen.

Mrs. Centlivre's *A Bickerstaff's Burying* (acted 1710) is an interesting continuation of the *Tempest* school. The main plot is derived from *Sinbad, the Sailor* rather than from Greek romance, but the way desert, or at least distant, island material is combined with realistic nautical details is suggestive of the prototype itself. Mrs. Take-it has been wrecked on the island of Casgar and has married the Emir Mezro. She has instructed her husband's niece, Lady Isabinda, in the superiority of everything English. The law compels the widow or widower to be buried alive with the deceased husband or wife, and she is kept in subservience by the Emir's feigning illness. A ship arrives in distress; the captain, who has known Lady Mezro in England, falls in love with Isabinda at first sight, and offers to kidnap both ladies aboard ship. Lady Mezro pretends to die, and is duly smuggled off in her coffin; the Emir, much relieved to discover that she is not dead, swears never to marry again. Scene I opens with the following setting:

A working Sea seen at a Distance, with the Appearance of a Head of a Ship bulging against a Rock: Mermaids rise and sing: Thunder and Lightning: Then the scene shuts.

Lady Mezro and her niece discuss the wreck of the ship. Then the mariners enter:

CAPTAIN Well, how fares the Ship, has she any Damage

BOATSWAIN Only the Leak, which the Carpenter has stop'd, Captain.

CAPT. That's well: I can't imagine what this Island produces!

BOAT. Monsters, I think; for they stare as if they never had any Commerce with Mankind or ever saw a Ship in their Lives.

CAPT. I question if ever they did, and wish it had not been our Fortune to have improv'd their Knowledge.

1ST SAILOR I wish so too; I hate making strange Land: Who the Devil knows where to find a Wench now?

BOAT. Here's a Dog, that two Hours ago, drown'd his necessary Orders with his Prayers, and now is roaring as loud for a Whore.

1ST SAILOR 'Tis our Custom, you know; out of Danger the Sailor must be merry, i'Faith; ha, ha.

2ND SAILOR Nell, at the Ship at Chatham, shall know this.

1ST SAILOR I care not a Rope's-End if she does: Why, what the Devil do you think I'll come into a strange Land, and not examine what Commodity it produces? No, no, Faith; Nick must know if the Females here be Fish or Flesh, before he puts off again.

Surely, the wreck on a rock near a desert island after a tempest; the miraculous element of the mermaids and the slight damage done the ship; the discussion of the disaster by spectators ashore; the suggestion of the possible discovery of monsters and fishy ones at that; the reference to prayers drowning out the orders; the suggestion of how the chance of marrying a lady goes to the First Sailor's head, as evidenced by his decision to rise in rank ("And I will be an Ambral too, for all you, and my Master here, shall be my Rear Ambral";[37] The master's only comment is, "Oh, your very humble servant, Mr. Admiral"); and possibly the earlier adventure of Lady Mezro in reaching the island by an incident not too different from the one which brought Prospero and Miranda—all indicate the influence of *The Tempest*. In the end, the First Sailor is scared by the law, and it is the Second Sailor who takes the lady to sea with him.

The technical commands are missing, since there is no occasion for them in any scene actually presented. The nautical atmosphere is here given, as so often in the plays of the *Plain Dealer* group, by salt water figures of speech. Says the First Sailor,

. . . foresake a fine Lady for *Nell?* That's quitting a Bowl of Punch for a Draught of Sea-water. (*Spitting*)

BOAT. I wonder what she saw in that ugly Phiz of thine, that's always dirty as the Hammock you swing in; and as seldom wash'd as your Shirt, which is not once a Quarter.

2ND SAILOR Ha, ha! Oh, she fell in Love with his Nose or his Legs.[38]

The captain becomes lyrical:

. . . Ha! your Skin's as smooth as the Sea in a Calm, and your Eyes outshine the Sun after a Storm; your Voice as sweet as Syrens Songs; and 'tis greater Pleasure to behold you, than Land after a dangerous Voyage.[39]

There is no suggestion of piracy, but a considerable one of general lawlessness. Over all is the flavor of sentimental patriotism that is to be so popular a hundred years later.

The *Fair Quaker, of Deal* (1710) is important as a link between Jonson's comedy and Smollett's fiction. The second title, *The Humours of the Navy*, makes it clear that Shadwell thought of himself as a member of the dramatic tribe of Ben. The play differs from any by Jonson in that a whole group of sailors are presented, several of them favorably. Worthy is the perfect hero, with little of the sailor about him. He shows some of the sentimental attitude toward his followers that is to characterize the sea hero of later drama and fiction.

So, thank Heaven I have at last reached my Native Land. Coxen, take care the Water be sent on Board with Expedition, and bid the Purser hasten to Dover for fresh Provisions, and let the Sick Men be set on Shore the next Trip: There's something for the Boat's Crew, go and refresh yourselves.[40]

To which the coxswain replies dutifully, if unnaturally,

All your Orders shall be punctually comply'd with.

He describes his fellow captains as, "Flip my Commadore, a most obstinate, positive, ignorant Wappineer-Tar," and Mizen, "a Sea Fop, of all Creatures the Most Ridiculous." There are one or two other officers, and some rough and ready tars.

The plot is negligible, although Mizen's plan to win Dorcas by carrying her aboard ship suggests the kidnapping episode. His principal aim is her fortune; and, after getting that, he may decide to heave her out of the cabin window, and report that she had a calenture and so jumped overboard. He is fooled into marrying a courtesan, and is glad to discover that the marriage, as in *The Silent Woman,* is invalid. The important element in the play is not the action, but the character studies and criticisms of naval institutions.

Flip has a good bit of the plain dealer about him:

ROVEWELL Most Noble Commadore, your humble Servant.
FLIP Noble, a Pox of Nobility I say; the best Commadores that ever went between the two Ends of a Ship have not a drop of Nobility in 'em, thank Heaven. . . . I have serv'd in every Office belonging to a Ship from Cook's Boy to a Commadore; and have all the Sea Jests by Heart from the Fore-Castle to the Great Cabin; and I love a sailor.[41]

He is accused of getting drunk once a week with each mess in the ship and, by the men, of punishing them later with

"Whips, Pickles, Guns, Gears, and Bilboes" for any impertinences of which they may have been guilty while intoxicated.[42]
He provides the drink and women for his men. The sailors explain that he ought to force the surgeon to cure them, at government expense, of diseases caught this way, since the doctor gets
more than half the pay for the entire ship's company, officers
and all. The marine officer complains:

... the old Dog had the Impudence to Confine me three Months to my
Cabin, only for knocking down a Boatswain's-Mate that had struck one
of my Marines. . . .

He is always expressing his contempt for Mizen, and his love
for the good old days of the Dutch wars. A trace of the *Tempest*
convention is suggested in his comment, "Sirrah, don't you
flinch your Ladle; he that will do that will run down into the
Hold in an Engagement, or say his Prayers in a Storm."[43]

Mizen is first introduced ordering a supply of perfume. His
cabin is furnished as nearly as possible like a drawing room,
and, when he has a visiting day, the conversation is chiefly
gossip.[44] He complains that Commodore Flip has broken forty
pounds worth of china in his cabin. He has plans to reform the
navy by making it more genteel, and hopes to substitute a
less harsh sounding technical vocabulary. Before he presents
his plan to parliament, he will see to it that the "Tar Captains"
are sent to the West Indies (where the fever will presumably do
the rest).[45] When at the end of the play he finds that he has
been fooled, he shows considerable ability in using nautical
language himself.

The characteristics of the sailors, and especially their love of
liquor and women, have been indicated above. They get drunk
and debate whether they shall throw the Purser, Boatswain, and
Bilboes overboard: "when the Captain and Purser whispers, our
Guts ought to grumble." The Coxswain tries to get out of going
with them to drown the constable or ravish all the women, but

they insist that they have "no Dispect of Persons."[46] One explains to Flip that he does not wish to get drunk as he always beats his wife when he is in that condition, and is going to see her for the first time in sixteen months. The Commodore says that he will send him aboard so that he will not see his wife for two months more. "Oh! then, Sir, I'll be drunk with all my heart."[47]

In addition to the comments already quoted, there are reflections on the heavy drinking among naval chaplains, on bribery and influence as methods of securing promotion, on the contrast between the bravery and the immorality of the sailors, and on Avery's mutiny and piracy. Worthy defends the Admiralty as men of honor, and generally favors existing conditions.

Injur'd Love (1711) contains a romantic story suggestive of the *Tempest* school, narrated as exposition. Thrivemore, returning home from the Indies with a fortune, is attacked by a pirate. His vessel is "shatter'd," and the captain killed, so that the next day

being blown upon a Desert Island, we had not hands enough to clear her from the Rocks, against which we bulg'd; two or three more and I, with much ado, sav'd our selves in the Boat.[48]

His share in a chest of treasure makes up for the loss of his fortune. With his last shot he saves two gentlemen from a boar. Captain Cruize sees their signal of distress, and brings them home to England. It develops that the two gentlemen are Fidelia and her companion, marooned on the island by Rashlove, the former's husband, who believes Fidelia unfaithful to him. After the usual cross purposes plot, all ends happily.

The captain's manners, perhaps because he is represented in the *dramatis personae* as endowed with a "polite Land Education," are good, and he does not boast of his frankness. It is true that he loses his temper with his unconscious rival, Scrape, but the provocation is great:

SCRAPE Pray, Captain, who are you in love with?
CAPT. With a Mare-maid. . . .
SCRAPE Oh Lord! a Mare-maid! Why then it's twenty to one but you have a God for your Rival, ha, ha.
CAPT. Yes; and am very much tempted to beat him into Stock-fish.
. . . .
SCRAPE . . . you Sea Voyagers carry your House about you and see nothing.
CAPT. And prithee what hast thou seen? Damn thee!
SCRAPE Something else, I hope, besides Sky and Water, Sea Elves, Porpusses and Whales. . . .[49]

The captain also rails at marriage:

Marriage! the very Word sounds of Chains, Shackles, and Fetters. Dear Liberty, I long to enjoy thy unconfined Privileges, and feast my Eyes upon this new Constellation of Beauties.[50]

It is almost immediately after proclaiming that he would "rather part with my Money than my Liberty" that he falls in love at first sight with Charmilla.

Johnson's *Successful Pyrate* (1713) is a queer mixture of Elizabethan romance and the not yet written *History of the Pirates*. The plot is based on some episodes in the life of Avery, but the material is expanded into a desert island romance. Arviragus, alias Averio, a noble pirate, returns to England, after distinguished service in the Dutch Wars, to find that his best friend has cheated him of his fortune and his mistress. He is then imprisoned for caning a superior officer, a coward. Disillusioned, he sets up a pirate kingdom on Madagascar. Zaida, daughter of the Mogul, is captured en route to be married, and in her train is a minor noble, Aranes, hopelessly in love with her, who is rather glad that the capture has prevented marriage. Arviragus falls in love with Zaida at first sight, and, because of jealousy, orders Aranes slain. The revolt of the sailor-subjects against a new rule that they must marry captive women is suppressed: this provides the humorous element in the drama. Arviragus discovers that Aranes is his own son by a noble Indian, Zelmane (remarkable reunion and recognition by means of a bracelet), and in the midst of his remorse is overjoyed to find that the young man still lives. He gives Zaida to his son, and abdicates in the latter's favor. There is considerable sentimental patriotism in the ex-ruler's pathetic wish to return to England.

Because of its romantic setting on the Island of Madagascar, and its general nautical background, this play may be grouped with the continuation of the *Tempest* school. The scene of the rebellious pirates, and their suppression, is nearer to Duke Stephano than to anything in the *Plain Dealer group*. Yet this play obviously owes something to the latter tradition, by this time well established. Admiral Boreale, late Lieutenant R.N., while not especially nautical, is blunt and honest. And the mob of sailors rail at marriage, insisting that one who admits his birth to be legitimate is a "son of a who--e,"[51] and praise drinking instead.

The Bravo Turn'd Bully (1740), according to the prologue, is based on an actual incident. The scene is Havana, and the story the escape from the clutches of the Don, of Jenkins, Merry, Manly, and Richwell, with their crews, by means of a trick. Jenkins is, on the basis of the reference to his taking "the Loss of an Ear worse than another man would take the Loss of his Head,"[52] an historical character. His chief characteristic is righteous indignation. Manly is the melodramatic sentimental hero who loves his wife, adores his country, prides himself on his honor, and, in a few minutes, runs the whole gamut of emotions from exultation to extreme despair. Richwell is an older and less emotional man. Merry is the plain dealer of the play, and takes part in repartee with another Fidelia, the

English companion of the Governor's lady. They make up their match so quickly that the rather pert heroine finds it necessary to apologize for her forwardness in the epilogue. There is what seems an echo of *The Rover* in Merry's calling her "that pretty Gypsy."[53] But aside from his drinking heavily in the first scene as a way of getting information from the Spaniards, Merry's character, while bold and resolute with flashes of humour, has none of the bad qualities of the rake suggested in the earlier plays. A scene of sailors dancing and singing in prison to celebrate their officers' visit is lugged in.[54]

Smollett's *The Reprisal* (1757) is a farce, and as such looks forward to the burlesque and music sea drama that is to culminate in the next century in *Black Eye'd Susan* and *Pinafore*. Yet, just as I shall have occasion to point out in connection with his novels, Smollett here shows considerable indebtedness to the Greek romance conventions. Heartly and Harriet, lovers, are captured in time of peace by Champignon, commander of a French frigate (kidnapping by pirates). He robs the prisoners, and makes love to Harriet (amorous captain). Harriet, like Riche's Silla, seeks to pass as Heartly's brother (change of identity). Heartly's escape results in the bringing of Lieutenant Lyon and a British tender (not exactly a miraculous rescue). Two comic Jacobite exiles in French service, Lieutenant Oclabber and Ensign Maclaymore, force the French commander to fight for a few minutes, but he surrenders in great fear as soon as he can. There is a suggestion that the entire naval strength of France comes from Irish and Scotch exiles. The ridicule of the French is carried far beyond the bounds of taste.

Although there are some scenes actually aboard ship, the technical language is so scanty, perhaps owing to the rapidity with which Champignon surrenders, that these can hardly be considered in the *Tempest* tradition. But there is a swearing boatswain, much adulterated, in the character of Ben Block, who gets drunk and resents the reprimand of Lieutenant Lyon:

> LYON But in the mean time, I shall have you to the gangway, you drunken swab.
>
> BLOCK Swab! I did swab the forecastle clear of the enemy, that I must confess.
>
> LYON None of your jaw, you lubber.
>
> BLOCK Lubber!—man and boy, twenty years in the service—lubber!—Ben Block was the man that taught thee, Tom Lyon, to hand, reef, and steer—so much for the service of Old England; but, go thy ways, Ben, thy timbers are crazy, thy planks are started, and thy bottom is foul. I have seen the day when thou wouldst have shown thy colours with the best o'un.[55]

Harriet interferes and makes peace, forcing Block to admit that Lyon is a "brisk" seaman. The whole play is overdrawn and abounds in burlesque characters and songs.

Mrs. Centlivre's *Basset Table* (1761) will suffice to close the plain dealer school, for the tendency in the direction of musical drama of the burlesque or sentimental sort was definitely under way by this time. Captain Hearty, called Captain Firebrand in the stage direction for his first entrance,[56] dresses his friend Lovely, an army officer, as a seaman, Captain Match, in order that the latter may win the daughter of Sir Richard Plainman, who will consent only to her marriage with a naval officer. Before learning of his friend's affair, the captain proposes to Sir Richard's learned daughter practically at first sight:

> Well, Madam, what think you of a cruizing Voyage towards the cape of Matrimony, your Father designs me for the Pilot; if you agree to it, we'll hoist Sail immediately. . . .[57]

As she is in love with Ensign Lovely, she sheers off; and, like Ben Legend, the worthy captain is rather relieved than otherwise to escape matrimony. His plot on behalf of his friend follows. He flirts a bit with Lady Reveler, who says of him in his absence,

What, the Sea Captain, Uncle? Faugh, I hate the Smell of Pitch and Tar; one that can entertain one with nothing but Fire and Smoke, Larboard and Starboard, and t'other Bowl of Punch; ha, ha, ha . . .[58]

but plays hero-worship in his presence. When her true lover, Lord Worthy, catches them together, the captain says that he has seen no woman worth fighting for since he came ashore:

But, Sir, if you have a mind to a Breathing here, tread upon my Toe, or speak but one Word in favour of the *French,* or against the Courage of our Fleet, and my Sword will start of itself to do its Master and my Country Justice.[59]

Elsewhere he characterizes himself as follows:

My word is this, I hate the *French,* love a handsome Woman, and a Bowl of Punch.[60]

The change of identity element is provided by the disguise of Lovely, who also shows the popular conception of the naval officer as a plain dealer:

I'm not for Compliments; 'tis a Land Language, I understand it not; Courage, Honesty, and Plain-dealing Truth, is the Learning of our Element; if you like that I am for ye. . . .[61]
I am rough and Storm-like in my Temper, unacquainted with the Effeminacy of Courts. . . .

One episode, presumably an elaboration of the similar incident in *Sir Harry Wildair,* gives its name somewhat illogically to the play: Captain Hearty, like Captain Fireball, comes from the card table in a passion over his losses:

. . . now the Devil blow my Head off if ever I saw the Cards run so; damn'em. . . . Fire and Gunpowder. . . . What the Devil had I to do among these Land-Rats?—Zounds, to lose forty Pounds for nothing, not so much as a wench for it.[62]

Murphy's *The Desert Island* (1762) is, according to the "Advertisement," based on a romantic Italian poem, the *Isola Disa-*

bitata, combined with various ingredients suggested by a friend of the author's, and concluded "with a drunken song by the Tars of *Old England.*" The plot is a rambling romantic one. Constantia and her little daughter Sylvia are landed on the Desert Island for refreshment, and are deserted for many years. Although the former still loves her husband, she believes he has marooned her intentionally; but, soon after the opening of the play, the husband, Ferdinand, and a friend, Henrico, land on the island to look for the women. Ferdinand explains that he was attacked by pirates just after the first landing on the island, and carried into slavery. After the remarkable reunion of the older couple, Henrico and Sylvia fall in love at first sight, and all ends happily. An element suggesting the new romance of the revolutionary period rather than the old of the Renaissance, is the interest in picturesque scenery displayed in the opening stage direction:

The scene represents a vale in the Desert Island, surrounded by rocks, caverns, grottos, flowering shrubs, exotic trees, and plants growing wild. On one side is a cavern in a rock, over the entrance of which appears, in large characters, an unfinished inscription. *Constantia* is discovered at work at the inscription, in a romantic habit of skins, leaves, and flowers; in her hand she holds a broken sword, and stands in act to finish the imperfect inscription.

There is no scene at sea, and no realistic nautical figure to spoil the nobility of this Arcadian picture. The men are conventionally perfect. It is clear that the Greek romance nautical play persists through the period along with the continuation of the *Tempest* and humours schools.

From 1660 to 1760, then, the sailor appears in the drama either as a rough and ready heart of oak against a background of actual nautical life, or as a subject for satire ashore, only occasionally admirable for his plain dealing in contrast with land hypocrisy. In each manifestation he appears as bold and rough, much given to wine and women; but in the former his courage is stressed and his recklessness admired, while in the latter even his admirable traits are caricatured. A notable fact is the absence from the drama of influence by *Robinson Crusoe* or other imitations of voyage narratives.

CHAPTER VII

THE SAILOR IN FICTION

1760-1802

About the middle of the eighteenth century a new-old influence began to make itself felt in fiction dealing with the sea,
as a result of the writings of Fielding and Smollett. These owe
more to the drama of the humours school than to the imitation
voyages, and hence can be distinguished from the latter without
much difficulty. As in the plays, the nautical incidents are thrown
into an essentially land story for the sake of variety, and the
emphasis is placed on character rather than on incident. The
imitation voyage exaggerated produces a journey to the Moon;
the naval episode exaggerated produces a caricature of a foppish
seaman, a cowardly seaman, or even of a courageous seaman.
The protagonists of the imitation voyages are adventurers, merchant captains, or buccaneers; of the naval episodes, naval officers or Jack Tars. Distant countries, desert islands, and imaginary kingdoms play a considerable part in the former; in the
latter the land becomes largely the edge of the sea, except that
England is important as a point of departure, and may be the
setting of the main tale in which the episode occurs. Details of
climate, inhabitants, and products give place to anecdotes of
cabin and forecastle. Whether slaver, privateersman, or buccaneer, the voyage hero is usually sentimentally pious, whereas
the attitude of the author of the episode may be cynical, and is
nearly always satirical.

Near the beginning of the century, the satirist Edward, or

Ned, Ward anticipated the application of the critical method to the presentation of maritime characters much as it was to be carried out in the naval episode. Whether he in turn was influenced by the "characters" of a still earlier period is hard to say. In his *Wooden World Dissected* he satirized most of the ranks of the ship's company, apparently in defence of the common sailor. His captain certainly belongs to the humours school, and may well be a forerunner of Smollett. He is of doubtful birth and interested only in making money. He never comes on deck if he can avoid it and refuses to lower his dignity by associating with his lieutenants. His wife is a shrew and unfaithful, so that he remains on his ship as much as possible, because he fears her more than a storm. He starves his crew by arrangement with his purser to line his own pockets: if they die, he can get more by pressing. He will do anything to avoid West India service because of the fever. He hates merchant captains because, by courtesy, they share his title, and fears the Admiralty.

The Boatswain—Is a Kind of a *Jack* with a Box, for let him but whistle once, and you have a hundred or more *Cartesian* Puppits, pop up upon Deck, and run about, and streight disappear again in an Instant. . . . His badge of Power, is his Bamboo . . . it has cur'd more of the Scurvy, than the Doctor, and made many a poor Cripple take up his Bed and Walk: Sometimes it makes the Lame to skip, and run up the Shrowds like a Monkey. . . .

And yet this same tool of his, is but a mere Sugar-candy Stick in Comparison to his Cat of Nine-Tails. . . . But were his Call, Stick, and Cat too, all thrown overboard, he yet would distinguish himself by his Throat; for no Ass in *Christendom* brays like himself; he varies his Notes to the Occasions, and sometimes it is so unaccountably terrible, that the poor simple Sort of Tars will run from it. . . .

He's a damn'd thundering Fellow . . . he dignifies all his Umbrays with the Title of Dog, Rogue or Rascal. . . . He mortally hates your Gentleman Volunteer . . . how frequently soever he damns himself, he is sure to damn others much oftener. In short, he's a Fellow that will throw away ten times more Oaths and Strokes in hoisting out a Barge, than in boarding an Enemy. But, Zounds, he'll cry, what would you have me do?[1]

As suggested before, this description, besides preparing the way for the characterizations in the naval episode, indicates that there was a considerable element of realism in the presentation of the swearing boatswain on the stage during the preceding century, despite the cold picture given in the sea grammars. Ward is not entirely alone in his attacks on contemporary naval administration, but his work is the only one easily accessible.[2] He is equally bitter toward lieutenants, midshipmen, and pursers.

It should be noticed that Smollett was not quite the first to make use of the humours method in presenting characters on the sea in fiction. Fielding's *Jonathan Wild* (1743), ordinarily classified as a continuation of the picaresque school, differs from the *English Rogue* in that the actual details of seafaring life are stressed instead of voyage material: there is a shipwreck on the coast of Africa with various adventures among the natives, but this part of the story is hazy as contrasted with the vivid nautical language of the sailors and other concrete details. We know from the *Journal of a Voyage to Lisbon* that the author was interested in the sea and its life, rather than in distant countries and voyage literature. It may almost be said that *Jonathan Wild,* and not the later *Roderick Random,* was the transition form from the imitation voyage to the naval episode, although of course it does not contain the excellent group of sea characters of the latter.

On the other hand, there is some attempt at presenting a gallery of sea figures. The villain-hero is of course only incidentally a mariner, but there is the rough and ready captain who "rapped out a hearty oath, and asked Wild if he had no more Christianity in him than to ravish a woman in a storm?"[3] and replied to Wild's threats with the obscenest form of con-

tempt; there is the brutal man-of-war captain who says in reply to Mrs. Heartfree's comment on his addresses, "Dresses,
d---n your dresses! I want to undress you,"[4] and his "virtuous and brave" lieutenant, who has been "twenty-five years
in that post without being able to obtain a ship, and [has]
seen several boys, the bastards of noblemen, put over his
head";[5] and there are the sailors who drink the brandy to save
it when they think they are lost, see their ship sink "with the
tenderness of a lover or a parent,"[6] and, as to women, think
"one color is as good as another."[7] Such characterizations appear infrequently in the imitation voyages.

The Greek romance elements are also present in goodly
numbers. When escorting Mrs. Heartfree to her husband in
France, Wild plays the part of the amorous captain, and is prevented from attacking her only by the actual captain.[8] Soon
after, they are captured by a Frenchman, a noble pirate, who
thinks the lady is Wild's wife (change of identity) and who, on
finding out the truth, sets Wild adrift in an open boat. Wild
jumps out of the boat in despair but, according to the author,
is saved mysteriously and miraculously. It develops later that
he merely climbs back into the boat: this is surely a burlesque
of the conventional miraculous rescue.[9] An English man of war
captures the French pirate, and the captain proves amorous:
he forces Mrs. Heartfree to come to his cabin when he is
drunk, and threatens to ravish her. She puts him off, and succeeds in getting him still more intoxicated, after which she
escapes from the cabin; in trying to follow he falls down the
steps, and dislocates his shoulder.[10] After a number of transfers from ship to ship, and the wreck referred to above, she rejoins her husband by a remarkable reunion. The naval episode
then is just as likely to contain Greek romance elements as is
the imitation voyage.

Smollett's *Roderick Random* (1749) is ordinarily considered the first great sea novel as distinct from imitation voyages. It contains in fact what I have called a naval episode, on rather a grand scale.[11] In a recent article Professor Ellison has tried to show Smollett's debt to Shakespeare, especially to the Falstaffian comedies, for his gallery of characters; but at the same time has admitted that the author derived his method almost entirely from the comedy of humours of Jonson and his successors: Smollett represents his characters "as the embodiment of a single dominant trait or ruling passion."[12] Captains Oakum and Whiffle, Mr. Morgan and Tom Bowling are too well known to require discussion in this study, but reference ought again to be made to the fact, pointed out by Commander Robinson, that Charles Shadwell's *Fair Quaker of Deal or the Humours of the Navy* is the transition between Jonson's comedy and Smollett's fiction. There is more than a hint of Captain Mizen, who keeps his cabin as nearly like a drawing room as possible and plans to reëdit technical sea language leaving out "your Larboard and Starboard, Hawsers, and Swabbs,"[13] in Smollett's sea fop, Captain Whiffle. The name occurs in the play, although applied to another character. The abuses complained about in both, graft on the part of the surgeon and purser, and the promotion of officers through interest rather than merit, are much the same. Shadwell's sailors get drunk and propose to throw overboard the purser, boatswain and bilboes, beat the mayor and corporation, and drown the constable, or to ravish all the women they meet, or break all the windows. Smollett's gallants get drunk and propose to "scour the hundreds, sweat the constable, maul the watch, and then reel soberly home to bed."[14]

The other characteristics identifying the naval episode are almost too obvious to require mention. The nautical characters are all of them officers and seamen of the Navy, and their activities take place chiefly at sea. The attitude of the author toward them is satirical. And, although the fact of their importance in the history of maritime fiction has given them false emphasis, the nautical incidents are merely thrown into a much longer story. The attack on Cartagena,[15] is part of the author's own experience, and is reproduced obviously as a bitter criticism of the management of the campaign.

Ironically enough, this novel, which has been adopted for ordinary purposes as the perfect example of the naval episode overlaps with the imitation voyage group, since one brief incident is borrowed from the account of a contemporary voyage. The romantic story of the hero's shipwreck on the estate of the girl with whom he is to fall in love at first sight, derives its details from Bulkeley and Cummins' *A Voyage to the South Seas* (1743). Roderick's enemy Crampley succeeds to the command of the ship on the death of the captain, an old man, who himself has been in command for only a short time.

We had been seven weeks at sea, when the gunner told the captain that, by his reckoning, we must be in soundings, and desired he would order the level lead to be heaved. Crampley swore he did not know how to keep the ship's way, for we were not within a hundred leagues of soundings, and therefore he would not give himself the trouble to cast the lead. Accordingly we continued our course all that afternoon and night, without shortening sail, although the gunner pretended to discover Scilly light, and next morning protested in form against the captain's conduct, for which he was put in confinement. We discovered no land all that day, and Crampley was still so infatuated as to neglect sounding; but at three o'clock in the morning the ship struck, and remained fast on a sandbank. This accident alarmed the whole crew; the boat was immediately hoisted out; but, as we could not discern which way the shore lay, we were obliged to wait for daylight. In the meantime the wind increased, and the waves beat against the sloop with such violence, that we expected she would have gone to pieces. The gunner was released and consulted. He advised the captain to cut away the mast, in order to lighten her; this expedient was performed without success. The sailors, seeing things in a desperate situation, according to custom, broke up the chests belonging to the officers, dressed themselves in their clothes, drank their liquors without ceremony; and drunkenness, tumult, and confusion ensued. In the midst of this uproar I went below, to secure my own effects; and found the carpenter's mate hewing down the purser's cabin with his hatchet, whistling all the while with great composure. When I asked his intention in so doing, he replied very calmly, "I only want to taste the purser's rum, that's all master." [The purser comes down and asks] what occasion he had for liquor, when, in all likelihood, he should be in eternity in a few minutes. "All's one for that," said the plunderer, "let us live while we can,"[16]

Crampley orders a boat out, gets in himself, and is rapidly followed by the crew. He tries to leave Random behind, but the latter forces his way in at the point of a pistol. On shore they fight a duel; Random is slugged from behind, robbed, and left for dead. Mention is made that the gunner saved the ship by floating her, but received no reward from the Admiralty.

The parallels with the voyage referred to above are numerous. In the first place, it seems more than a coincidence that the names used by Smollett in the chapter describing the wreck are Crampley and Tomlins, immediately suggestive of Bulkeley and Cummins. The death of Captain Kidd promotes Captain Cheap to the command of the "Wager," some time before the wreck, and he in turn is disabled by a dislocated shoulder.[17] The Master "could not see the Commodore's Light, tho' it was visible to every one else on the Quarter-Deck."[18] Bulkeley explains that, although he is gunner, he has charge of a watch: the implication is that this appointment entitles him to take the important place he assumes in the councils of the officers.[19] Without any such apology Smollett's gunner assumes an equal authority. Since the ship is in bad condition from a previous storm, Bulkeley urges the captain to stay off shore; but the captain insists that he must obey his orders, and adds that "there are no Soundings until you come within seven Leagues of the Land."[20] The argument is respectful but prolonged.

. . . at Half an Hour past Four this Morning, the Ship struck abaft
on a sunken Rock. . . . Launch'd the Barge, Cutter, and Yaul over the
Gunnel: cut the Main and Fore-Mast by the Board. . . . At Night it
blow'd very hard at North, with a great tumbling Sea; we expected
every Moment that the Ship would part. . . . They [some of the sailors]
began with broaching the Wine in the Lazaretto; then breaking open
Cabbins and Chests, arming themselves with Swords and Pistols, threaten-
ing to murder those who should oppose or question them: Being drunk
and mad with Liquor, they plunder'd Chests and Cabbins for Money
and other Things of Value, cloathed themselves in the richest apparel
they could find, and imagined themselves Lords Paramount.[21]

In addition to these fairly definite parallels there are a number of details in the *Voyage* that might have been adapted by
Smollett. Soon after the landing, the captain knocks down the
recalcitrant boatswain with his cane, "so that he was motion-
less, and to Appearance dead."[22] The "Lords Paramount" sober
up and are stripped of all their finery. The Captain is as un-
feeling toward the midshipman, Mr. Cozens, whom he wounds
and leaves to die in the open without surgical attention, as
Crampley is toward Tomlins in confining him until he dies of
fever. And, like the gunner who floats off the ship but receives
no recognition from the Admiralty, Bulkeley and Cummins,
after all their efforts, face a court-martial for mutiny when they
get back to England.

Since less than four pages of *Roderick Random* are covered
by this incident, it is presumably safe to say that it does not
invalidate the classification of that novel with those containing
naval episodes. The Greek romance elements are surprising, considering that the author claims to be writing a picaresque tale.
Random is kidnapped and carried aboard ship: this detail is
assimilated to the naval background by having a press gang
the instrument. He meets his mistress as the result of a shipwreck, and the lady with whom he takes service supposes that
he must have come ashore on the back of a whale or a dolphin.[23]

He has a remarkable reunion in Paraguay with his father, who explains that the report of his death grew out of a shipwreck from which, by a miraculous spar rescue, he alone was saved. There is even the suggestion of a formula storm, although this one does not result in destruction of a vessel.

By his own statement, Smollett is trying to write a picaresque tale,[24] so that here at least it is safe to relate the episodic structure and villain-hero to that source.

Kimber's *Joe Thompson* (1750) combines both the imitation voyage and naval episode methods. After a whole series of land adventures of the picaresque order, about a hundred pages along in Volume II, Joe Thompson goes to sea with Captain Social of H. M. S. "Hastings." A boatload of survivors from a ship which has blown up is saved, and among them the hero finds his old friend Prim. The latter tells of his sufferings under Captain Surly who, drunk most of the day, kicks and abuses him until he deserts into the woods at St. Augustine Bay, Madagascar. There follows a short desert island story. Prim is taken off by a British ship in which a mutiny has just been suppressed by setting the men ashore with their wages. Prim saves the ship by putting out a candle carelessly stuck in an open powder barrel in the magazine, but that crew is apparently fated, for later the burning tobacco dropped from the pipe of a sailor, who has gone to open a cask of rum, sets his chest afire and blows up the ship.

A few more incidents in the main narrative precede the next digression. The "Hastings" encounters a water spout off St. Helena and breaks it with a swivel gun. The roll of the ship following this knocks Thompson out of the cabin window, but he is saved by his servant. Captain Social dies suitably of gout of the stomach and is succeeded by Mr. Bentley, "a good officer." Thompson reaches his destination at Fort St. George on the Coast of Coromandel. After some land adventures, he starts home. He encounters another old friend, Diaper, who tells an ancient mariner story of being becalmed without food and water on a damaged vessel in the Pacific, and an equally exciting yarn concerning a mutiny. After various other adventures, including capture by a French privateer, a noble pirate, Thompson lands safely in France.

The method of presentation is clearly that of Smollett. Captains Social, Surly, and Clement belong to the school of Oakum and Whiffle. Scott, the boatswain who leads the rebellion in Diaper's story, "of a mutinous, domineering spirit, and particularly severe in the execution of his office,"[25] thus expresses himself concerning Diaper's dog:

"Damn me! how came this dog here. He's like his master, always peering and prying about, and be damned to him. I wish I could as easily dispatch him as I could his dog, and then we should have nothing to fear; but I'll be damned if I do not hide the precise son of a bitch some how or other notwithstanding!" Upon which he gave my dog a kick, who ran yelping away. . . .[26]

Like Jim Hawkins in *Treasure Island*, Diaper overhears the plot through awaking from a nap; he succeeds in getting the word to the officers, who gather ashore, and leads the mutineers into an ambush. Scott refuses to surrender, "So d---n ye, my lads, let us charge them directly!"[27] Diaper is forced to shoot the boatswain at close range, when the latter charges him with his empty gun. This tar suggests the "wood lion" of Elizabethan times.[28] A considerable number of the other figures are vividly presented.

There are a number of characters connected with the navy, and the details of the life on board ship are stressed in a critical fashion, although the attitude is usually favorable. On the other hand, as is shown by the summary, there is, in addition to the shipwreck-desert island episodes, a considerable element of voyage detail.

If the Greek romance tradition makes any contribution besides the series of remarkable reunions, it is in the storm early in Thompson's voyage which approaches the formula:

Propitious gales carried us without any remarkable occurrence, to the height of Cape Cantin. . . . The clouds on the western board began to blacken the skies, and a few melancholy drops wept a farewell to one of the finest days I had ever, methought, experienced: and now the lightning flashed, and the hoarse thunder growled over the concave vault with deafening roar, as if whole nature was meeting with a general dissolution, and presently the impetuous west wind raised the irritated billows mountains high . . . [our mainsail] was split into twenty pieces . . . [a eulogy on the courage of the sailors takes the place of the usual mention of fear]. . . . The horrid tumult upon deck, the piping of the boatswain and his mates, mingling with the howling of the winds, and the continual dashing of the waves, made such a confusion, as was sufficient to stun the head of any stranger to these uncouth and terrifying scenes.[29]

The captain however calls it "good seaman's weather."

About the same time appears in *Tom Jones Married* (2d ed. 1750), one of those brief characterizations of the sailor that become rather frequent in land fiction. I classify this with the naval episode because of its critical nature. Lord B---n says of the mariners, that they are

A Race of Men, who in all their actions would persuade us, that they are more than Mortals! They contemn *Heat* and *Cold, Hunger* and *Thirst:* They remain intrepid in the midst of the most astonishing Dangers, when both the Winds and the Seas are at War. And though Sheets of Lightning descend; the Moon be obscured; the Stars seem extinguished by the Tempest; all Things be filled with Horror and Despair; and the dangerous Rocks, and devouring Sands, seem ready to break their Ships in Pieces, and swallow them up; They meet them all with Resolution and Undaunted Courage.—But—I cannot hide their Faults.—Even in the very Moment of Destruction, when their Vessel strikes, and the rolling Waves rush greedily to devour them, these Men, who seem more indebted to Providence for their Safety, than other Men, mingle their very Prayers with Blasphemies: They will invoke the Name of God with Horror, calling upon him, at every trifling Moment, to destroy and reprobate them to Eternity: and as they have cast off Fear of God, so I can assure you, they regard no Man's Person. . . . [30]

One wonders whether the author evolved this after watching the first scene of the revised *Tempest*.

Peregrine Pickle (1751) adds a few more characters to Smollett's picture gallery, notably the grand figure of Hauser Trunnion, but nothing particular to his method. Here, as well as later, may be mentioned also *Sir Launcelot Greaves* (1760-1761) where Captain Crowe, master mariner and knight errant, is one of the best characters in the book. The author characterizes him as follows:

> Captain Crowe had commanded a merchant ship in the Mediterranean trade for many years, and saved some money by dint of frugality and traffic. He was an excellent seaman, brave, active, friendly in his way and scrupulously honest; but as little acquainted with the world as a sucking child; whimsical, impatient, and so impetuous, that he could not help breaking in upon the conversation, whatever it might be, with repeated interruptions, that seemed to burst from him by involuntary impulse. When he himself attempted to speak he never finished his period; but made such a number of abrupt transitions, that his discourse seemed to be an unconnected series of unfinished sentences, the meaning of which it was not easy to decipher.

Crowe has the conventionally low opinion of matrimony expressed by so many plain dealers:

> . . . a seafaring man may have a sweetheart in every port; but he should steer clear of a wife, as he would avoid a quickstand.—You see, brother, how this here Clewline lags astern in the wake of a snivelling b--h; otherwise he would never make a weft in his ensign for the loss of a child—odds heart! he could have done no more if he had sprung a top-mast, or started a timber!

When the pretended ghosts announce that they are spirits of his relatives from heaven, he replies:

> Ye lie, ye b--s of hell! ye are d--ned for heaving me out of my right, five fathom and a half by the head, in burning brimstone. Don't I see the blue flames come out of your hawse-holes?[31]

A brief sketch[32] of a sailor is inserted in *Young Scarron* (1752), possibly by Thomas Mozeen. A sturdy young mariner returns to his father's house after three years absence, tells interesting tales which are not recorded, and promises to aid his father financially. When he is paid off, he gradually drifts away and spends his money on riotous living, until he lands in Marshallsea for a note of hand given to "a Lady in Drury Lane." His friends visit the prison, and find him asleep, with his head in a courtesan's lap. The latter claims to be his wife and attacks his mother. Mr. Valentine buys him out, and takes him home to sober up. The young reprobate fools them into thinking he has still some money due, and departs with some of Valentine's property, leaving debts for his parents to pay. He is never heard of again.

The Life and History of a Pilgrim (1753) contains a realistic sketch of sailors at an inn in Barcelona. The hero is encouraged by an old salt in the following fashion:

S'blood, don't be cast down, Wind and Tide do not serve always alike, at the Stern To-day and at the Head To-morrow; if the Wind be in your teeth now, you must try t'other Tack, and may be, Messmate, the other Trip may be better; she won't always carry her Top and Top-Gallant Sail; we must sometimes reef a bit, and lie under her Fore-sail: S'blood, what if she's brought Gunnel to, Helm-a-lee and she is in her Geers. There's our Boatswain now, I remember him to fall over-board at *St. Kitts,* he swam ashore an half-drowned Rat, and now the Dog has a Skin as the best of us: Come, Messmate, drink about, Tide will be out before we shall be able to get half our Loading in.[33]

There is also a characterization of Captain Dowding,

. . . a morose and churlish Fellow. . . . Nothing in nature could better resemble the Monster in the inchanted Island, than the Monster on board the Little Robin of Bristol, never tractable when sober, but the most fawning Animal when he was drunk . . . he constantly fumigated his Nose with Tobacco, stuped his Entrails with Brandy, and had no more Desire for Conversation, than a Quaker, under the Inspiration of the Spirit, at a Silent meeting.[34]

When he discovers that he has lost his Algerine pass, he begins to drink heavily and swears he sees a whole fleet flying "the bloody flag, the black ensign and pennant, and the death's head."

In the *Duplessis Memoirs* there is storm and shipwreck, followed by the murder of the crew by Cornish wreckers. The description of the reaction of the mariners to danger carries on the old tradition:

Fain would I [the hero] have prevail'd with the Mariners to assist me in Prayer, for a Deliverance but . . . neither Precept or example could perswade those insensible Wretches to quit their Dram Bottles, which they swore would do them more Good by Half than all the Prayers in the Book. *A man could die but once, they said, and by G--d they'd die merrily* . . . nothing was to be heard but the most impious Oaths and horrid Blasphemies.[35]

Charles Johnstone's *Chrysal or the Adventures of a Guinea* (1760) contains a whole collection of sea portraits. There is the naval captain who accepts a bribe not to attack a Spanish galleon, insisting to his bellicose crew that she is a man of war.

The officers acted all the inconsistent outrages of madness. The men chewed the *quid*, damned their eyes and limbs for their bad luck, and went to work as usual. . . .[36]

This captain, sent to Coventry by his officers, bribes a higher official to escape punishment. Against this character, may be set the honest commander who is fined a year's pay because his ship's expenses for the voyage are too low.[37]

There are one or two other rogues; one coward who depends on his connection with the nobility to escape the consequences of running away in action, but is "broke" nevertheless; and what is evidently intended as an ideal figure, who serves out rum before the action, encourages the crew with talk of prize money and the honour of Old England, and displays courage himself. But the gem of the collection is the fop, lineal descendant of Mizen and Whiffle:

When I entered into the possession of my new master, he was lolling in a listless manner on a sofa in his state-room, where every art was exerted to counteract nature, and elude the mid-day heat, in one of the fiercest climates of the torrid zone. A gown of the thinnest silk hung loosely over his large limbs; the radiance of the sun was softened by shades of linen drawn before the open windows, and kept constantly wet, to cool the air as it entered through them; and every disagreeable savour was drowned in the most delicate perfumes.[38]

With these commanders are presented several tars, generally pictured favorably. One relieves the wife of another, a slave to duty in an almost literal sense since he has been turned over into another ship after a six years' voyage without receiving any of his pay or prize money.

Cheer away, sister, sister, cheer away: we'll bring up all this lee way next trip. Damn my eyes and limbs if I'll see a brother seaman's family at short allowance while I have a shilling. Come, heave a-head; I'll rig you and victual you and your children against your husband comes, to man you for a voyage home. I'll swing my hammock in the next birth [sic] and you shall cook the kettle, while I stay ashore.[39]

Another, in an inquisition prison in Lisbon, is hired to buy a ship, and does so, keeping careful account of the money.

I'll do it, though it was to hand the main-top-gallant sail in a storm at midnight, when the yard was broke in the slings, and it was not my watch; for if it was a man's watch, do you see, it would be but his duty; and there is no merit in a man's doing his duty—I am no flincher. I never say aye when I mean no. . . .[40]

He later comments complacently that there is still a little honesty left among the "tars of Old England."

In general, there is a great deal of sentimental patriotism expressed in terms of the honour and courage of Old England, but the greater number of figures presented are dishonorable and cowardly. On the other hand, suggestions are made that the administration of the navy is improving.

At least one romantic tale with a maritime background appears in *Chrysal*. Traffic, having cheated Amelia and married another woman, is sued by the former. She loses and goes to

Jamaica. Captured by the Spanish, she marries one of them. Traffic loses his money, becomes a buccaneer, and takes the town in which she lives. Her husband turns the tables, and Traffic, having been begged off from death by Amelia, is sentenced to the mines. The element of remarkable reunion is obvious.

The History of Jack Connor (1766) contains a rough and ready officer in "Captain Mizen, of the Superb man of war." He arranges with Loveit that the affections of the fair and frail Polly shall be transferred to himself for a monetary consideration.

S'blood, said the Captain, what's all this jawing for? I've done as coz desired, and o' has the papers in's pocket. Now d'ye see, an it be too little, there's twenty pieces more to turn the scale.—Now mistress, how say you? Shall we make the bargain and seal lips. . . . S'blood coz, she's a well built sloop, and will carry a huge deal of canvas.[41]

. . . Captain Mizen visited constantly, but seldom before one or two in the morning, and frequently half seas over, as he called it. . . . I was his pinnace, his frigate, and a thousand tender names, but on struggling, he has cried out.—That's right! Yard-arm and Yard-arm—S'blood, Poll, and you blow me up, by the world I'll clap the broad R on you.[42]

Captain Arundel, in the novel bearing his name (1776), is described as "a rough and martial figure above six feet high, his head bald to the crown, and a few grey curling locks in his neck, with a deep cut across his forehead, over which he wears a black patch . . . a face which defies *the winds of heaven* . . ."[43] He is made of

. . . precious materials, though of rough workmanship; in antient time, I am told, our sea officers were in general such as Captain Arundel is now; the modern class. . . . are more courtly, and no less courageous.

. . . he is the life and soul of our circle, but it requires a proper share of nerves to relish his conversation, for he talks as loud as if he was in a storm, and his laugh is a perfect feu de joie; he has a thousand sea-tricks which he practises on Lord S. and a set of jokes ready made for the occasion that I dare say have a great deal of humour in their own language, but to me were perfectly unintelligible.[44]

Needless to say different characters make these varying reports.
He hopes his nephew does not intend "to grow a flashy fellow
and learn to turn up [his] nose at a tar jacket,"[45] and mentions
that sailors "venture [their] lifes for Old England." He is promoted to admiral. This character serves the same purpose as
the one which was becoming so popular as an eccentric in the
drama.

His coach is a "large old tumbril" with six horses. Two sailors
in "scarlet jackets" are on the box. Two more in "flowered cot-
ton waistcoats with long silk handkerchiefs round their necks"
act as postillions. Inside are Arundel, a Scotch earl, now a captain, and "two noble boys in midshipman's uniform." When a
party goes for a ride in a wherry, the admiral takes the helm,
and keeps "roaring to them all the way from behind us, not without a due proportion of such phrases as had novelty at least to
recommend them."[46]

One of the other characters of the story is also a naval officer,
a young earl, who restores the family fortunes by capturing
prizes at sea. He is endowed with all the romantic virtues, and
has no nautical flavor at all.

Fanny Burney's *Evelina* (1778) presents a naval character,
Captain Mirvan, against a land background as a subject for
satire and contempt. The heroine says that he is "surly, vulgar,
and disagreeable."[47] He comments on the ill-shaped nose of
his daughter, whom he has not seen for seven years, threatens to throw the unfortunate Madame Duval out of the coach
window into the rain, gets great enjoyment from her falling into
the mud, and actually lays violent hands on her. His comments on the opera are "gross" and disapproving; but he considers *Love for Love* "one of the best comedies in the language,"
and admires Sailor Ben because he is a *man*.[48] He delights in
cruel practical jokes, and laughs uproariously whenever they
succeed, as when the fop, Mr. Lovel, is bitten in the ear by the

monkey, which the captain has introduced as Lovel's "messmate" and brother.[49]

The fop contends that he has no "sea-phrases" to explain
London to the captain, but the latter uses little nautical language himself. He speaks rudely and bluntly, with an occasional mistake in grammar such as "that there," and many
ejaculations such as " 'Fore George," "Ods my life," and "By
Jingo." There seems to be just a touch of archaism in his
"ben't" and "pr'ythee," a flavor given by other nautical characters, particularly in the drama. In plain dealer fashion, he
prides himself on his bluntness and honesty, despises the
French, and considers the English landsmen little better, with
their absurd costumes, servile flattery, and monkey-like manners: "before long, we shall hear the very sailors talking that
lingo, and never see a swabber without a bag and a sword."[50]

Scott's *The Adventures of a Rupee* (1783) presents two naval
portraits. One is of a hypocritical first mate.

We generally draw the sailor boisterous in his behaviour, but honest and
generous in his intentions. It was quite the reverse with this officer. His
hair fell in ringlets on his shoulders, and he wore a black coat, with
every other part of dress suitable to its decent gravity. . . . His face by
no means handsome, was contracted into a heavenly meekness, mixed with
self complacency, and his modest eye never ventured to look upon any
person with confidence; but, to mark the humility of its master, was
constantly fixed on its parent earth. . . . He made love in the softest note
of his scale.[51]

The other is of a foremast hand who goes ashore at Portsmouth, and in a short time spends six years pay on drink and
women. He saves the rupee to give to an old sweetheart, Moll
Black (is she any relative of Chrysal's Black Moll of Wapping?). When his money is gone, he becomes homesick to see
his mother, and sets out on foot. He helps a traveller by carrying
a child:

Messmate . . . we can make but little way in this here weather; but if you will hand me your ballast there, you may ride somewhat lighter.[52]

At the inn he sleeps with the landlord's daughter, and at London spends the rupee for rum with some shipmates. The rupee comments on his lack of observation in the countries he has visited:

. . . he saw the men in India were black, that the Dutch had canals, and the Chinese red and white houses.[53]

This blindness of the tar is mentioned as early as Ward, and as late as Cardinal Newman.

One vivid incident occurs at sea. The mate described above makes an excuse to visit a young woman in her cabin after she has retired, and attempts to ravish her (amorous captain). Her calls for help result in the mate's being found by the other passengers and sailors in a ridiculous situation. Her maid shouts fire, and a stout old woman is drenched by a sailor who is endeavoring to extinguish the supposed blaze.[54] This is clearly a modification of the inn episode so common in novels of the Fielding school, derived apparently from *Don Quixote*. The captain protects her thereafter; the mate takes his revenge by pretending to the other passengers that he has had an affair with her.[55]

Eugenius (second edition 1786) contains, among a group of eccentric characters in a Welsh village, a retired Lieutenant Bombketch, otherwise called Admiral Bembo according to a village custom by which the local attorney is known as the chief justice, and so on. He has in his court a stone mastiff painted to look like life, and ready to jump (surely an improvement on the American iron deer of a later period!). He also has imitation rabbits and hares, and an owl over the door. Six demi-culverins line his terrace. His friends joke about his failure to know the difference between the prayer book and the Bible, and tell a story of how he read the marriage service, by mistake for the appropriate prayer, during a storm in the Bay of Biscay.

Jonathan Corncob (1787), that rollicking burlesque at the expense of the Americans, has almost equally bitter satire on the British navy. The ship to which Jonathan escapes from a Boston jail is commanded by "a d---d smart officer."

Nobody, (said he) can assert that Captain Furnace is not a seaman, for he d---ns his eyes, chews tobacco, and is an excellent hand at making a sea-pye. He is also allowed to be a good officer for when it blows hard, he makes more noise than the boatswain and gun-tackles together. When he drinks a great deal of strong grog, which is generally every night, you would suppose the liquor he swallows to be the spirit of contradiction. On the passage to America, whenever he had taken his dose, and we were in the neighborhood of a rock or shoal, he was sure, spite of all remonstrance, to sail directly for it . . .![56]

He flogs men for failing to hear his commands in a storm. He nearly allows the ship to burn by refusing to listen to news of a fire since it does not come through the proper channel. He loses two landsmen overboard by forcing them aloft in a heavy sea, and, when Corncob refuses to go, orders the dozen lashes which were the limit for one offense, and then adds three sets more for technical offenses involved in the refusal. An old sailor says rather proudly that this is "a little sample of the discipline of the navy."[57]

There is also the cowardly Captain Quid, who, with much shouting of unintelligible commands back and forth, surrenders to an American privateer, the "Picaroon," after a litany of, "He has sixteen guns, and we only fourteen." "I have been at sea forty years, man and boy, and never met with so obstinate a fellow."[58] A grim irony lies in the fact that the American skipper is afraid of a king's ship and intends himself to surrender after a little bluffing. Quid is much frightened by a storm, and wakes Corncob to pray. Courtmartialed for cowardice, he is acquitted by a group of captains with whom he has influence.

A sailor prays, "Lord have mercy upon us!" all the night of the storm, and then, as soon as he is assured that the weather is clearing up, responds,

Is it, by G--? if that's the case, Jack, Ile lend you a hand [to steal some liquor] with all my heart. A drop of brandy will do me a great deal of good, for this d--n'd praying has made my throat as dry as a chafing mat.[59]

When the ship finally goes to pieces, twenty-two drunken sailors are drowned.

There is a little satire on the more serious naval fiction in the descriptions of sea battles. In one, "our mizzan-top-gallant stay-sail bowline and smoke-sail haleyards were shot away."[60] In another, a gun becomes so hot it scorches the captain three hours afterward. The big-'fraid-little-'fraid contest has already been referred to. Corncob also recognizes the formula storm convention:

I beg the reader will consider me as at sea in a gale of wind, or, as most historians call it, a storm or tempest. As I do not write by the sheet, I will not employ half a dozen pages in a description of it, for a tempest has been so often described, that it is now very generally understood. . . .[61]

He goes on to tell how the sailors threaten to throw him overboard for whistling in the wind.

Lord Thornby in *The Disappointed Heir* (1796) has passed many years in the naval service before unexpectedly coming into his title. He is "the true British tar . . ." endowed with "good sense, good nature, plainness of manners, with sincerity, honor and bravery." When a friend gets drunk, he sends word to the latter's family that the guest will "take a birth" with his lordship for the night.[62] A young lady describes an admiral as "such a great big ugly man, and used such *very* wicked words."[63]

In *Berkeley Hall* (1796) there is an old commodore who talks in sea metaphors, and stresses the order and cleanliness of the navy as a good background for the training of a youth.

He asserts that "at *sea* he has' a fair chance of rising by his own merit. . . ."[64] An old tar explains that the lack of respect which a green sailor shows for visitors from ashore is due to his still being a landlubber.

Thirty years, Sir, man and boy, and in sixteen capital actions, and was never known to [complain] in the cause of Old England. . . . I never balk the can; but never take a *skin-full* except when off duty and ashore. We must be content, your reverence knows, we can't expect to lead the *life of angels here below, and get groggy every day.*[65]

There are a number of stories of sea fights told by the commodore. In Volume I are tales by highly improbable Indian princes of fantastic voyages to the pole. These are dull and totally unrealistic: they represent as far a remove as possible from the imitation voyages.

During the last two decades of the century, naval figures and incidents become so common in the increasing volume of novels that it is difficult, and probably valueless, to try to discuss any large number of them. *Henry Willoughby* (1798) carries on the tradition of Smollett in presenting a satirical view of naval life. Sir Cyclops Dunstaville, Bart., combines the characteristics of both the bully and the coward. His frigate is called "the hell afloat."

If we submitted with patience to the blows, kicks, and unjust censures of our officers, out patient acquiescence was construed into sulkiness; but if on the contrary, we expressed the least resentment, or ventured to murmur at the ill treatment we received, then our behaviour was termed mutiny. In both cases, a flogging with a cat-o'-nine tails was the sure reward of the offending party.[66]

In a storm, after the vessel has lost two masts, and is leaking badly, the captain and all the officers go below and seek the seclusion that the cabin grants, while one midshipman, who tears off the uniform of which he is ashamed, works with the crew to save the ship. As soon as the danger is passed, the officers reassert their authority by reprimanding the midshipman and giving a dozen lashes to a seaman who asks for a glass of grog.

There is another bully, the natural son of an admiral, "with the pride and ambition of his father, and the ignorance and depravity of his mother." After reading his commission, he promises four dozen lashes for any offence great or small.[67] At Port Royal, Jamaica, he will not allow the awnings up or the ports open, nor will he permit anyone on deck. Nearly every night two or three men suffocate. Fever and dysentery develop, and thirty of the crew die within a few days.

Set against these brutal figures is the usual ideal one, Captain Laniard, of the "Bellona," who has risen by merit and is strict, but kind and just. He lays his ship "on the Frenchman's lee beam, near enough to see the buckles in their shoes."[68] He refuses to receive back a cowardly lieutenant, the son of a nobleman, who has interest enough to get himself promoted after being courtmartialed for cowardice.

There is a vivid description of the activities of the press gang. The hero sleeps in a hammock over a pawn shop because of poverty. The wife of his master, angry at being scorned, informs on him as a sailor. He is taken, but protests that he is a landsman.

None of your damned palaver! [said the lieutenant who commanded the party], I could swear you have been as long at sea as I have, if it was only for the natural way in which you turn out of your hammock.[69]

He is carried on board a tender, brought before the "king of the hold," and cheated by sailors whom he pays to act as messengers. He faints from the bad air. Brought before the regulating captain, he insists that he has never been to sea before:

Damn your eyes! . . . do you think to get to windward of us with your damned Canterbury stories? . . . if I had my will, you should be keel-hauled instantly. . . .[70]

A friend explains that he must buy his way out.

Contrasted with this bitter presentation is the romantic *Sailor Boy* (1800). The hero, Edward Fortescue, is endowed with all the virtues. Saved from a French mob by Captain Bloomfield, he becomes a midshipman on that equally perfect officer's vessel. Fortescue sets out for England in command of a captured privateer, but is taken by the French, escapes to England, and is immediately seized by a press gang. Carried before the regulating officer, he is excused from service because of his youth.[71] He rejoins Bloomfield as a lieutenant although he has not served his six years as midshipman. After many adventures, the hero has a cowardly lieutenant who wishes to surrender the ship put in irons, takes command himself, and captures a French ship. He transfers his men to the prize, gallantly saving his fever-stricken captain as the British vessel sinks. After some other battles, Bloomfield recovers his senses, and they proceed home. Fortescue is made a captain for his exploits, finds in a great naval battle that the dying admiral is his long-lost father, discovers a wealthy long-lost uncle on a recaptured Indiaman, and finds out that he is a nobleman. Surely this career is successful.

The tars are only mildly profane, and fairly burble with sentimental patriotism about the "honour of Old England." The only realtisic touch is their insistence that Admiral Sir William, the hero's father, be consigned to the waves immediately after his death, lest keeping the corpse aboard bring bad luck.[72] The whole story is one long remarkable reunion.

Meantime the popularity of Greek romance material is also indicated by incidents in other novels. In De Vere's *Salerno* (1770) the Princess Julia is kidnapped at the altar by Turkish rovers and sold to the Bassa. Later the ship on which the lovers are going to Italy is captured by a French captain who dismisses them politely. *In Northern Memoirs or the History of a Scotch Family* there is the account of a girl who, decoyed on shipboard, is carried to Leghorn by an amorous captain and held prisoner in an attempt to force 'ner to marry him. Her rescuer carries her off on another shi_J after helping her to escape by means of rope ladder and sleeping potion. Celestina in *The Scotch Marine* dresses in men's clothes and enlists in the marines to be near her lover, although he does not penetrate her disguise. After numerous adventures they are wrecked on a desert island, separated from each other by the French ships which rescue them, go through many incidents of capture and recapture, and in the end, with great originality and many apologies, marry other people.

The last novel to be discussed is John Davis's *The Post Captain or the Wooden Walls Well Manned* (1802). This excellent tale is rather short and, although in the Smollett vein, confines itself to the adventures of three naval officers, Captain Brilliant, Lieutenant Hurricane, and Midshipman Echo. Like plays of the *Tempest* school, the opening scene creates atmosphere by showing a series of nautical activities accompanied by the technical commands.

The lieutenant went upon the deck. "Mr. Echo," said he to a midshipman, "send the after-guard aft here, to hoist the main-topsail."

"Aye, aye, sir," said Mr. Echo, who in concert with half-a-dozen other weekly-account gentlemen, thus vociferated for several minutes at the break of the quarter-deck: "Boatswain's mate! boatswain's mate! I say, you boatswain's mate, send the after-guard aft here to the main-topsail-haliards. Corporal of marines! send the marines aft on the quarter-deck to clap on the main-topsail-haliards. Master at arms! go down below and send all idlers up! Send all idlers up! Do you hear, there, master at arms? Send all idlers up! . . ."[73]

An old merchant and his young wife, Mr. and Mrs. Factor, are picked up from a ship that has recently been plundered by a Frenchman. The captain, although in love with Cassandra back in Wales, kisses and caresses Mrs. Factor until she is forced to protest that her husband will catch them. The lieutenant is also struck by her beauty. Brilliant rides into Wales and elopes

back to Portsmouth with Cassandra. Meanwhile Mr. Factor
has died and Hurricane has married the beauteous Flora, his
relict. The latter is almost driven to leave her husband in a
passing man of war, by the tales of his earlier marriages and
amorous exploits with which his shipmates regale her. In a sea
fight of the conventional type, the British board and capture a
French man of war from their own sinking vessel. Ashore, Echo
and the dashing Captain Tempest, an Irishman, who is as much
interested in his bride's fortune as in her beauty, elope with
their respective sweethearts to Gretna Green. Various jollities
follow and the story ends on a note of general domestic happi-
ness.

Although there are several rather vividly drawn eccentric
land characters, the naval heroes are not carefully distinguished
from one another. Brilliant is represented as something of a
plain dealer, with a considerable fondness for coarse humour.
Hurricane is rather a ladies' man. Captain Tempest is a comic
opera Irishman. Except youth, Echo has little to mark him off
from the others. All constantly use nautical metaphors, of which
Brilliant's rhapsody over Cassandra's miniature is a fair sample:

Such top-lights! Or can any form be more ravishing? Such a pair of
cat-heads! And, oh! what hair! By ---, one might take a sheep-shank
in it![74]

To Lord Fiddlefaddle, his rival in love, who has just paid the
usual compliments of the time, the worthy captain replies:

And I, sir, am Lord Fiddlefaddle's most humble-come-tumble out of the
maintop into the lower hold!—I would not wish to fall further.[75]

His commands to his gun crews at the beginning of the action
are refreshingly free from the "honour of Old England!" "Keep
yourselves cool, my lads! Mind the heave of the sea! Now, strike
it into her!"[76] And his comment on the dead master is simple

and sincere, despite its nautical trappings: "The soul of as good a seaman as ever took hold of the helm of a vessel, is gone aloft to heaven!"[77]

Despite the fact that the author calls *The Post Captain* "a view of naval society and manners," the thin thread of plot which runs through it goes back to the Greek romance tradition with which this study begins. Hurricane and Echo both fall in love at first sight; Brilliant feels it incumbent upon him to act the amorous captain as far as is permitted by his really loyal and honest nature; Flora is temporarily kidnapped aboard ship; and the double elopement to Gretna Green involves change of identity and remarkable reunion.

As in the chapter on the imitation voyage, generalizations concerning the naval episode are difficult to make. As late as *Henry Willoughby* there is bitter criticism of naval administration and officers, such as occurs back in Smollett. On the other hand, the sentimental characterization of the seaman with all the virtues which effeminate landsmen lack, apparently increases as time goes on. This presentation parallels the similar one in the drama.

Chapter VIII

THE SAILOR IN THE DRAMA

1760-1800

From about 1760 to the end of the century, there are an increasing number of naval plays tending generally in the direction of comic opera, but difficult to classify. The dramatic value of most of them is not high, and except in preparing the way for Jerrold's *Black Ey'd Susan* and Gilbert's *Pinafore*, the presentation of the sailor is not significant. Four groups may be distinguished. Neo-classical comedy continues the humours school with the sailor an officer ashore, often a plain dealer. Sentimental comedy usually presents a heart of oak close to a shipwreck of the *Tempest* kind, either described or implied. The musical pieces seem to have developed from the sailors dancing with pipe and can, and often contain a variation of the theme of the unexpected return of an honest mariner just in time to rescue his sweetheart from the clutches of an old but wealthy suitor (Thomas and Sally). And some plays show the influence of contemporary naval exploits.[1]

The first group contains naval officers of varying character, sometimes alone, sometimes attended by loyal tars of Old England. In Colman's *The Jealous Wife* (1761) appears that charming ruffian, Captain O'Cutter, R.N., who, appointed a regulating captain through the influence of Lord Trinket, tries to return the favor by pressing some noisy grooms. Although the honest officer does not know it, the victims are the father and lover of Harrit [sic], the heroine, whom his lordship is planning to kidnap while her natural protectors are on the tender. The captain interchanges two letters accidentally, and exposes the plot: "Devil burn me, not I, I never rade at all." He is something of a swashbuckler: "Little Terence O'Cutter never fails, fait, when a troat is to be cut."[2] He gives a vivid description of a press gang fight entirely in terms of a naval engagement, apparently admiring the courage of his opponents, although one of them wounds his "starboard eye." Captain Cape, in Murphy's *The Old Maid* of the same year, shows little nautical flavor on the other hand, unless his tenacity of purpose in refusing the old maid after she has jilted him for a younger man and been disappointed in her turn, be proof of the plain dealer characteristic.

Captain Loyd, in Griffith's *School for Rakes* (1769), is a blunt old salt, here intended apparently as something of a bore. He uses sea metaphors upon all occasions:

. . . if she had applied to me, she shou'd have been far enough from her guardians by this, we'd have run gunnel to, all the way. . . .[3]

He forces his way into Sir William Evans' house, an episode that may have come ultimately from *The Rover*. Of similar nature, but more interesting, is Commodore [sic] Capsterne in Francklin's *The Contrast* (1776). He forces his way into the house through a crowd of servants: "D---n you all, I will come up; the fleet's arrived, and I must salute the admiral." His chief nautical oath is "Split my topsails!" and like some of the other naval figures he has a saw of his own: "If I say it I'll do't. that's the humour of Commodore Capsterne."[4]

Captain Allspice, in Dent's *The Candidate* (1783), resents the suggestion (false) that Gander has come down to contest his election to parliament, after the former has made his canvass:

Look ye, Sir, I am a man of few words, and must know whether you are Sir Gregory Gander or not. Damn me, I always like to look ahead before I sail.[5]

Captain Freeman, a retired naval officer, in Dent's farce *Too Civil by Half* (1783), asks for the hand of Sir Toby Treacle's daughter Nancy, using sea metaphors, since Sir Toby prides himself on his command of nautical language. The latter thinks the captain is asking for the command of the ship, also named "Nancy," which he is building for the government. When he realizes his mistake, he forbids the match because he has another suitor in mind. The captain takes advantage of a mere compliment, and occupies the house, like a pirate boarding, says Sir Toby: this episode is evidently becoming a convention. He makes the servants drunk, holds a masquerade, and by the fortunate coincidence that his costume fools the father into thinking him the other suitor, marries the girl with the father's consent. The captain's bluntness seems to be acquired for the occasion.

Pilon's *Fair American* (1785) contains some highly sentimental passages, and a romantic story of the American Revolution; but the naval element is provided by a retired admiral, Cable Dreadnaught, who has served under Hawke and sailed around the world with Anson. He has turned his house into a man of war and has an entourage of crippled ex-sailors. His friend Bale speaks rather favorably of him:

. . . I think he's a very good looking man for his age—to be sure you may know by his walk that he has been more used to the quarter-deck than the drawing-room—then perhaps you'll say he's tann'd, and has got a few scars in his countenance; but these are Valour's credentials, and the old Admiral looks the nobler for them.[6]

Mrs. Wilmot, the widow of a naval officer, adds some plain dealer characteristics:

He is the true English seaman; rough as the element on which he once fought the battles of his country; but there is a tenderness of heart and a greatness of soul about him, not always found under a more polished out-side. He is a stranger to dissimulation himself, and abhors it in others.— But indeed I have often observed, that the manners of British seamen are peculiar to themselves; as if there was something that mended the heart, and purified the mind, in the very air of the ocean.[7]

The admiral soliloquizes on marriage and concludes, as several mariners have done before, that he is fairly well satisfied to lose the heroine to a younger rival. Toward the end of the play, Bale indicates that he hopes to marry the admiral's rather attractive old maid sister.

Admiral Cleveland in Richardson's *The Fugitive* is also a plain dealer. Asked whether sailors every pray at sea, he replies, "Why, what should we pray for? Except, when there's danger in the wind, and then, to be sure, that alters the case." He also resents a statement that he is ignorant of his duty:

Ignorance of duty!—why, you palavering whipper snapper, am I to be taught my duty after having had the command of a fleet, by such a sneaking son of a whore as you?

He later glows with pride at English virtue, however:

. . . they may say what they will about the degeneracy of the times and the falling off of our morals, and all that; but, to my thinking, we improve in every thing except in fighting, and in that—though we may equal—damn me, if we can better the good old model of our forefathers.[8]

This play also contains a girl disguised in men's clothes and, a popular element in naval drama after Murphy's play of that name, an old maid.

Cumberland's *The Brothers* (1767) continues the *Tempest* school. The first scene opens on

A rocky shore, with a fisherman's cabbin in the cliff: a violent tempest with thunder and lightning: a ship discovered stranded on the coast. The characters enter after having looked out of their cabbin, as if waiting for the abatement of the storm.

It develops that Belfield Junior, Captain Ironsides, and the crew of the "Charming Sally" privateer, have been wrecked on the coast of Cornwall, near the country home of Belfield Senior (remarkable reunion). With them incognito (change of identity) is the latter's wife, Violetta, who has been rescued by the privateer from a wrecked packet. All come ashore in a boat, with most of the treasure of the privateer. Belfield Junior arrives just in time to save his sweetheart, Sophia, from a forced marriage with his brother, already married to Violetta, whom he has abandoned (Thomas and Sally episode). The villain, forced into a corner, repents, and makes everything right in the end.

Captain Ironsides is a rough and ready old salt, accompanied by a chorus of sentimentally loyal and patriotic sailors:

OMNES [*as the captain and master, who have stayed aboard to take final leave of the Sally by drinking as much as possible, come ashore*] Huzza, huzza, huzza!

1ST SAIL. Long life to your honour! welcome ashore noble captain.

2ND SAIL. Avast there, Jack; stand clear and let his old honour pass; bless his heart, he looks chearly howsomever; let the world wag as it will, he'll never flinch.

3RD SAIL. Not he; he's true English oak to the heart of him; and a fine old seaman-like figure he is.

IRONSIDES Ah, messmates, we're all a ground: I have been taking a parting cup with the charming Sally—She's gone; but the stoutest bark must have an end; master here and I did all we cou'd to lighten her; we took leave of her in an officer-like manner.

1ST SAIL. Hang sorrow; we know the worst on't, 'tis only taking a fresh cruize; and for my part I'll sail with Captain Ironsides as far as there's water to carry me.[9]

He "boards" the house of a friend, much against the will of Lady Dove, who despises sailors: "Foh! I shan't get the scent of his tar-jacket out of my nostrils this fortnight." He also has the plain dealer tendency to rail at love:

Pshaw, you're a fool, Bob; these wenches will be the undoing of you; a plague of 'em altogether, say I; what are they good for but to spoil company, and keep brave fellows from their duty? o' my conscience, they do more mischief to the king's navy in one twelve month, than the French have done in ten.[10]

There is a reminiscence of the *Tempest* school in the details of the wreck:

1ST SAIL. Here's a pretty spot of work! plague on't, what a night this has been! I thought this damn'd lee-shore wou'd catch us at last.

2ND SAIL. Why 'twas unpossible to claw her off; well, there's an end of her—The charming Sally Privateer!—Pour Soul; a better sea-boat never swam upon the salt sea.

3RD SAIL. I knew we shou'd have no luck after we took up that woman there from the packet that sank along side of us.[11]

The captain accuses the master of not luffing in time. The latter defends himself on the ground that the wind changed suddenly.

SKIFF Well, I cou'd have swore—

CAPT. Ay, so you cou'd, Skiff, and so you did, pretty roundly too.[12]

This discussion has at least a suggestion of the technical commands in *The Tempest*. Cumberland's other nautical plays have some of the same elements in them.

Birch's *The Smugglers* (1796) contains a somewhat similar situation. Captain Pendant, having lost his ship in battle, is on the way home with his booty in another, when the vessel runs aground on the coast of Cornwall, just as in *The Brothers*. He and his loyal follower, Trim, land with the treasure but are destitute otherwise, and the captain is ill. He is relieved by his own daughter (remarkable reunion) without realizing it (change of identity?) and is saved by Trim from losing his treasure to the smugglers. The daughter's lover appears at the opportune time, and all ends happily, with Trim about to marry the daughter's maid.

That the *Tempest* influence persists to the end of the century is indicated by the production of Waldron's *Virgin Queen*, a sequel to *The Tempest*, in 1797. This play is something of a jumble. The Europeans leave the island, taking with them Caliban at his earnest desire, although the sailors feel that he and Prospero will bring them bad luck. With the help of Sycorax,

who is freed by the drowning of the book, the rebel lords plot
to destroy the provisions so that the ship must put in at the
first land, a beautiful island where Caliban and Sycorax are in-
vulnerable and powerful. On this island are Claribel and Abdallah, King of Tunis, prisoners of Hyrca, a sorceress in love
with Abdallah. The loyal party goes hunting and the rebels, having captured the women, fall out over them until finally Caliban
gets Miranda, and Trinculo Claribel. Hyrca and Sycorax form
a league. Hobgoblins burn the ship, and are going to burn the
loyal party with it; but just in time Ariel arrives with a host
of spirits, the rod and book, and a rescue fleet. The rebels,
by Heaven's decree, are marooned on the island.

Despite the attempt to imitate Shakespeare, the verse has a
neo-classical sound and many end-stopped lines; the sailors
are distinctly less nautical (and interesting); and Claribel's
power through her virginity derives from *Comus,* rather than
from anything by the earlier writer. The Abdallah episode probably reflects contemporary romantic interest in pseudo-oriental
material. One quotation will show how the boatswain has de-
teriorated:

Yare! yare! bare a hand with that stowage; here's a fresh breeze sprung
up, and as fair for Italy as heart can wish. . . . as for Duke Prospero,
I'm a lubber if I think him a jot better than an old wizard!"[13]

Two of Cross's "dramatic works" based on voyage material
are pantomimes with some operatic features: *Blackbeard or the
Captive Princess* is derived from *The History of the Pirates,*
and *Sir Francis Drake and the Iron Arm* from legends of Drake.
It will be sufficient to examine the former. The scene opens in
the pirate ship's cabin, with Blackbeard and his principal officers singing over their grog. William and Nancy, evidently borrowed from the Thomas and Sally convention, are present,
Nancy disguised as a sailor (change of identity). A vessel
flying the mogul's colors appears and all rush out, except

Nancy, who reveals herself to William. There follows a scene
'tween decks in which the mogul's ship surrenders, and the
mogul's daughter, Ismene, is brought aboard. All the prisoners
are taken ashore to Blackbeard's fort from which the important
ones succeed in escaping with the aid of Blackbeard's wife,
who is rightly jealous of Ismene (amorous captain). A British
ship attacks Blackbeard's, and sends a scroll aboard, "The
Enemy is British and will die or conquer." Blackbeard gives a
scroll to Caesar, his favorite negro, "Should the Enemy prove
victorious, blow up the Ship."[14] Abdullah, Ismene's follower,
stabs Caesar, however, before he can carry out his intention.
The last scene shows a hand to hand fight between Blackbeard
and Lieutenant Maynard, first with pistols, then cutlasses.
Wounded, Maynard falls back in the arms of a sailor. Abdullah
throws Blackbeard overboard and the pirates strike.

With this should be compared the account of Blackbeard in
Johnson. The oriental episode seems to have been elaborated
from the casual mention of the capture of the Mogul's daughter
in the story of Avery. In Cross, the ships are named the "Pearl"
and the "Revenge." In Johnson, Maynard has two, the "Pearl"
and the "Lime," while Blackbeard's is the "Revenge." The episode of the scroll is stated thus: Blackbeard says,

Damnation seize my Soul if I give you Quarters, or take any from you.
In Answer to which, Mr. Maynard told him, That he expected no Quarters from him, nor should he give him any.[15]

Later Johnson reports that the pirate

. . . had posted a resolute Fellow, a Negroe, whom he had bred up, with
a lighted Match, in the Powder-Room, with Commands to blow up
when he sould give him Orders . . . & when the Negroe found how it
went with Black-beard, he could Hardly be perswaded from that rash
Action, by Two Prisoners that were then in the Hold of the Sloop.[16]

A pirate named Caesar is listed among the prisoners taken by
the king's ship, along with the Israel Hands, whose name gets
into Stevenson's *Treasure Island.*

The conclusion is not quite the same: Blackbeard, although wounded,

... stood his Ground, and Fought with great Fury, till he receiv'd five & 20 Wounds, & 5 of them by Shot. At length, as he was cocking another Pistol, having fir'd several before, he fell down dead ... [others] much wounded, jumped over-board, & call'd out for Quarters.[17]

The anonymous *Female Volunteer* (1801) is of no great importance as nautical drama. The title rôle is that of a minor character who disguises herself as a soldier (change of identity) in order to accompany her husband on service in Ireland. The main plot tells how Pensive, an officer, is washed overboard in a storm, is rescued after some time on a rock (desert island?), and returns to his hermit's cabin in time to save Emma, his love, from attempted suicide. He finds that his shrewish wife is dead and that he may marry Emma. He announces that he is a person of fortune in retirement and all ends happily. The author claims to be an ex-sailor, introduces some sentimental patriotic songs, and pictures an old salt with a wooden leg, Ned Brace, who serves as a kind of chorus to the play. For all his sentimental patriotism, Ned is a lineal descendent of the swearing boatswain:

Whew! an herring-faced Son of a Sea-calf! split my Topsails, if I would not keel-hawl the Rascal! Don't we know that he turn'd tail and sheer'd off at Bunker's Hill....[18]

This is too good to be true of course. One bit of contributory evidence to the hypothesis of the formula storm appears in Ned's discussion with Syntax the schoolmaster:

SYNTAX. An horrible tempest indeed, Mr. Ned, it has been: it reminds me very much of the Hurricane, d'ye observe me, that drove Aeneas, and his fleet into the Port of Carthage, as described by Virgil.

After humorous comments at cross purposes, Ned becomes offended at the school-master's reflections on Dido's character, since he once served in a ship of that name. The storm referred to is elsewhere described in language suggestive of the formula:

Scarce had the transports, which convey'd the Corps,
Weighing from Portland Roads, mid-channel gain'd,
E're Darkness veil'd the Heav'n and from our sight
Obscur'd the day! In sudden gusts, the wind
From diff'rent points burst with an hollow murmur,
Like distant Thunder! Midst contending waves,
Dashing in dire collision, as the force
Of adverse squalls impell'd, the trembling Ship
Impetuous borne, baffled the Pilot's skill,
Suspended *Hope,* and daunted ev'n the *Brave!*[19]

There is no wreck or spar rescue, however, although the hero's landing on his rock may be classed as miraculous.

The naval comic opera does not need to detain us long. As far back as *The Tempest,* Trinculo and Stephano are represented as singing a sea song to comfort themselves on the strange island. It will be remembered also that sailors in *The World Toss'd at Tennis* come in dancing and singing with pipe and can. Sailor Ben in *Love for Love* is not the only officer who entertains in similar fashion during the later period; and Commodore Broadsides in Griffith's *Variety* is not the only retired captain who delights in roaring his own songs. Furthermore, occasional references in the voyage narratives indicate that the sailors actually amused themselves in this way.[20] As time went on, music and dancing, the usual things in certain kinds of Elizabethan drama, came to be essential elements, whether suitable or not, in plays that contained naval officers or sailors; in fact, the sailors sometimes appear to be introduced for the express purpose of singing and dancing.

Toward the end of the eighteenth century plays with a considerable musical element were very popular. Some are called operas; some are called farces. The hero is either a perfect romantic naval officer, followed by an equally exaggerated heart of oak, or the heart of oak himself. Obviously there must be considerable borrowing from the *Tempest* school of drama, althrough the operatic versions of that play belong to a higher type, and stress other elements. The plot often involves the winning of the girl at the expense of an unsuitable, but wealthy, land suitor.

Some of these operas may be mentioned, although the study of them belongs with the next century. *Thomas and Sally* (1760) presents a sentimental tar, who returns to his love just as the Squire is about to attack her. Having protected her from the latter, Thomas takes her to the church to be married. He uses many nautical expressions, stresses sentimental patriotism, and discusses the hardships and plain dealing of the sailor. *A Pill for the Doctor* (1790) represents Sailor Ben as coming back with "six hats full of money" just in time to save his love Polly from being forced by her parents to marry rich Dr. Lotion, sixty-three years old. He offers to divide his wealth with his friend William, the squire, out of pure generosity, and aids the latter to win Lydia. The doctor is fooled into marrying Dorothy, his mistress of ten years. The play ends with the triple wedding and general jollity. In *Auld Robin Gray* (1794) Jemmy, having gone to sea to make his fortune, is wrecked on a coast, and finds a chest of treasure. He comes home in time to prevent Jenny from marrying Auld Robin Gray, who amid an "Oh yoe" chorus of sailors, is reconciled. Hoare's *No Song, No Supper* opens on the coast of Cornwall just after a shipwreck, this one complicated by a mutiny. Robin, the heart of oak, has saved Frederick by means of a spar rescue. The latter has a remarkable reunion with his sweetheart, Louisa; and a keg of gold, around which Robin dances a hornpipe, helps to forward the action to a pleasant conclusion.

The following speech indicates the attitude of sentimental patriotism so common in these plays:

That [risking life] is no concern to a British sailor: he has his life in keeping for his King, his country, and friend, and for them he will cheerfully lay it down, whether scorching beneath the line, or freezing under the North Pole. . . .

Davies' *The Man of Honour* has many comic opera elements. The principal purpose seems to be to contrast the sailor with the landsman, much to the disadvantage of the latter. Captain Firmly saves Nancy from a pirate and wins her in the end amid many songs. One of the tars remarks:

Damnme, messmates, if I don't feel my blood rise, when I tread upon English ground.

Another proclaims that they will show "what mettle there is in a few of the boys of old England."

1ST SAILOR You'll be with us, I hope, Captain.
CAPTAIN Ay 'till death.
1ST SAILOR Generous!
2ND SAILOR Ay, and brave as generous.
CAPTAIN Nay, my lads, there's no necessity of praising a British tar to make him act like a man—[21]

Brewer's *Bannian Day* (1796), a more elaborate drama, is entitled a musical entertainment. The scene is Plymouth. Lieutenant Goodwill has married against his father's consent, and, despite the assistance of a loyal family retainer, Jack Hawser, is enduring a bannian day, i.e., short commons indeed. The irate father disguises himself as a money lender, becomes acquainted with the charming young wife, and takes them both to his bosom. Jack is successful in winning his Polly, and promises never to get tipsy again: his earlier view, however, is well represented in his comment,

Lord! if the English Channel was but filled with [grog], I can't help thinking how often I should stoop down to the lee-scuppers to take a sup; ecod I shou'd never pump the ship out;[22]

His explains, "I drank to drown the troubles of life." He also proclaims the nobility of the British tar:

What! foresake the standard; no, Sir, an English sailor's never missing when his commander's in danger, or his friend's in distress.[23]

Since the plays containing references to contemporary naval history are often operatic, and since some of the legitimate dramas contain such references, the last group is difficult to distinguish definitely. The setting is frequently Portsmouth, or some other port town, and an actual event is used as a peg on which to hang more or less unsuitable comic material. Some of the titles suggest the influence of *News from Plymouth*.

Stevens' *A Trip to Portsmouth* (1773) describes the main event of the opera in the following terms:

. . . a King of Great Britain reviewing his Royal Navy; and encouraging, by his presence, his honest-hearted sailors, is such a picture, that any Englishman must exult in. It has long been wished for, and the accomplishment of it must give universal satisfaction.[24]

This scene is reserved for the close. Of the sailors, one of the principal characters says, "Is it not a pity they should be so brave, and yet so thoughtless?" One stanza of the many so-called sailor songs announces:

> What's got at sea, we spend on shore,
> With sweethearts or our wives;—
> And then, my boys, hoist sail for more;
> Thus passes sailors lives.

One tar says to another, "Belay that, Jack, why you know no more of manners, than as thof you had never been at sea."[25] Jack describes a hunt in sea terms, much as does Captain Porpuss in *Sir Barnaby Whigg*.

Pilon's *Illumination* (1779) uses the celebration in honor of the acquittal of Admiral Keppel in the same way. This drama is a farce rather than an opera, but the plot is similar. A glazier, Skylight, with some friends, has been out breaking windows during the excitement aroused by the celebration. Quillet, an attorney's clerk, waits until the glazier is drunk, rescues him from a supposed press gang, of his own hiring, and wins the girl as a reward.

Meanwhile, Neville's *Plymouth in an Uproar* presents the rescue of the heroine by an impossibly gentle press gang, from an attempted kidnapping by Lord Heartless. The fun is provided in the capture of Sukey, the heroine's maid, disguised, apparently for no reason at all, in men's clothes, and in the perpetually intoxicated, but otherwise noble hearted, Sailor Ben. The historical event is the expected attack on the port by the French, and the whole ends in a maudlin gush of patriotism. Andrews' *Fire and Water* (1780) is based on the attempt of one Jack the Painter to burn the dockyard in 1776. Frederick, a midshipman, rows ashore to warn the town of an expected French attack; and, while there, saves the docks from destruction and his sweetheart from the French spy.

Pearce's *Arrived at Portsmouth* (1794) is notable because it does not contain an old salt. Captain Pendant comes into Portsmouth, and, amid many expressions of sentimental patriotism concerning an impossibly perfect navy, wins the girl. The concluding scene shows the high street illuminated in honor of victory, and sailors singing and dancing the hornpipe.

In summing up this dramatic period, it is fairly safe to say that most of the elements contributed earlier by the *Tempest* and humours schools persist to the end of the century, although they appear in all sorts of combinations. Plain dealers, shipwrecks, hornpipes, saccharine patriotism, and drunken hearts of oak are all jumbled together in a kind of burgoo. One or two special developments may be noted. In the first place the plain dealer tends to become a retired naval officer, often a commodore or admiral, rather than a captain on leave. Sometimes he has a peculiar establishment reflecting his long life at sea, a detail derived perhaps from Smollett's Trunnion, or Sterne's

Uncle Toby, and fairly common in fiction. Again, as occasionally in fiction, a rather superfluous old maid is often associated with the naval officer. In fact, for the first time since the pastoral plays and Arcadian novels of the Elizabethan period, nautical fiction and drama come close together; but the former is on the ascent to the masterpieces of Scott and his successors, while the latter, save for the comic opera development, is on the decline, and must wait over a hundred years for an O'Neill to lift it into literature again.

Before closing, it may be well to summarize the ground covered in this study. As stated in the beginning, my aim has been to survey the presentation of the sailor in English fiction and drama from 1550 to 1800; and, despite necessary digressions into narrative technique and stage conventions, this aim I have kept constantly in mind. After a brief account of the narratives of actual voyages, I have discussed the creative writing in some detail. From 1550 to 1600, sea incidents appeared chiefly in the fiction modelled on the Greek pastoral romance; but, with the decline of Arcadian fiction in the next half century, such episodes were presented chiefly in the drama. I have tried to distinguish two groups of plays: the *Tempest* school, showing scenes at sea; and the humours school, presenting a captain ashore as a subject for ridicule. From the Restoration to about 1760, prose fiction dealing with the sea imitated the accounts of actual voyages; and the drama continued, with less definite separation into types, the two schools mentioned above. About 1760, fiction turned to life in the Navy. Drama, meanwhile developed many nautical types, of which perhaps the most important was the musical entertainment.

As to the sailor himself, he appears in many guises. I have tried to distinguish, for convenience in discussion, the noble pirate, polite and bloodthirsty, the swearing boatswain, blunt and brave, the humours captain, thoroughly despicable, the plain dealer, misanthropic and honest, the merchant skipper, pious and practical, and the heart of oak, rough and loyal; but I know that these classifications are largely arbitrary. My general conclusion is that the English sailor, and possibly any sailor from Socrates' jurymen to Grand Admiral von Tirpitz, is much the same sort of person in all ages; and that differing presentations in literature are chiefly due to changing views as to which of his characteristics are virtues, and which vices. The literary figure in each age represents a more or less unconscious compromise between the practically unchanging mariner of fact and the literary convention already established ashore.

Several lines of investigation leading off the main course have been sufficiently tempting to deserve mention. Mr. H. W. Krieger of the Smithsonian Institution attacks the legend of hidden treasure: "I don't believe there ever was enough pirate gold buried to outfit one good-sized fishing schooner."[26] Then, how did the Nibelungen hoard, or whatever it was, get associated with Captain Kidd? And, for that matter, what is the origin of the Jolly Roger and cryptogram? No student of folklore has made a thorough investigation of what seem to be fragments of primitive ritual existing, even today, in such ceremonies as mustering a ship into commission;[27] nor has any philologist made a special study of the growth and structure of nautical language, actual and literary. Has Caliban become the silk-hatted, missionary-eating, South Sea Islander of the comic strip? These and other problems, together with the history of the literary sailor from 1800 to the present, must be left for future study.

NOTES

Notes and Bibliography are reduced to the smallest compass conformable with a fair presentation of the material covered. Unless otherwise specified, notes refer to editions listed in the Bibliography. I have diverged from customary usage in occasionally including page references for plays where there is no line numbering.

CHAPTER I

1. Robinson and Leyland, *The British Tar in Fact and Fiction*. London, 1909. Preface, p. xvii.

2. *Ibid.*, Preface, p. xi.

3. *Ibid.*, p. 54.

4. *Ibid.*, p. 55; Ralegh, *History of the World*, Bk. IV, chap. ii, p. 4.

5. Robinson and Leyland, *op. cit.*, p. 62.

6. *Ibid.*, p. 86.

7. *Ibid.*, p. 48; cf. Manly, *Chaucer's Canterbury Tales* (1928), p. 534, note to line 649 of Prologue.

8. Robinson and Leyland, *op. cit.*, p. 261.

9. *Ibid.*, p. 188; Ravenscroft, *The Canterbury Guests*, II, ix, p. 24.

10. Robinson and Leyland, *op. cit.*, p. 172.

11. Secord, *Studies in the Narrative Method of Defoe*, 1924.

12. Unpublished Harvard Ph.D. Diss. Parts have appeared as "Warner and the Voyagers," MP, XX, 2, pp. 113-47; "Drayton and the Voyagers," PMLA, XXXVIII (1923); "Shakespeare's Use of the Voyagers in the *Tempest*," PMLA, XLI, pp. 688-726; see also "George Gascoigne and the Siege of Famagusta," MLN, XLIII, pp. 297-99.

13. *Desert Islands, or Robinson Crusoe*. New York, 1930.

14. Professor Chinard considers 1550 the date before which "rien ne nous autorise à supposer que l'Amérique excita beaucoup d'intérêt, en dehors d'un milieu tout spécial de marins et d'armateurs." *L'exotisme américain dans la littérature française au XVIe siècle*, 1911; cf. Parks, George.

15. *See* Chapter VII *below*.

16. Lowes, *The Road to Xanadu*, pp. 48 ff.

17. Hakluyt, Richard, *The Principal Navigations, Voyages, Traffiques, and Discoveries of the English Nation,* ed. Masefield, 1927, V, 286.
18. *Albion's England,* Chap. LXII, p. 634.
19. *Op. cit.,* II, 1.
20. Hakluyt, *Voyages,* II, 98.
21. *Ibid.,* I, 233.
22. *Ibid.,* II, 227.
23. *Ibid.,* IV, 375.
24. *Ibid.,* VII, 62.
25. *Ibid.,* IV, 298; I, 312; V, 155.
26. *Ibid.,* V, 155.
27. *Ibid.,* I, 339.
28. *Ibid.,* I, 339.
29. *Ibid.,* IV, 293-94.
30. *Ibid.,* IV, 294.
31. *Ibid.,* V, 133.
32. *Ibid.,* V, 214.
33. *Ibid.,* V, 249.
34. *Ibid.,* V, 315; this occurs with definite ref. to London Bridge, also *Ibid.,* V, 241.
35. *Ibid.,* VI, 123.
36. *Ibid.,* IV, 296.
37. *Ibid.,* VII, 217.
38. *Ibid.,* VIII, 304.
39. *Ibid.,* VI, 350.
40. *Ibid.,* VI, 339.
41. *Ibid.,* II, 393.
42. *Ibid.,* IV, 244.
43. *Ibid.,* II, 267.
44. *Ibid.,* V, 147.
45. *Ibid.,* V, 341.
46. *Ibid.,* II, 225.
47. Purchas, *His Pilgrimes,* 1905-7 ed., XIX, 201.
48. *Ibid.,* XVI, 187.
49. Hakluyt, *Voyages,* VIII, 126.
50. *Ibid.,* IV, 146.
51. *Ibid.,* VIII, 101.
52. *Ibid.,* V, 20.
53. *Ibid.,* IV, 255.

54. Hakluyt, *Voyages,* VIII, 43.
55. *Ibid.,* VIII, 152.
56. *Ibid.,* V, 266.
57. *Ibid.,* VI, 49.
58. *Ibid.,* III, 39-40.
59. *Ibid.,* II, 221.
60. *Ibid.,* I, 237.
61. *Ibid.,* I, 331.
62. Purchas, *Pilgrimes,* XVII, 60.
63. *Ibid.,* III, 275.
64. *Ibid.,* III, 525-26.
65. *Ibid.,* XX, 53.

Chapter II

1. Teonge, *Diary,* p. 41.
2. *Ibid.,* p. 29.
3. *Ibid.,* p. 36.
4. Esquemeling, *op. cit.,* p. 200.
5. Dampier, *Voyages,* Preface.
6. Rogers, *A Cruising Voyage Round the World,* p. 1.
7. Dampier, *op. cit.,* part I, 17.
8. Rogers, *op. cit.,* p. 187.
9. *Ibid.,* p. 32.
10. Johnson, *op. cit.,* pp. 21-35.
11. Shelvocke, *A Voyage round the World,* p. 207.
12. *Ibid.,* p. 73; Lowes, *Road to Xanadu,* pp. 223-28.
13. Bulkeley and Cummins, *A Voyage to the South Seas,* Preface, p. xxix.
14. Byron, *The Narrative of the Honorable John Byron,* p. 113.
15. Morris, *A Narrative . . . of the Wager,* p. 16.
16. Anonymous, *An Affecting Narrative of . . . His Majesty's Ship Wager,* p. 16.
17. Anson, *Voyage,* p. 76.
18. Cook, *Voyages,* p. 5.
19. *Ibid.,* p. 71.
20. Boswell, *Life of Samuel Johnson,* Everyman ed., I, 478.
21. *Ibid.,* II, 9.
22. Teonge, *Diary,* p. 124.

23. Teonge, *Diary*, p. 39.
24. *Ibid.*, p. 138.
25. *Ibid.*, p. 220.
26. *Ibid.*, p. 248.
27. *Ibid.*, p. 79.
28. *Ibid.*, p. 219.
29. *Ibid.*, p. 39.
30. *Ibid.*, p. 121.
31. Esquemeling, *Buccaneers of America*, p. 144.
32. *Ibid.*, p. 207.
33. *Ibid.*, part III, Chaps. VI-VII *passim*.
34. *Ibid.*, p. 218.
35. *Ibid.*, p. 140.
36. *Ibid.*, pp. 220-21.
37. *Ibid.*, p. 292.
38. *Ibid.*, p. 136.
39. *Ibid.*, p. 144.
40. *Ibid.*, p. 329.
41. *Ibid.*, p. 330.
42. *Ibid.*, p. 336.
43. *Ibid.*, p. 408.
44. *Ibid.*, p. 435.
45. *Ibid.*, p. 274.
46. *Ibid.*, p. 320.
47. *Ibid.*, p. 404.
48. *Ibid.*, p. 433.
49. *Ibid.*, p. 283.
50. *Ibid.*, p. 398.
51. *Ibid.*, p. 447.
52. *Ibid.*, p. 411.
53. *Ibid.*, p. 495.
54. Dampier, *Voyages*, I, 371.
55. *Ibid.*, I, 366 ff.
56. Rogers, *Cruising Voyage*, p. 4.
57. *Ibid.*, pp. 9-10.
58. *Ibid.*, p. 19.
59. *Ibid.*, p. 78.
60. *Ibid.*, p. 119.
61. *Ibid.*, p. 8.

62. Rogers, *Cruising Voyage*, p. 5.
63. *Ibid.*, p. 131.
64. *Ibid.*, p. 185.
65. *Ibid.*, p. 205.
66. *Ibid.*, p. 129.
67. *Ibid.*, p. 130.
68. Shelvocke, *Voyage round the World*, p. 2.
69. *Ibid.*, p. 4.
70. *Ibid.*, p. 7.
71. *Ibid.*, p. 9.
72. *Ibid.*, p. 12.
73. *Ibid.*, p. 16.
74. *Ibid.*, p. 19.
75. *Ibid.*, p. 25.
76. *Ibid.*, p. 73.
77. *Ibid.*, p. 205.
78. *Ibid.*, p. 120.
79. Byron, *Narrative*, Preface, p. vii.
80. *Ibid.*, p. 125.
81. Bulkeley and Cummins, *Voyage to the South Seas*, p. 19.
82. *Ibid.*, p. 21.
83. *Ibid.*, p. 22; Byron, *Narrative*, p. 43.
84. Anonymous, *Narrative of the Wager*, pp. 35-36.
85. *Ibid.*, p. 79.
86. *Ibid.*, p. 20.
87. *Ibid.*, p. 25.
88. Bulkeley and Cummins, *op. cit.*, p. 108.
89. Morris, *Affecting Narrative of the Wager*, p. 44.
90. Anonymous, *Narrative of the Wager*, p. 32.
91. Bulkeley and Cummins, *op. cit.*, p. 77.
92. *Ibid.*, p. 45.
93. *Ibid.*, p. 90.
94. *Ibid.*, p. 149.
95. Walter, *Anson's Voyage*, Bk. I, chap. 1, *passim*.
96. *Ibid.*, p. 81.
97. *Ibid.*, p. 30.
98. *Ibid.*, p. 180.
99. *Ibid.*, p. 180.
100. Cook, *Voyages*, p. 1.

101. Cook, *Voyages,* p. 47.
102. *Ibid.,* p. 102.
103. *Ibid.,* p. 96.
104. *Ibid.,* p. 134.
105. *Ibid.,* p. 211.

CHAPTER III

1. *Clitophon and Leucippe,* Bk. II, chap. 18.
2. Longus, *Daphnis and Chloe* (Loeb Classical Lib.), pp. 67-74.
3. *Aeneid,* I, lines 82-108.
4. *Clitophon and Leucippe,* Bk. III, chaps. 1-4.
5. Cf. *Odyssey,* V, 350-450; Masefield's Preface to Lubbock, *Adventures by Sea from the Art of Old Time;* Hakluyt, *Voyages,* III, 258; Dampier, *Voyages,* Bk. II, chap. 6, etc.
6. *Clitophon and Leucippe,* Bk. III, chap. 5.
7. *Daphnis and Chloe,* p. 44.
8. *Clitophon and Leucippe,* Bk. V, chap. 8.
9. *Ibid.,* Bk. V, chap. 17.
10. *Ibid.,* Bk. I, chap. 7.
11. *Aethiopica,* Bk. II, chap. 23.
12. *Ibid.,* Bk. V, chaps. 19-25.
13. *Greek Romances in Elizabethan Prose Fiction,* p. 461.
14. Sidney, *Arcadia,* I, 5.
15. *Ibid.,* II, 159-60.
16. *Ibid.,* I, 38 ff.; II, 249-51.
17. *Ibid.,* I, chap. 12.
18. *Greene,* Works, IX, 15-16.
19. *Ibid.,* VII, 24.
20. *Ibid.,* II, 173-74.
21. Riche, *His Farewell to Militarie profession,* pp. 72-74.
22. Lyly, *Euphues and His England,* pp. 230-31.
23. Nash, *Jack Wilton,* p. 25.
24. *Ibid.,* p. 31.
25. *Ibid.,* p. 24; *see* contemporary prints.
26. *Ibid.,* p. 8.
27. Nash, *Pierce Penilesse,* p. 25.
28. Greene, *Notable Discovery of Coosnage,* p. 47.
29. Hakluyt, *Voyages,* V, 242.

30. Hakluyt, *Voyages*, III, 7.
31. *Ibid.*, V, 41.
32. *Hyckescorner*, lines 301-401.
33. Greene, *Friar Bacon and Friar Bungay*, II, iv, lines 80 ff.
34. Marston, *Fawn*, III, i, lines 140 ff.
35. Jonson, *Staple of News*, III, i.
36. *Clyomon and Clamydes*, Sc. viii.
37. Greene, *Looking Glass for London and England*, IV, i, lines 1310 ff.
38. Marston, *Antonio and Mellida*, I, i, lines 209 ff.
39. *Posies, Masque for Viscount Montacute*, p. 75.
40. Gascoigne, *Dulce Bellum Inexpertis*, stanzas 105-8.
41. Markham, *Tragedy of Sir Richard Grinvile*, p. 42.
42. Fitzgeffrey, *Drake*, stanza 11.
43. Deloney, *A Joyful New Ballad*, lines 91 ff.
44. *MP*, XIX, 2, pp. 143-62.
45. *e.g.* Patterson, J. E., *The Sea's Anthology*.
46. *2 Henry VI*, IV, i, lines 25-43.
47. *King Leir*, scene xxiii, lines 1990 ff.
48. *Taming of the Shrew*, I, ii, lines 48-9; lines 204-8.
49. *Ibid.*, II, i, lines 282-83.
50. *Ibid.*, III, ii, lines 161-82.

Chapter IV

1. *Twelfth Night*, I, ii, lines 8-15.
2. *Gesta Romanorum*, Cap. 2.
3. *Pericles*, III, 1, lines, 43-53.
4. Cf. Hakluyt, *Voyages*, VIII, 132.
5. Heywood, *Fortune by Land and Sea*, IV, iv.
6. Daborne, *Christian Turn'd Turk*, lines 280 ff., p. 199, Acts not numbered.
7. *Ibid.*, pp. 195-96.
8. *Ibid.*, lines 286 ff., p. 199.
9. "Shakspere's Use of the Voyagers in *The Tempest*," *PMLA*, XLI, 688-728.
10. Purchas, *Pilgrimes*, XIX, 6 *n*.
11. Cawley, *Loc. cit.*, p. 691 *n*.
12. Rae, "A Source for the Storm in *The Tempest*," *MP*, XVII, 279-286.

13. *Tempest*, I, i and I, ii combined.

14. Purchas, *Pilgrimes*, XIX, 12; *Tempest*, II, ii lines 130-31.

15. Purchas, *Pilgrimes*, XIX, 7.

16. Hakluyt, *Voyages*, VII, 162.

17. *Damon and Pithias*, ll. 150 ff.

18. *Custom of the Country*, II, ii.

19. "Zur Quellenfrage von Fletchers *The Sea Voyage*," *Anglia*, XXXIII, 343, "Warner gab Fletcher das Plot des Stückes, daher die Flucht der Portugiesen, die Trennung der Gatten; ihre Landung auf der dürren und der unfruchtbaren Insel, die Erlösung des Mannes und die glückliche Vereinigung der Gatten."

20. Fletcher, *The Sea Voyage*, I, i.

21. *Ibid.*, I, i; *Tempest*, II, ii.

22. *Tempest*, I, ii.

23. *Sea Voyage*, III, i.

24. *Tempest*, II, i, line 315.

25. *Ibid.*, III, ii, lines 133-34.

26. *Sea Voyage*, I, i, p. 36.

27. *Double Marriage*, III, i.

28. *The Prisoners*, IV, iii.

29. *Ibid.*, IV, iv.

30. *Ibid.*, IV, iii.

31. *The Broken Heart*, II, i.

32. *As You Like It*, IV, i, line 21.

33. *Family of Love*, III, ii, lines 102 ff.

34. Heywood, *English Traveller*, II, ii.

35. Massinger, *The City Madam*, II, iii.

36. Middleton, *Blurt, Master Constable*, III, iii.

37. *White Devil*, V, i.

38. *Ibid.*, V, i.

39. *Anything for a Quiet Life;* Middleton praises travel however in *Sir Robert Sherley*, Bullen, VIII, 305.

40. Marston, *Mountebank's Masque*, p. 430.

41. Marston, *Insatiate Countess*, II, ii, line 82.

42. Massinger, *Guardian*, II, ii.

43. Tourneur, *Atheist's Tragedy*, III, i.

44. Middleton, *Black Book*, Bullen ed., VIII, 13.

45. Overbury, *Miscellaneous Works*, pp. 113 ff.

46. Middleton, *Phoenix*, I, ii, lines 1 ff.

47. Middleton, *Phoenix*, II, ii, lineŝ 201 ff.

48. The kidnapping plot is probably ultimately from Greek romance material, cf. "A Source for the Petronel-Winifred Plot," Curtis, *MP*, V, 105-8.

49. *The Silent Woman*, IV, ii, lines 1 ff.

50. *Staple of News*, IV, i.

51. Middleton, *World Toss'd at Tennis*, lines 622 ff.

52. *Ibid.*, lines 671 ff.

53. Before 1625, pub. 1661.

54. *News from Plymouth*, II, ii, p. 137.

55. Heywood's *Fair Maid of the West* should perhaps be mentioned in a chapter on Elizabethan nautical drama, since it contains mariners and scenes at sea. Save for one command, "Board! Board! Amain for England!" IV, iv, the presentation is entirely colorless.

CHAPTER V

1. Secord, *Studies in the Narrative Method of Defoe*, p. 12.

2. Atkinson, *The Extraordinary Voyage in French Lit. before 1700*, pp. 162.

Professor Eddy reviews the classifications used by other critics for the various kinds of voyage narrative. *Gulliver's Travels: A Critical Study*, pp. 12-13. He challenges Professor Atkinson's use of the adjective "extraordinary" in a limited sense, on the ground that the setting of this group of voyages is realistic; and suggests that the term may be more appropriately applied to the group which he himself calls "fantastic." The difficulty lies in the fact that, in discussing the voyages, one must use as technical terms words which have long been employed in a general sense (cf. my own attempt to distinguish between the imitation voyage and the naval episode, Chapter VII); and in the fact that a single voyage may contain details borrowed from many different sources. I am inclined to defend any usage that is carefully distinguished by definition.

3. Atkinson, *The Extraordinary Voyage in French Lit. 1700-1720*, pp. 6-7.

4. *Isle of Pines*, Ford ed., p. 85. This novel is ascribed to Henry Neville 1620-1694, but not by Mr. Ford.

5. Atkinson, "A French Desert Island Novel of 1708," PMLA XXXVI, 509-28.

6. *The Development of the English Novel*, pp. 27-28.

7. *The Development of the English Novel*, p. 12.

8. Not the title of the edition used in this study, but an unconscious reminiscence of Lamb's love for the book; see *Christ's Hospital Five and Thirty Years Ago*.

9. *English Rogue*, p. 233.

10. *Ibid.*, p. 238.

11. *Ibid.*, pp. 245-46.

12. *Linschoten*, pp. 248 ff.; *English Rogue*, pp. 250 ff.

13. *Linschoten*, p. 99; *English Rogue*, pp. 246-47.

14. *Linschoten*, p. 98; *English Rogue*, p. 247.

15. Atkinson, *Ext. Voyage before 1700*, p. 162.

16. *Isle of Pines*, p. 56.

17. *Ibid.*, p. 60.

18. *Ibid.*, p. 70.

19. *Ibid.*, p. 85.

20. *Ibid.*, pp. 62-63.

21. Head, *Floating Island*, p. 5.

22. *Ibid.*, p. 13.

23. Knox, *op. cit.*, p. 331.

24. *Captain Singleton*, p. 158.

25. Secord, *Defoe*, p. 107.

26. *Ibid.*, p. 33.

27. *Ibid.*, p. 32.

28. *Enstehungsgeschichte von Defoes "Robinson Crusoe."*

29. *Falconer*, III, 179.

30. *Boyle*, pp. 10-11; *Falconer*, I, p. 12.

31. *Boyle*, pp. 111, 129, 254; *Falconer*, I, pp. 40-51.

32. *Boyle*, p. 472; *Falconer*, I, p. 60.

33. *Boyle*, p. 449; *Falconer*, p. 43.

34. *Boyle*, p. 398; *Falconer*, II, p. 40.

35. *Boyle*, p. 474; *Falconer*, II, p. 10.

36. *Boyle*, p. 196; *Falconer*, II, p. 57.

37. *Boyle*, p. 142; *Falconer*, II, p. 57.

38. *Buccaneers*, pp. 335-36.

39. *Ibid.*, p. 336 n.

40. *Falconer*, I, 37.

41. *Ibid.*, II, 6-7.

42. *Ashton's Memorial*, pp. 121-41.

43. *Anglia*, XV, 345-89.

44. Eddy, *Gulliver's Travels: A Critical Study.* Princeton, 1923. MLN. XXXVII, 353 ff., 416 ff.; XXXVIII, 345 ff.

45. *Gulliver's Travels,* Preface, p. xxvi.

46. *Ibid.,* p. 312.

47. *Ibid.,* p. 74. cf. Collins, *Jonathan Swift,* 1902, pp. 107-8.

48. *Falconer,* I, 47-48; *Boyle,* pp. 23-24, 155.

49. *Falconer,* III, 110; *Boyle,* p. 25.

50. *Boyle,* p. 5: I cannot accept the hypothesis that Chetwood was the author of both.

51. *Ibid.,* p. 85.

52. *Ibid.,* p. 157.

53. *Ibid.,* p. 174.

54. *Ibid.,* p. 84.

55. In a note to his *Road to Xanadu,* p. 459, Professor Lowes gives a list of references to parallel passages. He evidently did not know that *The Hermit* is ascribed to Longueville by the Widener Library, and assumed that a later edition was the only one at Harvard.

56. *Hermit,* p. 54.

57. *Ibid.,* pp. 79-81.

58. *Ibid.,* p. 81.

59. *Ibid.,* pp. 153-54.

60. Brunt, *Cacklogallinia,* pp. 24-28.

61. *Isle of Pines,* p. 63; *John Daniel,* p. 26.

62. *Isle of Pines,* p. 63; *John Daniel,* p. 26.

63. *Isle of Pines,* p. 63; *John Daniel,* p. 27.

64. *Isle of Pines,* p. 64; *John Daniel,* p. 26.

65. *John Daniel,* pp. 21-24.

66. *Boyle,* p. 25; *David Price,* p. 71.

67. *Boyle,* p. 83; *David Price,* p. 71.

68. *Boyle,* p. 110; *David Price,* pp. 183 ff.

CHAPTER VI

1. Montague Summers, *Shakespeare Adaptations,* Introduction, pp. xli-lii.

2. Dramatis Personae.

3. *Tempest,* I, i, lines 39-40.

4. Davenant's *Tempest,* I, i.

5. *Ibid.,* III, i.

6. Davenant's *Tempest*, II, i.

7. Masefield, *Sea Life in Nelson's Time*, p. 204: I cannot explain the existence of this custom side by side with the superstition that women cause storms.

8. *Plain Dealer*, I, i, lines 145-46.

9. *Ibid.*, I, i, lines 1-5.

10. *Ibid.*, II, i, lines 992-98.

11. *Ibid.*, I, i, lines 171-74.

12. *Ibid.*, II, i, *passim*.

13. Behn, *The Rover*, V, i, p. 65.

14. *Ibid.*, V, i, p. 65.

15. *Ibid.*, I, i, p. 11.

16. *Ibid.*, V, i, p. 11.

17. *Ibid.*, V, i, p. 61.

18. Otway, *Cheats of Scapin*, p. 207.

19. *Sir Barbaby Whigg*, I, i, p. 2.

20. *Ibid.*, I, i, p. 5.

21. *Ibid.*, II, i, p. 20.

22. *Ibid.*, V, ii, p. 20.

23. *Love for Love*, III, vii.

24. *Ibid.*, III, vi.

25. *Ibid.*, III, vii.

26. *Ibid.*, IV, xiii.

27. *Cant. Guests*, IV, ii, p. 41.

28. *Ibid.*, I, vi, p. 9.

29. *Ibid.*, III, v, p. 35.

30. *Ibid.*, I, vi, p. 9.

31. *Ibid.*, II, ix, pp. 24-25.

32. *Ibid.*, V, iii, p. 54.

33. *Sir Harry Wildair*, I, i.

34. *Ibid.*, IV, i.

35. *Ibid.*, II, ii.

36. *Gibraltar*, IV, i, p. 44.

37. Centlivre, *A Bickerstaff's Burying*, Sc. i, p. 276.

38. Sc. i, p. 269.

38. *Ibid.*, Sc. i, p. 269.

39. *Ibid.*, Sc. i, p. 272.

40. *Fair Quaker*, I, i, p. 1.

41. *Ibid.*, I, i, p. 4.

42. *Fair Quaker,* I, i, p. 15.

43. *Ibid.,* III, i, p. 35.

44. *Ibid.,* I, i, p. 9.

45. *Ibid.,* II, i, p. 25.

46. *Ibid.,* III, i, p. 38.

47. *Ibid.,* III, i, p. 35.

48. *Injur'd Love,* I, i, p. 6.

49. *Ibid.,* III, i, p. 31.

50. *Ibid.,* I, i, p. 2.

51. *Successful Pyrate,* III, i, p. 37.

52. *Bravo,* Sc. iv, p. 21.

53. *Ibid.,* Sc. v, p. 23.

54. *Ibid.,* Sc. vii, p. 35.

55. *Reprisal,* II, xv.

56. Is this, like the gambling scene, a reminiscence of *Sir Harry Wildair?*

57. *Basset Table,* II, i.

58. *Ibid.,* I, i.

59. *Ibid.,* II, i.

60. *Ibid.,* II, i.

61. *Ibid.,* III, i.

62. *Ibid.,* LV, i.

CHAPTER VII

1. *Wooden World Dissected,* pp. 76-81. See W. A. Eddy, "Ned Ward and Lilliput," *Notes and Queries,* CLVIII, 148-49, for influence of Ward on Swift.

2. Cf. Selection from the rare Braithwaite's *Whimzies, British Tar,* p. 95.

3. *Jonathan Wild,* p. 122.

4. *Ibid.,* p. 240.

5. *Ibid.,* p. 241.

6. *Ibid.,* p. 242.

7. *Ibid.,* p. 260.

8. *Ibid.,* p. 121.

9. *Ibid.,* p. 126.

10. *Ibid.,* p. 240.

11. *Roderick Random,* pp. 142-211 out of 428 pages in all.

12. "Elizabethan Drama and the Works of Smollett," PMLA, xliv, pp. 842-62.
13. *Fair Quaker*, I, i, p. 9.
14. *Roderick Random*, p. 272.
15. *Ibid.*, Chaps. XXXI-XXXIV; cf. Ford, *Admiral Vernon and the Navy . . . a Critical Reply to Smollett.*
16. *Roderick Random*, pp. 209-10.
17. Bulkeley and Cummins, *Voyage to the South Sea*, p. 6.
18. *Ibid.*, p. 11.
19. *Ibid.*, p. 5.
20. *Ibid.*, p. 10.
21. *Ibid.*, pp. 12-13.
22. *Ibid.*, p. 16.
23. *Roderick Random*, p. 219.
24. *Ibid.*, Preface, p. 4.
25. *Joe Thompson*, II, 174.
26. *Ibid.*, II, 174.
27. *Ibid.*, II, 175.
28. Hakluyt, *Voyages*, III, 39.
29. *Joe Thompson*, II, 142-43.
30. *Tom Jones Married*, pp. 100-1.
31. *Sir Launcelot Greaves, Works.* Saintsbury ed., X, pp. 2, 233, 76.
32. *Young Scarron*, pp. 46 ff.
33. *History of a Pilgrim*, pp. 409-10.
34. *Ibid.*, pp. 466-67.
35. *Duplessis Memoires*, pp. 39-40.
36. *Chrysal*, I, 63.
37. *Ibid.*, I, 78.
38. *Ibid.*, II, 244.
39. *Ibid.*, I, 185.
40. *Ibid.*, II, 233.
41. *Jack Connor*, I, 348.
42. *Ibid.*, I, 349.
43. *Arundel*, II, 64.
44. *Ibid.*, II, 216.
45. *Ibid.*, I, 349.
46. *Ibid.*, II, 217.
47. *Evelina*, p. 35.
48. *Ibid.*, p. 91.

49. *Evelina,* pp. 471-474.
50. *Ibid.,* p. 130.
51. *Adventures of a Rupee,* pp. 69-71.
52. *Ibid.,* p. 95.
53. *Ibid.,* p. 112.
54. *Ibid.,* pp. 72-73.
55. *Ibid.,* p. 74.
56. *Jonathan Corncob,* pp. 73-74.
57. *Ibid.,* p. 43.
58. *Ibid.,* p. 153.
59. *Ibid.,* p. 196.
60. *Ibid.,* p. 31.
61. *Ibid.,* p. 189.
62. *Disappointed Heir,* I, 56.
63. *Ibid.,* I, 113.
64. *Berkeley Hall,* II, 130.
65. *Ibid.,* II, 152.
66. *Henry Willoughby,* I, 162-63.
67. *Ibid.,* I, 180-81.
68. *Ibid.,* I, 174.
69. *Ibid.,* I, 133.
70. *Ibid.,* I, 142-43.
71. *The Sailor Boy,* I, 72.
72. *Ibid.,* II, 219.
73. *Post Captain,* pp. 3-4.
74. *Ibid.,* p. 2.
75. *Ibid.,* p. 40.
76. *Ibid.,* p. 113.
77. *Ibid.,* pp. 115-16.

Chapter VIII

1. I am indebted to Professor A. H. Thorndike for the groupings used in this chapter.
2. Colman, *The Jealous Wife,* III, i, p. 57.
3. Griffith, *The School for Rakes,* IV, i, p. 63.
4. Francklin, *The Contrast,* I, i, p. 25.
5. Dent, *The Candidate,* II, iii, p. 27.
6. Pilon, *The Fair American,* I, i, p. 18.

7. Pilon, *The Fair American,* III, i, p. 56.

8. Richardson, *The Fugitive,* I, iv, p. 12.

9. Cumberland, *The Brothers,* I, i, p. 9.

10. *Ibid.,* I, x, p. 11.

11. *Ibid.,* I, iii, p. 3.

12. *Ibid.,* I, ix, p. 10.

13. Waldron, *Virgin Queen,* I, ii, p. 7.

14. Cross, *Blackbeard,* Sc. xx, p. 43.

15. Johnson, *History of the Pirates,* p. 29.

16. *Ibid.,* p. 31.

17. *Ibid.,* p. 30.

18. *Female Volunteer,* I, ii, p. 14.

19. *Ibid.,* III, ii.

20. Hakluyt, *Voyages,* VIII, 93; Cook, *Voyages,* p. 138.

21. Davies, *Man of Honor,* II, ii, p. 393.

22. Brewer, *Bannian Day,* I, iii, p. 8; II, v, p. 33.

23. *Ibid.,* I, i, p. 2.

24. Stevens *A Trip to Portsmouth,* Sc. ii, p. 26.

25. Scene not numbered, p. 29, *ibid.,*

26. United Press Dispatch, June 9, 1928. My attempts to secure a personal statement from Mr. Krieger have failed.

27. Dr. Rappoport explains the christening of ships with a bottle of wine as going back to the pagan custom of placing the vessel under the care of a particular god by pouring a libation at launching. *Superstitions of Sailors,* p. 268.

BIBLIOGRAPHY

With a few exceptions, I have listed in the Bibliography only works actually cited in the text and notes; and I have omitted those of general significance, e.g., Chaucer's *Canterbury Tales*. The works are classified under four heads: (A) critical and historical works written since 1800; (B) literature of travel written before 1800; (C) prose fiction; (D) drama and poetry. I have subdivided the last into collections and single editions.

CRITICAL AND HISTORICAL

ATKINSON, GEOFFROY. The Extraordinary Voyage in French Literature before 1700. New York, 1920.

————. The Extraordinary Voyage in French Literature 1700 to 1720. Paris, 1922.

————. A French Desert Island Novel of 1708. PMLA, XXXVI, 1921.

————. La Littérature géographique de la Renaissance. Paris, 1927.

————. Les Relations de voyages du XVIIe siècle et l'évolution des idées, Paris, n.d.

BAKER, HARRY T. The Relation of Shakspere's *Pericles* to George Wilkins's Novel, *The Painfull Adventures of Pericles, Prince of Tyre*. PMLA, XXIII, 100-18, 1908.

BASKERVILL, CHARLES READ. Play-Lists and Afterpieces of the Mid-Eighteenth Century, MP, XXIII, 445-64, 1926.

BERNBAUM, ERNEST. The Mary Carleton Narratives 1663-1673, a missing Chapter in the History of the English Novel. Cambridge, 1914.

BORKOWSKY, TH. Quellen zu Swifts Gulliver. Anglia, XV, 345-89, 1893.

CAWLEY, ROBERT RALSTON. Drayton and the Voyagers. PMLA, XXXVIII, 1923.

————. George Gascoigne and the Siege of Famagusta. MLN, XLIII, 297-99.

————. The Influence of the Voyagers in Non-Dramatic English Literature between 1550 and 1650 with Occasional References to the Drama. Harvard Univ. unpublished Ph.D. dissertation, 1921.

————. Shakspere's Use of the Voyagers in *The Tempest*. PMLA, XLI, 688-726, 1926.

————. Warner and the Voyagers. MP, XX, 113-47, 1922.

CHINARD, GILBERT. L'Amérique et le rêve exotique dans la littérature française au XVIIe et au XVIIIe siècle. Paris, 1913.

————. L'Exotisme américain dans la littérature française au XVIe siècle d'après Rabelais, Ronsard, Montaigne . . . Paris, 1911.

CLOWES, WM. LAIRD. The Royal Navy, a history from the Earliest Times to the Present. 5 vols. [actually 7], London, 1897.

CORBETT, SIR J. S. Drake and the Tudor Navy. 2 vols., London, 1898.

CROSS, W. L. The Development of the English Novel. London, 1902.

CURTIS, HARLOW DUNHAM. A Source of the Petronel-Winifred Plot in Eastward Hoe. MP, V, 105-08, 1907.

DOTTIN, PAUL. Daniel De Foe et ses romans. 3 vols., Paris, 1924.

EDDY, WILLIAM ALFRED. Gulliver's Travels: a Critical Study. Princeton Univ., 1923.

ELLISON, LEE MONROE. Elizabethan Drama and the Works of Smollett. PMLA, XLIV, 842-62, 1929.

FORD, DOUGLAS. Admiral Vernon and the Navy. A Memoir and a Vindication. London, 1907.

HUGHES, MERRITT Y. Spenser's Debt to the Greek Romances. MP, XXXIII, 67-77, 1925.

JACOBI, GUSTAV ADOLF. Zur quellenfrage von Fletchers The Sea Voyage. Anglia, XXXIII, 332-43, 1910.

KOLLMANN, W. Nashs Unfortunate Traveller und Heads English Rogue, die Beiden Hauptvertreter des Englishen Schelmenromans, Anglia, XXII, 81-140, 1899.

LAUGHTON, L. G. C. See Shakespear's England.

LOWES, JOHN LIVINGSTON. The Road to Xanadu, a Study in the Ways of the Imagination. New York, 1927.

LUBBOCK, BASIL. Adventures by Sea from Art of Old Time. Preface by Masefield. London, 1925.

MANN, WILLIAM EDWARD. Robinson Crusoe en France, étude sur l'influence de cette œuvre dans la littérature française. Paris, 1916.

MASEFIELD, JOHN. Sea Life in Nelson's Time, London, n.d. [1905]

————. Preface to Adventures, etc. (See Lubbock.)

PARKS, GEORGE BRUNER. Richard Hakluyt and the English Voyages. New York, 1928.

PETHERICK, EDWARD AUGUSTUS. Catalogue of the York Gate Library . . . an index to the literature of Geography, Maritime and Inland Discovery, Commerce, and Colonization. London, 1886.

RAPPOPORT, ANGELO S. Superstitions of Sailors. London, 1928.

REA, JOHN D. A Source for the Storm in *The Tempest*. MP, XVII, 279-86, 1919.

ROBINSON, COMMANDER C. N. and LEYLAND, JOHN. The British Tar in Fact and Fiction, London, 1909. Vol. IV, chap. iv, The Literature of the Sea; chap. v, Seafaring and Travel. Cambridge Hist. Eng. Lit.

ROSS, ERNEST C. The Development of the English Sea Novel from Defoe to Conrad. Univ. of Virginia Ph.D. dissertation, n.d. [1927?].

SCHNEIDER, ARNO. Die Entwickelung des Seeromans in England im 17. und 18. Jahrhundert. Univ. of Leipzig dissertation, 1901.

SECORD, A. W. Studies in the Narrative Method of Defoe. Univ. of Illinois Ph.D. dissertation, 1924.

Shakespeare's England, Oxford, 1917, I, chap. v, The Navy, by L. G. C. Laughton.

STEPHENSON, H. T. Shakespeare's London. New York, 1906.

THORNDIKE, ASHLEY HORACE. English Comedy. New York, 1929.

————. Shakespeare in America, Parts of the Annual Shakespeare Lecture of the British Academy, delivered July 6, 1927. Shakespeare Association Bull., III, 1928.

————.Tragedy. New York, 1908.

TRAILL, H. D. [ed.] Social England. 6 vols., London, 1909.

TRENEER, ANNE. The Sea in English Literature from Beowulf to Donne. Liverpool, 1926.

TURBERVILLE, A. S. English Men and Manners of the Eighteenth Century. Oxford, 1926.

WACKWITZ, FREDERICH. Enstehungsgeschichte von D. Defoes *Robinson Crusoe*. Berlin, 1909.

WHALL, W. B. Shakespeare's Sea Terms Explained. London, 1910.

WHITNEY, LOIS. Spenser's Use of the Literature of Travel in the *Faerie Queene*, MP, XIX, 143-62, 1921.

WOLFF, SAMUEL LEE. Greek Romances in Elizabethan Prose Fiction. New York, 1912.

WYCHERLY, GEORGE. The Buccaneers of the Pacific. Indianapolis, 1928.

LITERATURE OF TRAVEL

ANONYMOUS. An Affecting Narrative of the Unfortunate Voyage and Catastrophe of his Majesty's Ship Wager. London, 1751.

BOTELER, NATHANIEL. Six Dialogues about Sea-Services between an High Admiral and a Captain at Sea. London, 1685.

BUCKINGHAM, DUKE OF. A Satire on Sea Officers by Sir H. S. in Miscellaneous Works of George Late Duke of Buckingham. 2 vols. London, I, 1707; II, 1705 [sic].

BULKELEY, JOHN, and CUMMINS, JOHN. A Voyage to the South Seas in his Majesty's ship Wager in the years 1740-41. (ed. by D. Howden Smith), New York, 1927.

BYRON, HONOURABLE JOHN. The Narrative of. 2d ed., London, 1768.

CORBETT, JULIAN S. [editor] Papers relating to the Navy during the Spanish War 1585-1587. London, 1898.

CORYATE, THOMAS. Coryate's Crudities, Hastilie gobled up in five Moneths Travells in France, Savoy, Italy, Rhetia. . . . 2 vols. Glasgow, 1905.

[COOK, JAMES.] Captain Cook's Voyages of Discovery London, 1906. [Only the second narrative is by Cook.]

COOKE, EDWARD. Voyage to the South Seas, and round the World in 1708-11. London, 1712.

DAMPIER, CAPT. WILLIAM. A New Voyage Round the World. 2 vols., London, I, 1703; II, 1705.

ESQUEMELING, JOHN. The Bucaniers of America, or a True Account of the most remarkable Assaults committed upon the Coasts of the West Indies by the bucaniers of Jamaica and Tortuga. (edited by W. S. Stallybrass), London, n.d. [1st ed. 1684].

FALCONER, WILLIAM. The Poetical Works of Wm. Falconer with the Life of the Author. London, n.d. [1798].

HAKLUYT, RICHARD. The Principal Navigations Voyages Traffiques & Discoveries of the English Nation. . . . (edited by John Masefield.) 8 vols., New York, 1927.

HOLINSHEAD, RAPHAEL. Chronicles of England, Scotland, and Ireland. 6 vols., London, 1807.

JOHNSON, CAPT. CHARLES. A General History of the Pirates, ed. by Philip Gosse. 2 vols. Kensington, I, 1925; II, 1927.

KNOX, CAPT. ROBERT. An Historical Relation of Ceylon. Selection in An English Garner, II, Westminster, 1903.

LINSCHOTEN, JOHN HUYGHEN VAN. The Voyage to the East Indies from the Old English Translation of 1598. 2 vols., London, 1885.

MAVOR, WILLIAM. Historical Account of the Most Celebrated Voyages, Travels, and Discoveries. 25 vols., London, 1796.

MORRIS, ISAAC. A Narrative of the Dangers and Distresses which befel Isaac Morris and Seven more of the Crew belonging to the "Wager" Store-Ship. . . . London, 1756.

OVERBURY, SIR THOMAS. A Sailor, in Miscellaneous Works in Verse and Prose, with Memoirs of his Life. London, 1756.

PURCHAS, SAMUEL. Hakluytus Posthumus or Purchas His Pilgrimes. 20 vols., Glasgow, 1905-7.

RAMUSIO, GIOVANNI BAPTISTA. Delle Navigationi et Viaggi. 3 vols., Venetia, 1588.

ROGERS, CAPT. WOODES. A Cruising Voyage round the World . . . begun 1708, and finished 1711. Containing . . . an Account of Alexander Selkirk's living alone four Years and four Months in an Island. ed. by G. E. Manwaring. New York, 1928.

SHELVOCKE, CAPT. GEORGE. A Voyage round the World. Perform'd in the Years 1719, 20, 21, 22. London, 1726.

SMITH, CAPT. JOHN. Works, ed. by Edw. Arber. Limited Library Edition [London], n.d.

TEONGE, HENRY. Diary of Henry Teonge, Chaplain on Board H.M.'s Ships "Assistance," "Bristol," and "Royal Oak" 1675-1679. ed. by G. E. Manwaring. New York, 1927.

WALTER, RICHARD. A Voyage round the World in the Years 1740-44 by Lord Anson. (Everyman Lib.) New York, 1911.

[WARD, EDWARD.] The Wooden World Dissected. By a Lover of Mathematicks. [2d ed.], London, 1708.

PROSE FICTION

ACHILLES TATIUS. [Clitophon and Leucippe] tr. by S. Gaselee, London, 1917. (Loeb Classical Library.)

ANONYMOUS. The Adventures of Alonso. 2 vols., London, 1775.

———. Berkeley Hall: or the Pupil of Experience. 3 vols., London, 1796.

———.The Castle of Saint Donats or the History of Jack Smith. 3 vols., London, 1798.

———. Henry Willoughby, a Novel. 2 vols., London, 1798.

———. The History of Tom Jones in his Married State. [2d ed.], London, 1750.

———. Northern Memoirs or the History of a Scotch Family, Written by a Lady. 2 vols., London, n.d.

————. The Sailor Boy, a Novel. London, 1800.

————. The Scotch Marine or Memoirs of the Life of Celestina. London, n.d.

————. The Voyages and Adventures of Captain Robert Boyle. . . . The Voyage, Shipwreck, and Miraculous Preservation of Richard Castelman, Gent. London, 1726.

BARCLAY, JOHN. Barclay his Argenis or the Loves of Polyarchus & Argenis Faithfully Translated out of Latin into English by Kingsmill Long. . . . London, 1636.

BARNARD, JOHN. Ashton's Memorial an History of the Strange Adventures and Signal Deliverances of Mr. Phillip Ashton. Boston N.E., 1725.

[BROWNE, JOHN]. The Life and Adventures of Mr. Francis Clive. 2 vols., Dublin, 1764.

BRUNT, CAPT. SAMUEL. A Voyage to Cacklogallinia. London, 1727.

BURNEY, FANNY. Evelina or the History of a young Lady's Entrance into the World. New York, 1920.

[CHETWOOD, WILLIAM RUFUS]. The Voyages, Dangerous Adventures and imminent Escapes of Captain Richard Falconer. . . . London, 1720.

CORNCOB, JONATHAN [?]. Adventures, Written by Himself. London, 1787.

[CUMBERLAND, RICHARD]. Arundel, by the author of the Observer. 2 vols., London, 1789.

DAVIS, JOHN. The Post-Captain or the Wooden Walls Well Manned, a View of Naval Society and Manners. London, 1928.

DEKKER, THOMAS. Newes from Hell, in Non-Dramatic Works. Huth Lib., II, London, 1885.

————. The Wonderful Yeare 1603. London, 1924.

DEFOE, DANIEL. Romances and Narratives of. ed. by George Aitken. London, 1895.

————. The Life, Adventures, and Piracies of the Famous Captain Singleton. (Everyman Lib.) London, 1906.

DE VERE, MARQUIS. The Life and Adventures of the Prince of Salerno. London, 1770.

DU PLESSIS, ————— [?]. Du Plessis's Memoirs or Variety of Adventures. 2 vols., Dublin, 1757.

FAULCONER, HERVEY [?]. The Mother-in-Law or the Innocent Sufferer, Adventures of Hervey Faulconer. 2 vols., London, 1757.

FIELDING, HENRY. Jonathan Wild the Great, in Works. Jenson Society ed., X, 1905.

FORD, CHAUNCEY WORTHINGTON [editor]. The Isle of Pines, an Essay in Bibliography. Boston, 1920.

[GARNIER, CHARLES G. T.] Voyages Imaginaires, Songes, Visions, et Romans Cabalistiques. 39 vols., Amsterdam, 1787.

GODWIN, BISHOP FRANCIS. The Voyage of Domingo Gonzales to the Moon. *Anglia*, X, 428-56. [1st ed. 1638.]

GOMERSALL, A. The Disappointed Heir or Memoires of the Ormond Family. 2 vols., Exeter, 1796.

[GRAVES, RICHARD]. Eugenius or Anecdotes of the Golden Vale. 2 vols., (2d ed.) London, 1786.

GREENE, ROBERT. Alcida: Greene's Metamorphosis, in The Life and Complete Works. Huth Library, IX, London, 1881-83.

――――. A Notable Discovery of Coosnage. London, 1923.

――――. Greene's Pandosto, or Dorastus and Fawnia. London, 1907.

――――. Philomela, the Lady Fitzwater's Nightingale, in Archaica. ed. by Sir E. Brydges, I, London, 1815.

HEAD, RICHARD, and KIRKMAN, FRANCIS. The English Rogue described in the Life of Meriton Latroon, a Witty Extravagant. London, 1928.

[HEAD, RICHARD]. The Floating Island: or a New Discovery Relating to the strange Adventures on a late Voyage from Lambethana to Villa Franca alias Ramallia to the Eastward of Terra del Templo: By three Ships, Viz. The Pay-naught, Excuse, Least-in-Sight Under the Conduct of Captain *Robert Owe-much* . . . Published by Frank Careless, one of the Discoverers. [London], 1673.

HELIODORUS. An Aethiopian History. (Underdowne's Translation of 1587), ed. by George Saintsbury, London, n.d.

HUBBARD, LUCIUS L. [editor]. The Narrative of the El-Ho Sjouke Gabbes (Krinke Kesmes) by Hendrik Smeeks [1708]. Ann Arbor, 1921.

JOHNSTONE, CAPT. CHARLES. Chrysal or the Adventures of a Guinea by an Adept. 3 vols., London, 1821.

KIMBER, MR. [EDWARD]. The Life and Adventures of Joe Thompson, A Narrative founded on Fact. 2 vols., London, 1783.

LEGUAT, FRANÇOIS. Voyages to Rodriguez, Mauritius, Java, and Cape of Good Hope. London, 1891.

LODGE, THOMAS. The Margarite of America, (reprinted from 1596 ed.). ed. by J. O. Halliwell, London, 1859.

――――. Rosalynde or Euphues Golden Legacy. ed. by E. C. Baldwin, New York, 1910.

[LONGUEVILLE, PETER]. The Hermit: or, the Unparalled [sic] Sufferings and Surprising Adventures of Mr. Philip Quarll, an Englishman. Westminster, 1727.

LYLY, JOHN. Euphues: the Anatomy of Wit: Euphues and His England, ed. by Croll and Clemons, London, 1916.

MORRIS, RALPH. The Life and Astonishing Adventures of John Daniel. London, 1926.

[MOZEEN, THOMAS]. Young Scarron. London, 1752.

NASHE, THOMAS. Pierce Penilesse, His Supplication to the Divell. [1592], London, 1924.

————. The Unfortunate Traveller or the Life of Jack Wilton. New York, 1920.

PALTOCK, ROBERT. The Life and Adventures of Peter Wilkins: a Cornishman, ed. by A. H. Bullen, (Everyman Lib.) London, n.d.

PRICE, DAVID [?]. A Genuine Account of the Life and Transactions of Howell ap David Price Written by Himself. London, 1752.

RICHE, BARNABY. Apolonius and Silla, in Riche his Farewell to the Militarie profession. [Reprinted from 1581 ed.], London, 1846.

[SCOTT, HELENUS]. The Adventures of a Rupee. London, 1783.

SIDDONS, HENRY. Virtuous Poverty, a Tale. London, 1804.

SIDNEY, SIR PHILIP. The Countess of Pembroke's Arcadia. ed. by E. A. Baker, London, n.d.

SWIFT, JONATHAN. Gulliver's Travels. ed. by Rupert Taylor, (Modern Readers Series) New York, 1927.

W------, G------. The Life and History of a Pilgrim. Dublin, 1753.

WANDER, JACK [?]. Adventures Written by Himself, London, n.d.

[VAIRASSE D'ALAIS, DENIS]. L'Histoire des sévarambes, peuples qui habitent une parties du troisième continent communément appellé la terre australe . . . in Voyages Imaginaires, Vol. v.

[VAUGHAN, GODFREY?]. The History of Jack Connor. 2 vols., Dublin, 1766.

DRAMA AND POETRY

I. COLLECTIONS

BEAUMONT and FLETCHER. Cambridge English Classics. ed. by A. R. Waller, 10 vols., Cambridge, 1906.

BEHN, MRS. APHRA. Plays, Histories, and Novels of the Ingenious. 6 vols., London, 1871.

CENTLIVRE, MRS. Dramatic Works. 3 vols., London, 1872.

————. Works. 3 vols., London, 1761.

CHAPMAN, GEORGE. Plays and Poems. ed. by Thomas Marc Parrott. 3 vols., London, 1914.

CIBBER, COLLEY. Dramatic Works. 4 vols., London, 1760.

CONGREVE, WILLIAM. Comedies. ed. by J. W. Krutch, New York, 1927.

CROSS, J. C. Dramatic Works. 2 vols., London, 1812.

D'AVENANT, SIR WILLIAM. Dramatic Works. 5 vols., Edinburgh, 1873.

DEKKER, THOMAS. Dramatic Works. 4 vols., London, 1873.

DELONEY, THOMAS. Works. ed. by F. O. Mann, Oxford, 1912.

DODSLEY, R. [editor]. Old English Plays, Revised W. C. Hazlitt, 15 vols., London, 1874-76.

DRAYTON, MICHAEL. Complete Works. ed. by Rev. Richard Hooper, 3 vols., London, 1876. [Not complete].

FARQUHAR, GEORGE. Dramatic Works. 2 vols., London, 1892.

FIRTH, C. H. [editor]. Naval Songs and Ballads. Printed for the Navy Records Society, London, 1908.

FITZGEOFFREY, REV. CHARLES. Poems. ed. by G. Grosart [London?], 1881.

FORD, JOHN. Dramatic Works, in Two Volumes, ed. by W. Gifford, London, 1826.

GASCOIGNE, GEORGE. The Glasse of Government, etc. ed. by J. W. Cunliffe, Cambridge, 1910.

———. The Posies. ed. by J. W. Cunliffe, Cambridge, 1907.

GREENE, ROBERT. Plays and Poems. ed. by J. Churton Collins, 2 vols., Oxford, 1905.

HEYWOOD, THOMAS. Dramatic Works. ed. by J. P. Collier, 2 vols., 1853.

LINNECAR, RICHARD. Miscellaneous Works. Leeds, 1789.

MANLY, JOHN MATTHEWS. Specimens of Pre-Shakespearean Drama. 2 vols., New York, [1897].

MARSTON, JOHN. Works. ed. by A. H. Bullen, 3 vols., London, 1887.

MASSINGER, PHILIP. Best Plays of the Old Dramatists. Mermaid Series, 2 vols., London, n.d.

MIDDLETON, THOMAS. Works. ed. by A. H. Bullen, 8 vols., London, 1885.

OTWAY, THOMAS. Complete Works. ed. by Montague Summers, 3 vols., Bloomsbury, 1926.

PEELE, GEORGE. Works. ed. by A. H. Bullen, 2 vols., London, 1888.

SOUTHERNE, THOMAS. Works. 2 vols., London, 1721.

WEBSTER, JOHN, and TOURNEUR, CYRIL. [Works.] Mermaid Series, London, 1893.

II. INDIVIDUAL PLAYS AND POEMS

ANONYMOUS. The Brave turn'd Bully or, The Depredators. London, 1740.

———. Injur'd Love or, The Lady's Satisfaction, a Comedy. London, [1711].

———. The Peruvian, a Comic Opera in three acts. London, 1786.

———. A Pill for the Doctor: or, The Triple Wedding, a Musical Entertainment. London, 1790.

———. Thomas and Sally or the Sailor's Return, a Musical Entertainment. London, [1760].

ANDREWS, MILES PETER. Fire and Water, a Comic Opera in Two Acts. London, 1780.

ARNOLD, JUN. S. Auld Robin Gray, a Pastoral Entertainment in Two Acts. London, 1794.

[ATKINSON, JOSEPH]. The Mutual Deception, a Comedy. London, 1785.

BEHN, MRS. [APHRA] ANN. The Rover or the Banish't Cavaliers. London, 1697.

BICKERSTAFF, ISAAC. The Plain Dealer, a comedy, in five acts. Altered from Wycherly, London, 1786.

BIRCH, SAMUEL. The Smugglers, a Musical Drama in two acts. London, 1796.

BREWER, GEORGE. Bannian Day, a Musical Entertainment. London, 1796.

COLMAN, GEORGE. The Jealous Wife, a Comedy. London, n.d. [Reprint 1777 ed.]

CUMBERLAND, RICHARD. The Brothers, a Comedy. London, 1767.

———. The Sailor's Daughter, a Comedy in five acts. London, 1804.

———. The West Indian, a Comedy. London, 1792.

DABORNE, ROBERT. A Christian turn'd Turke, ed. by A. E. H. Swaen, in Anglia, XX, 153-255.

DENNIS, MR. [JOHN]. Gibraltar or, the Spanish Adventure, a Comedy. London, 1705.

DENT, JOHN. Too Civil by Half, a Farce in two acts. London, 1783.

———. The Candidate, a Farce in two acts. London, 1782.

DURFEY, THOMAS, Gent. Sir Barnaby Whigg: or, No wit like a Womans, a Comedy. London, 1681.

[FRANCKLIN, THOMAS]. The Contrast, a Comedy in two acts. London, 1776.

[GRIFFITH, MRS. ELIZABETH]. The School for Rakes, a Comedy. London, 1769.

[GRIFFITH, RICHARD]. Variety, a Comedy in five acts. Dublin, 1782.

HIGDEN, HENRY. The Wary Widow or Sir Noisy Parrot. London, 1693.

HOARE, PRINCE. No Song, No Supper, a Musical entertainment in two acts. London, n.d.

JOHNSON, CHA[RLES]. The Successful Pyrate, a Play. London, 1713.

KILLIGREW, THOMAS. The Prisoners a Tragae-Comedy [sic], London, 1640.

[MALLET, DAVID]. Britannia, a Masque. London, 1755.

MARKHAM, GERVASE. The Most Honorable Tragedie of Sir Richard Grinvile, Knight. Edinburgh, 1886. [Reprint of 1595 ed.].

MOTTEUX, (?). Beauty in Distress, a Tragedy. London, 1698.

[MOTTLEY, JOHN]. The Widow Bewitch'd, a Comedy. London, 1730.

[MURPHY, ARTHUR]. The Desert Island, a Dramatic Poem in Three Acts. London, 1762.

MURPHY, [E. L.]. The Old Maid, a Comedy in two acts. London, 1761.

[NEVILLE, EDWARD]. Plymouth in an Uproar, a Musical Farce. London, 1779.

ODELL, [THOMAS]. The Smugglers, a Farce of Three Acts. London, 1729.

[PEARCE, WILLIAM]. Arrived at Portsmouth, an Operatic Drama in two acts. London, 1794.

"PHILO-NAUTICUS." The Female Volunteer or, the Dawning of Peace, a drama in three acts. London, 1801.

PILON, F. The Fair American, a Comic Opera in Three Acts. Dublin, 1785.

————. Illumination or The Glazier's Conspiracy, a Prelude. London, 1779.

POCOCK, I. "For England, Ho!" a Melo-dramatic opera in two acts. London, 1814.

RAVENSCROFT, EDWARD. The Canterbury Guests or a Bargain Broken, a Comedy. London, 1695.

REYNOLDS, FREDERICK. Delays and Blunders, a Comedy in five acts. London, 1803.

RICHARDSON, JOSEPH. The Fugitive, a Comedy. London, 1792.

[SHADWELL, CHARLES]. The Fair Quaker of Deal or, The Humours of the Navy, a Comedy. London, 1710.

[STEVENS, GEORGE]. The Trip to Portsmouth, a Comic sketch of one act with songs. London [1773].

[WALDRON, FRANCIS]. The Virgin Queen, a Drama in five acts attempted as a sequel to Shakespeare's Tempest. [London], 1797.

WYCHERLY, WILLIAM. The Country Wife and The Plain Dealer. ed. by G. B. Churchill, Boston [1924].

INDEX